6 00 029026 6

KT-384-596

DATE DUE FOR RETURN

UNIVERSITY LIBRARY

- 1 FEB 2000

SEM HALL 32

This book may be recalled before the above date

90014

Lord Acton
Historian of Liberty

Robert L. Schuettinger

Open Court
La Salle, Illinois

Chapter Two, "Education and Travel," was first published as "The Education of Lord Acton" in *Toward Liberty*, essays in honor of Ludwig von Mises on the occasion of his 90th birthday, September 29, 1971 (Menlo Park, California: Institute for Humane Studies, Inc., 1971), Vol. II, pp. 334-46. Reprinted by permission.

Copyright © Open Court Publishing Company 1976

All rights reserved for all countries. No part of this book may be reproduced by any means without the written permission of the publishers.

Printed in the United States of America

Library of Congress Cataloging in Publication Data

Schuettinger, Robert Lindsay, 1936-
    Lord Acton: historian of liberty.

    Bibliography: p.
    1. Acton, John Emerich Edward Dalberg Acton, Baron, 1834-1902.
D15.A25S38   1975   907'.2'024 [B]   74-20792
ISBN 0-87548-294-5

For F. A. von Hayek

Contents

Preface

A life of Lord Acton must be primarily the biography of a mind since Acton was, above all, a historian of ideas. It was ideas—both good and bad—which he believed were the moving forces of history. As Lord Keynes was to say in our own time, practical men who may rarely read a book are, if truth were known, the slaves of some long-dead scribbler.

Acton has justly been called the magistrate of modern history. It is in that combined role of teacher-judge that he offers lessons for us. If he were alive today, he would undoubtedly remind us of his most important lesson—always to be wary of that *absolute* power that corrupts absolutely. Power, like liberty, is in itself neutral—it can serve us or dominate us; in democracies, at least, how it is used is up to us. He would tell us to watch out for the concentration of power, especially the *personification* of authority in one man or one institution.

"Nothing causes more error and unfairness in men's views of history," he once wrote, "than the interest which is inspired by individual characters. The most absolute devotion to certain ideas and opinions is less dangerous, for they may be perfectly true, while no character is perfectly good; and the allegiance which is paid to doctrine is less blind and less unreasoning than that in which loyalty or friendship usurp the place of reason and duty. . . . An indiscriminate admiration and jealousy of criticism marks the feelings of a sect and a party toward its leaders" (*The Home and Foreign Review,* January 1863, p. 219).

Again and again, he shows us how practical men who hold ideas in contempt and regard principles with amusement serve their masters ill when they act as courtiers rather than as honest advisers. He tells us how one of Napoleon's officers rejoiced that he "had the prudence, on certain occasions, to suppress a just and useful remark" (*The Chronicle,* 20 April 1867, p. 99). Those in Washington and London and elsewhere, who today pride themselves on their political pragmatism, could do worse than to read even a few pages of Acton before setting off to their busy offices to face the pressures of day-to-day politics.

It is clear, I believe, that Acton does have something to teach us. There is, unfortunately, no definitive biography of Acton and no complete edition of his works. *Lord Acton: A Study in Conscience and Politics,* by the eminent Victorian scholar, Miss Gertrude Himmelfarb, is a work of thorough scholarship and considerable insight. Since it was published in 1952, however, a substantial amount of new work on Acton and his papers has been done. Perhaps the most important contribution to Acton studies in recent years has been the first complete and accurate edition of his correspondence with his coeditor, Richard Simpson. Fr. Damian McElrath and Josef Altholz have corrected, to the great benefit of modern readers, the incomplete and often misleading edition first compiled by Abbot Francis Gasquet, who attempted (from the best of motives) to obscure Acton's true views of persons and institutions within the Catholic Church. Other scholars, whose work is noted in the bibliography, have carried forward Acton scholarship in our time.

In 1942, F. E. Lally published a study of some of Acton's writings, but did not intend a full biography. G. Fasnacht has given us a work on Acton's political philosophy which, while useful, makes little attempt at serious analysis. Most recently, Archbishop David Mathew has published *Lord Acton and His Times*, which, while interesting, is more concerned with the Victorian world in general than with Acton in particular.

I first conceived the idea of writing a new study of Lord Acton and his thought in conversations with my adviser in the Committee on Social Thought of the University of Chicago. The dedication is a small gesture toward an intellectual debt that can never be repaid. Professor F. A. von Hayek has done as much as, and probably more than, any other single individual to keep alive the ideals of Lord Acton in this century.

The late Professor James Wilkie Nisbet welcomed me as a visiting member in the Department of Political Economy in the University of St. Andrews and made it possible for me to consult the chief repository of Acton papers in the Anderson Room of Cambridge University. He gave generously of his time and advice to me (as he did to generations of students and colleagues alike). For many obligations, I am happy to have this opportunity to say thank you to a genuinely great teacher.

Professor Norman Gash of the St. Andrews Department of Modern History extended invaluable counsel in the preparation of this manuscript; for two years I had the fortunate privilege of learning from one of the distinguished historians of the English-speaking world.

This book would never have been written were it not for the great assistance of the Volker, Relm, and Earhart foundations in enabling me to study political philosophy not only under F. A. von Hayek at the University of Chicago but also with Sir Isaiah Berlin, O.M., at Exeter College of Oxford University. For this I owe special thanks to Richard A. Ware of the Relm Foundation. I was able to complete this book on schedule thanks to a grant from the Heritage Foundation of Washington, D.C.

I should also mention with gratitude the staffs of the libraries of the British Museum, Cambridge University, Oxford University, St. Andrews University, and the Catholic University of America. Congressman Steven Symms of Idaho was kind enough to delegate to me his privileges in the Library of Congress.

Every student of Acton is indebted to the masterly work of Gertrude Himmelfarb, Fr. Damian McElrath, and Sir Herbert Butterfield. Douglas and Mia Woodruff were kind enough to extend to me the hospitality of their lovely home in Abingdon where the largest store of Lord Acton's personal papers are kept. I benefited greatly from the ideas and suggestions of Mr. Woodruff and also from the thoughts of the late Professor George Peabody Gooch, who knew Lord Acton well as a younger colleague in the 1890s at Cambridge.

My editors at Open Court, Richard S. Wheeler and Dale E. Howard, firmly and surely brought the manuscript into its final form. It is also a pleasure to acknowledge the assistance, given at various times, of Larry Abblitt, Isaiah Berlin, Randolph Boehm, Stuart M. Butler, André Carus, Edwin J. Feulner, Jr., David Franke, Herbert Frankel, Charles W. Hallberg, Russell Kirk, Carol Levitsky, Noel E. Parmentel, Jr., John and Marcia Petre, Madsen Pirie, Nora Pratt, William Richmond, and J. Kevin Woods.

Needless to say, all the faults of this work are mine and not theirs.

Robert Lindsay Schuettinger

Lord Acton

1. A Historian Who Made History

The relevance of Lord Acton to the twentieth century, according to one of his editors, "comes from his prophetic preoccupation with the very questions with which the twentieth century has found itself preoccupied. The great objects of his studies in history were the moral ends of government, the relations of politics to morality, and these are the questions which bitter experience has forced our age to think about more urgently than the Victorians needed to do."[1]

The great historian of liberty and educator of both Catholics and liberals was never in his life a stranger to the pathways of power, both sacred and profane. For over forty years he was a member of one or the other of the houses of Parliament. He traveled through the rough-and-tumble world of polemical journalism, as well as the most merciless lists of all, the back alleyways of academic and ecclesiastical intrigue. Still, he did not know firsthand the very worst in human nature; his reading in the Dark Ages could not have prepared him for the twentieth century, which had to experience what Acton tried so tirelessly to prevent.

The future Lord Acton was born in Naples on 10 January 1834, and baptized John Emerich Edward Dalberg-Acton. His grandfather, Sir John Acton, was both an English baronet and the prime minister of the Kingdom of the Two Sicilies. He was also, as it was delicately put, the confidant of his Bourbon queen. The prime minister had chosen to transfer his religious and political allegiances simultaneously, forsaking both the Anglican Christianity and political ties of his fathers for the Romanism of his employers.

Sir John Acton's eldest son, Sir Ferdinand Richard Acton, was to marry Marie Pelline de Dalberg, the devoutly Catholic heiress of an ancient and distinguished Bavarian house. This lady's own father, the duc de Dalberg, was also a peer of France and had represented Louis XVIII at the Congress of Vienna in the company, of course, of the bishop of Auton, better known as Talleyrand.

An Italian birthplace, an English father, a French-German-Italian mother, a supranational religion, and scores of relatives in high places in church and state in most of the nations of Europe inevitably stamped the character of John Dalberg-Acton for the remainder of his life.

In later years it was perfectly commonplace for him to sit at dinner with his family in one of his English or Bavarian or French country houses and talk in German with his wife, in English with his children, in Italian with his mother-in-law, in French with his sister-in-law, and perhaps in Spanish or Swedish with a guest.

He wore his cosmopolitanism, however, with an easy grace, just as he did his aristocratic upbringing and his own intellectual powers. His wit and love of good talk, as well as his powerful personality, made him a welcome companion wherever he went, from New York to Moscow. James Bryce, an ambassador to the United States and himself a notable scholar not unfamiliar with the great men of his time, once recorded a conversation with Acton in terms that would smack of ingenuousness were they to come from any lesser personage. The former cabinet minister and ambassador wrote in his *Studies in Contemporary Biography:*

> Twenty years ago, late at night, in his library at Cannes Acton expounded to me his view of how such a history of Liberty might be written, and in what wise it might be made the central thread of all history. He spoke for six or seven minutes only; but he spoke like a man inspired, seeming as if, from some mountain summit high in the air, he saw beneath him the far winding path of human progress from dim Cimmerian shores of prehistoric shadow into the fuller yet broken and fitful light of the modern time. The eloquence was splendid, but greater than the eloquence was the penetrating vision which discerned through all events and in all ages the play of those moral forces, now creating, now destroying, always transmuting, which had moulded and remoulded institutions, and had given to the human spirit its ceaselessly-changing forms of energy. It was as if the whole landscape of history had been suddenly lit up by a burst of sunlight. I have never heard from any other lips any discourse like this. . . .[2]

His absolute moral standards, however, which recognized no extenuating circumstances and made no allowances for time or place, often made him a difficult companion. It should be said that he did not always hold this view of the world. Until he entered his early thirties, Acton was proud to acknowledge himself a disciple of Burke and scorned ideologues and such single-minded people as the American abolitionists.[3] To the mature Acton, however, a man who condoned a moral lapse in a politician for "reasons of state" was as guilty as the sinner himself.

He once made his views on this subject unmistakably clear in his most famous letter, written to his good friend

Mandell Creighton, Anglican bishop of London and himself an eminent historian.

> I cannot accept your canon [he wrote] that we are to judge Pope and King unlike other men, with a favourable presumption that they did no wrong. If there is any presumption, it is the other way against holders of power, increasing as the power increases. Historic responsibility has to make up for want of legal responsibility. Power tends to corrupt and absolute power corrupts absolutely. Great men are almost always bad men, even when they exercise influence and not authority. There is no worse heresy than that the office sanctifies the holder of it. That is the point at which the negation of Catholicism and the negation of Liberalism meet and keep high festival, and the end learns to justify the means.[4]

In his inaugural lecture on the study of history, delivered when he accepted the Regius Professorship of Modern History at Cambridge University, he exhorted his students above all "never to debase the moral currency or to lower the standard of rectitude."[5] He often complained, as might be expected, that he was "absolutely alone" in his "essential ethical position." His Catholic friends, he said, did not understand his liberalism and his liberal friends did not appreciate his Catholicism. As he grew older he came to feel more isolated. "I never," he once said, "had any contemporaries." Still, his rather stiff-necked personality did not prevent him from living all his life at the center of political, ecclesiastical, and literary society both in Britain and on the Continent.

His physical appearance must have made almost as permanent an impression on those he met as his prodigious store of knowledge. The American poet James Russell Lowell remarked that Acton was one of the few men he had ever met "the inside of whose head more than keeps the promise of the out—and in his case that is saying a great deal."

His wide forehead, magnificent black beard (grown at an early age), and piercing blue eyes gave him the appearance of one of those ecclesiastical statesmen, handed down to us by Titian, whose mingled power and subtlety have earned the admiring gaze of four centuries. A deep, sonorous voice fully complemented this physical impression.

There can be little doubt that Acton exerted a magnetic attraction upon all who knew him. John Pollock, a distinguished scholar in the law and in his own way as sophisticated an observer as Viscount Bryce, once described himself as "enthralled" upon hearing Acton lecture.

> There was a magnetic quality in Acton's voice and a light in his eye that compelled obedience from the mind. Never before had a young man come into the presence of such intensity of conviction as was shown by every word Lord Acton spoke. It took possession of the whole being, and seemed to enfold it in its own burning flame.... More than all else, it was perhaps this conviction that gave to Lord Acton's Lectures their amazing force and vivacity. He pronounced each sentence as if he were feeling it, poising it lightly, and uttering it with measured deliberation. His feeling passed to the audience which sat enthralled. It was in truth an emotional performance of the highest order ... a wonderful work of art, such as in all likelihood will never again be witnessed.[6]

Although his style of lecturing and writing was usually restrained, even solemn, he sometimes could give free rein to a mordant wit that was always there, not far from the surface. Of a professor of history more famous for his political activities than his scholarship, Acton once remarked, "His lectures are indeed not entirely unhistorical, for he has borrowed quite discriminatingly from Tocqueville." Of another writer he noted, "Ideas, if they occur to him, he rejects like temptations to sin." Of a French historian who busied himself writing books glorifying Louis Napoleon (a type of scholar present in every age) he said, "He will have a fair grievance if he fails to obtain from a discriminating government some acknowledgment of the services which mere historical science will find it hard to appreciate."[7]

While Acton could be splendidly just, on occasion he could toss off thoughtless or even absurd *obiter dicta*. He maintained, for instance, that the idea (which is certainly debatable) that small states are inclined to petty tyrannies was "a silly thing that vulgar people say." He often said that George Eliot was the greatest of all modern novelists.[8] For this opinion, however, he had an excuse: Eliot and Acton were close friends for many years.

Even as a young man he had a reputation for knowing everyone and everything worth knowing. He was as much at home in the papal court as at Windsor Castle, in charming little rooms in the Faubourg St. Germain as in the county seats of philistine Tory squires. A list of his good friends reads like a *Who's Who* of the nineteenth century, ranging from Cardinal Newman and Jowett of Balliol to Premier Marco Minghetti of Italy and the Empress Frederick of Germany. Gladstone, even in the years when he was prime minister, often said that he could not get enough of Acton's company.

Much as he loved society, Acton's first passion was his books; he devoured an average of ten a day, as often in German or French as in English.[9] And yet, friends often lived in the same house with him for a week without ever seeing him so much as look at a newspaper. Despite his erudition, he was far from being a dryasdust. He slipped easily into an attitude of disengaged leisure and always took a lively interest in gossip and goings-on of all sorts, from cabinet crises and club scandals to marriages and garden parties. Loving good food and riding often in the country, he was an excellent judge of both wine and horses. He was as likely to be found in the raffishly elegant rooms of Brooks's—the favorite club of Whig grandees since the days of Pitt and Fox—as he was in the more sober halls of the Athenaeum, London, haunt of scholars and divines. Acton, as might be expected, liked clubs; in the words of Samuel Johnson, he was "a very clubbable man." He belonged to several, among them the Dilettanti, Grillions, the Literary Society, and The Club (founded by Johnson, Burke, Goldsmith, and Reynolds). Each of these little worlds reflected another side of his protean personality. For all his many interests, however, his chief delight was reading—his friends said it was almost a physical appetite.

Henry Sidgwick, himself a leading light of Victorian scholarship, was far from alone in saying that "however much you knew about anything, Acton was certain to know more." The historian G. P. Gooch, however, who knew Acton at the turn of the century when he himself was a young man, gives us what is doubtless a more detached and realistic view. Acton, he thought, had only an average educated man's knowledge of the natural sciences, cared little for pure literature and the arts, and was an oracle only on later medieval and modern history.[10] This estimate of the range of Acton's powers (which are still considerable) is corroborated by the list of one hundred best books that Acton once recommended as reading for the young university graduate. In the list there is only one poet, Dante, and no novelists; almost all of the works are in history, philosophy, theology, or politics. If Acton was not a truly universal man, it would still be fair to say that he was an authority on more subjects than almost all of his peers.

His multitude of interests, his preference for research at the expense of writing, and his perfectionism combined to prevent him from publishing even one volume in his lifetime. His projected masterwork, *The History of Liberty*, came to be known as the greatest book that was never written. He himself would ironically refer to it as *The*

Madonna of the Future, after the story by Henry James.
The notion that he published little, however, is a mis-
conception. In fact, a bibliography of his essays, reviews,
and articles consists of thirty-two closely printed pages.[11]
Mary Gladstone, the prime minister's daughter, applied to
Acton himself, Acton's judgment of Burke: that systems of
scientific thought have been built upon the crumbs that fell
from his table.[12]

Like Tocqueville, he never tired of exposing the dangers
in the new creeds that were sweeping away the old—in un-
checked democracy, in unbridled nationalism, in un-
mitigated racism, in uncritical progressivism, in a secular
materialism that had no time for such "words" as freedom,
honor, and morality. In essay after essay he prophesied the
horrors that would afflict the twentieth century unless
these great forces were tamed by civilization and
Christianity. "State absolutism," he wrote, ". . . is the
modern danger against which neither representative
government nor democracy can defend us. . . . If we do not
bear this in mind, we shall be led constantly astray by
forms to overlook the substance, to confound freedom of
speech with freedom of action, to think that right is safer
against majorities than against tyrants."[13]

With Burke and Tocqueville, he was convinced that a
liberal and just government could not long exist unless it
were founded on moral principles: on reverence for God
and respect for the rights and dignity of men. "It is by conscience," he maintained, "that religion has served the
cause of freedom. . . . Our conscience exists and acts for
ourselves. It exists in each of us. It is enough for oneself,
not for another. It respects the consciences of others.
Therefore it tends to restrict authority and to enlarge liberty. . . . Liberalism is ultimately founded on the idea of conscience. . . .[14]

Throughout his life, these were his two great concerns:
freedom *and* morality. He was absolutely convinced that

one could not exist without the other and that both were required for the fulfillment of man's purpose on this earth.

He inherited his religion along with his titles and illustrious names, but he perfected his faith through years of study and a lifetime of searching his conscience. His creed, like his liberalism, was not a matter of tradition or mere habit.

His paternal ancestors, in fact, were neither Catholics nor Whigs. They were High Tory Anglicans and proudly so; as ready to suffer for their beliefs when necessary as they were to benefit from them when possible. The Acton family is recorded as occupying their estate of Aldenham in Shropshire at least as far back as the beginning of the fourteenth century. During the Civil War they were resolutely Cavalier and High Church. For his pains, a Richard Acton was removed as lord mayor of London by the House of Commons. Charles I was not a man to forget loyalty, however, and the ousted lord mayor became the first of a long line of baronets. The third baronet, Sir Edward Acton, was among those who formally opposed the granting of the crown of England to "the Dutchman William" and his wife Mary.

In the eighteenth century, a younger and somewhat less austere branch of the family migrated to France and then to Italy. The first Lord Acton's grandfather, General (and Admiral) Sir John Acton, entered the service of the Bourbon sovereigns of Naples. The king's faculties, both physical and mental, were unfortunately in less than perfect condition. General Acton gallantly assumed many of the duties of his monarch and quickly rose from minister of war to prime minister, making use of all his talents to do so. He returned the queen's affections by remaining a bachelor until the age of sixty-three when, fortified with a papal dispensation, he married his niece and proceeded to insure the continuance of his recently inherited baronetcy.

In 1801 his first son, who was to succeed him as Sir Ferdinand Richard Edward Acton, was born. His second son, Lord Acton's uncle, was to become in due time a prince of the Church as Charles Edward, Cardinal Acton. Sir Ferdinand and his brother were both sent to England for their education, first at Westminster and then at Magdalene College, Cambridge. After the birth of his own son (the future Lord Acton) in Naples, Sir Ferdinand moved his family to Paris, where they took a house in the Faubourg St. Honoré. The Actons got on well in Paris and soon became part of a circle around the aging Talleyrand, whose caustic wit was still the delight of those bystanders not the subject of it.

Sir Ferdinand apparently lacked the political skills of his father, however. He never achieved more than a minor post about the new king of the Two Sicilies, who did not suffer from the incapacities of his predecessor and was capable of fulfilling his own responsibilities. The young baronet did inherit a taste for sumptuous living and, managing on his own to develop a seemly interest in literature, spent some time in building up a library. Early in 1837, when his only child was but three years old, Sir Ferdinand died unexpectedly of pneumonia at his Paris home. His son succeeded him as Sir John Dalberg-Acton, eighth baronet and master of Aldenham.

Acton's mother, of course, was a Dalberg, a member of a family who were the premier dukes of the Holy Roman Empire. Occupying the same position in Germany that the Howards, dukes of Norfolk, held in England, their rank was second only to the imperial family itself. At his coronation in 1494, the Emperor Maximilian I had granted the Dalbergs the right to be knighted before all others. At every coronation since, the phrase *Ist kein Dalberg da?* was heard; if any Dalberg were present, he would receive his knighthood first. There was even a legend, doubtless apocryphal, that the Dalbergs were directly descended from a relation of the Savior himself who had entered the

Roman army and emigrated from Palestine to the Rhine Valley to found the ducal estate of Herrnsheim. It is little wonder that Acton's maternal grandfather was uneasy about his daughter merging her quarterings with those of a mere baronet of scarcely two centuries' standing. The duke even attempted to have his prospective son-in-law created a peer of the United Kingdom, but when this last-ditch effort to keep faith with his ancestors failed, the *grand seigneur* accepted the inevitable with good grace. Unhappily, as matters turned out, the marriage was to be a short one.

In 1840, three years after the death of Sir Ferdinand, Lady Dalberg-Acton married again. Sir John Acton's stepfather was an old family friend who was presumably more acceptable to the fastidious duke; he was the eldest son of Earl Granville, the British ambassador in Paris. Lord George Leveson (as he then was), later the second Earl Granville, was to supply yet another tradition to Acton's already diverse background.

The Leveson-Gowers, who were related to the dukes of Devonshire, had long been prominent in the Whig aristocracy of England and therefore in diplomacy and in politics. Lord Leveson was to hold several of the great offices of state and was foreign minister in the governments of Lord John Russell and William Gladstone. The three families, the Actons, the Dalbergs, and the Leveson-Gowers, had first met in Paris where Lord Leveson's father, the first Earl Granville, was in charge of Her Majesty's embassy. Educated at Eton and Christ Church, Oxford, Lord Leveson was undersecretary for foreign affairs in the Whig ministry of Lord Melbourne at the time of his engagement to Lady Acton.

At first religious differences led to difficulties. Lord Leveson was a member of the Church of England; Lady Acton was a pious Roman Catholic. The engagement, in fact, was once broken because Lady Acton insisted that any children of the marriage be brought up as Catholics. The differences were reconciled, however, and Lord Leveson's sister, Lady Georgiana Fullerton, was so much impressed with Lady Acton's attitude toward religion that she converted to Catholicism herself. Acton's stepfather, however, was himself little troubled by religious scruples and in the end his Anglicanism was to have almost no influence on Acton. The general transcendental attitude of the great Whig families, in fact, was well expressed by their prime minister of the time, Viscount Melbourne, who once nonchalantly said that if he could not be called a pillar of the church, he was at least a buttress of it, since he strongly supported it from the outside.

If Leveson's rather vague ideas about the next world were to have little effect on his stepson, his more definite views about this world were to dominate Acton's political thinking for many years. The Anglican-Whig hierarchy, to which Leveson belonged and from which his political and social ideas were derived, had ruled Britain and her empire with few interruptions for almost a century-and-a-half. This group was a circle of some fifty interrelated great families who prided themselves on their liberal broad-mindedness and their disinterested devotion to duty while at the same time resting secure on their base of inherited privilege and power.

Charles James Fox and the early Burke were their intellectual mentors; they believed firmly in the cause of the people while distrusting democracy; they supported the Hanoverian dynasty and despised the king (regardless of who he was at the moment); they worshipped progress and hated change; they admired science and loathed talk of railroads and bridges. Above all else, they were an easygoing, pleasure-loving, tolerant lot; their one passion was a fear of *enthusiasm*. In politics, they were not indifferent to principles—they were positively opposed to them. As the arch-Whig Melbourne was to remark to his cabinet more than once, "It doesn't matter what we say so long as we all say the same thing."

Leveson fully shared this Burkean aversion to ideology or abstract principles that so characterized this party. So did John Acton; Burke's speeches, he said at the outset of his journalistic career in 1859, were "the law and the prophets."[15] (Several years later, he was to modify his earlier views as he became convinced that absolute moral values must prevail in politics as in religion.) Although generally on the conservative side of the Whig party, both Leveson and Acton, like their guide Edmund Burke, believed strongly in religious toleration and in free trade, policies that were held by only a part of the Whig coalition. Although both Leveson and Acton sincerely believed in toleration on grounds of principle, they obviously could not have done otherwise, at least insofar as Catholic emancipation was concerned. In the same way, it was easier for the Leveson-Gower group to side with the radical wing, led by Cobden and Bright, on the issue of free trade than it was for most of their party. The Leveson-Gower wealth, as it happened, was derived mainly from manufacturing and mining and not from the land; in this respect, they were a rarity among their own class. Aside from the issues of toleration and free trade, however, both Leveson and Acton had little in common with the radicals. Neither one could ever be accused of having Cobden's "essentially bourgeois way of looking at things," as Acton was later contemptuously to call it. In Acton's writings, the economic motive was generally ignored; like most men used to spending money without a thought of where it came from, he had little understanding of the attitudes of businessmen and workers.

Although he learned a good deal about the world and politics from his stepfather, Acton was ultimately to develop in his own way in his own time. The young baronet certainly admired the easy Regency manners of his diplomatic guardian and sympathized with his amiable and very human loyalty to his party. Such characteristics, however, were not so prominent in Acton's own serious and already more rigid temperament.

His education must have had much to do with this. Acton's schooling, in four countries (Saint Nicolas in France, Oscott in England, the University of Edinburgh in Scotland, and the University of Munich in Bavaria) was fully as cosmopolitan as his family life. Unlike the prevailing atmosphere of the English country houses of the time, the dominant values of his teachers were religious and not secular. Following the movements of his parents between their homes in Aldenham, Paris, Naples, Herrnsheim, and London, Acton soon learned to speak French fluently and was duly entered in the preparatory seminary of Saint Nicolas du Chardonnet in Paris in the year 1842.

Notes

[1] Lord Acton, *Essays on Church and State*, ed. Douglas Woodruff, p. 6.

[2] James Bryce, *Studies in Contemporary Biography*, pp. 396-97.

[3] See Lord Acton, *Essays on Freedom and Power*, ed. Gertrude Himmelfarb, p. 246. Acton was one of those rare individuals whose views become more idealistic and less moderate as they grow older.

[4] Ibid., p. 364.

[5] Lord Acton, "Inaugural Lecture on the Study of History," *Lectures in Modern History*, ed. John N. Figgis and Reginald V. Laurence, republished in *The Rise of the Free State*, p. 26.

[6] John Pollock, "Lord Acton at Cambridge," *Independent Review*, II (April 1904): 366.

[7] Lord Acton, *The History of Freedom and Other Essays*, ed. John N. Figgis and Reginald V. Laurence, p. xi.

[8]Clement Shorter, "Lord Acton's Hundred Best Books," *Pall Mall Magazine*, XXXVI, no. 147 (July 1905): 3.

[9]See Herman Finer, "Acton as Historian and Political Scientist," *Journal of Politics*, X (1948): 603. Professor Finer maintains that Acton probably read about twenty thousand volumes in his lifetime.

[10]G. P. Gooch, *History and Historians in the Nineteenth Century*, p. 365.

[11]See the bibliography of Acton's works.

[12]George E. Fasnacht, *Acton's Political Philosophy*, p. 222.

[13]*Rambler*, II (1860): 397.

[14]Acton manuscripts in the Cambridge University Library: Add. MSS. 4901, p. 357; p. 254; p. 20. (Throughout these notes, Add. MSS. refers to the Cambridge collection.)

[15]Lord Acton, *The Correspondence of Lord Acton and Richard Simpson*, ed. Josef Altholz and Fr. Damian McElrath, 1:149.

2. Education and Travel

Acton's first teacher was Monsignor Felix Dupanloup. Like the other two priests who were to influence his intellectual development, Cardinal Wiseman and Professor Döllinger, Dupanloup was a prominent theologian, with ideas of his own on how Peter's bark ought to be piloted. As the clerical spokesman for the liberal wing of French Catholicism, he was deeply involved in the attempt to reconcile the liberal state with the Catholic Church. At the Vatican Council he was to be part of the minority faction that held the definition of papal infallibility to be inopportune. Although liberal, his place in the Church seemed secure; he had been tutor to the royal princes and had received much acclaim for his part in the deathbed reconciliation of Talleyrand with Rome. (When the wiliest of diplomats was about to receive the last rites, he calmly turned his palms downward and said, "Remember, I am a bishop.")

In 1849, the liberal monsignor was to be elevated to the see of Orléans. A few years later Bishop Dupanloup was elected to the French Academy; at about the same time he helped to reorganize the liberal Catholic journal Le

Correspondant. He had been a friend and confessor to both the Dalbergs and the Actons and had assisted at the death of Sir Ferdinand Acton. His mother's frequent visits to Paris, Acton later said, were for the dual purpose of visiting her dressmaker and going to confession to Fr. Dupanloup.

When Acton entered St. Nicolas in 1842, Fr. Dupanloup, as the new supervisor, had just changed the rules to permit enrollment of boys who did not intend to enter holy orders. Acton remained at the school for only nine months, however. Since Acton was expected to matriculate at Cambridge, as his father and uncle had done before him, the family thought it more suitable that his preparatory education should be in England. Accordingly, he was sent to St. Mary's, Oscott, an institution which liked to boast that it was now what Eton once was: a school for Catholic gentlemen. Their official announcement, in fact, promised to teach all those branches of learning "becoming *either* a scholar *or* a gentleman" [emphasis supplied].

At the time, the college was under the presidency of the Right Reverend Nicholas Wiseman, titular bishop of Melipotamus and destined to wear a cardinal's hat. Dr. Henry Weedall, his predecessor, who was largely responsible for the growth of the college, was now in charge of the preparatory school. Through a series of moves in the ecclesiastical hierarchy, in which Acton's uncle (then Monsignor Acton) was involved, Dr. Weedall found himself, in his last years, in this relatively humble office. He was an elderly Catholic gentleman who belonged to the old world when Catholics desired nothing more than to be left in peace. He was thought to be too unassuming and lacking in aggressiveness. This was definitely not the mood of the militant Bishop Wiseman, who felt that "We are like the Jews returned to Jerusalem or like the first family after the Flood—we have to reconstruct everything."[1]

The future cardinal had arrived at Oscott shortly after the beginning of the Oxford Movement. Wiseman looked upon this intellectual faction within the Church of England as the foothold upon which he and his Church would build in order to gradually reconvert Britain to the orthodox faith. As things turned out, many of the leaders of the Oxford Movement, which had its origins in the publication of the famous *Tracts of the Times* in 1833, remained High Church Anglicans and did not go over to the Roman communion, despite their sympathies with the ancient church. John Keble and Dr. Edward Pusey, for instance, though they did much to widen the Anglican understanding of the Church of Rome, did not make the final break. John Henry Newman, of course, did take the Roman sacraments and was received into the Church at Oscott while Acton was still a student there in October of 1845. The most distinguished of English converts took up residence in the old college buildings, renamed Maryvale.

Encouraged by the small but steady trickle of converts who moved from Oxford to Oscott, Wiseman was convinced that Britain would soon be a Catholic nation once again and that Oscott, strategically placed as it was, was to be the prime mover in this turning point of history. Acton later recalled that Wiseman seemed to take personal satisfaction at each new "conquest" for Rome: "The converts used to appear among us and he seemed to exhibit their scalps."[2]

Some of the less farsighted of the Catholic parents and neighboring clergy sometimes thought that the good bishop was not giving enough of his attention to the job he was being paid for, namely, the education of his young charges. To these men of little faith, Wiseman haughtily replied:

> Among the providential agencies that seemed justly timed, and even necessary for it [the reconversion of England], appeared to me the erection of this noble

college, in the very heart of England. Often in my
darkest days and hours, feeling as if alone in my
hopes, have I walked in front of it, and casting my eyes
toward it, exclaimed to myself, "No, it was not to
educate a few boys that this was erected, but to be the
rallying point of the yet silent but vast movement
towards the Catholic Church, which has commenced
and must prosper." I felt as assured of this as if the
word of prophecy had spoken it.[3]

Through the outer-directed efforts of its president,
Oscott was visited by a continual train of distinguished
men—English nobility, French royalty, famous statesmen
both sacred and profane, philosophers, and theologians.
As Acton later recalled, "We used to see [Wiseman] with
Lord Shrewsbury, with O'Connell, with Father Mathew,
with a Mesopotamian patriarch, with Newman . . . and we
had a feeling that Oscott, next to Pekin, was a centre of the
world."[4]

The faculty of Oscott was by no means provincial; it was
drawn from a wide variety of sources. There were, of
course, many Oxford converts, some earlier Cambridge
converts (including the vice-president, Henry Logan, a
Scotsman by birth), Irish Catholics, local Midland clergy,
and some others whom Wiseman had brought with him
from Rome. Acton thought later that Wiseman failed to in-
tegrate properly these diverse elements or to inspire them
in any one direction. "The point is," Acton wrote, "that he
was an all-round person, and we did not clearly see his
drift."[5] Wiseman himself was an ultramontane, that is, he
belonged to that party in the Church which favored centralization of power in the papacy (so called from the
phrase "beyond the mountains," i.e., Rome). He
sometimes had visitors to Oscott, however, who would lecture on both points of view within the Church; for instance,
he once invited Vincenzo Gioberti, well known for his
belief in the separation of Church and State, and on

another occasion invited one of Gioberti's principal opponents, Antonio Rosmini.

In later life, Acton was to be rather critical of his old school; but while he was there, he seems to have been perfectly content and made great progress academically. He sent the following letter to his mother (he was ten years old).

> "Dearest Mamma,—I received your letter this morning and shall tell you what you told me—nothing but good news. . . . I am now happier here than I have ever been. I am very much liked by the boys, and excell in two principal things: I am the best chess player of all the boys, except four, and I am the best pick-pocket (of pocket handkerchiefs) ever known. . . . I am a perfect linguist, knowing perfectly—that is, so as to be able to speak them—English, French, German, and can almost speak Latin. I can speak a few words of Chinese, Greek, Italian, Spanish and Irish. I also know Chemistry, Astronomy, Mechanics, and many other sciences, but do not know botany. I am very happy here and perfectly reconciled to the thoughts of stopping here seven more years. —I am in a hurry, therefore good-bye,

> Caesar Agamemnon John Dalberg Acton"[6]

In 1848 at the age of fourteen, Acton left Oscott and spent the next two years at the University of Edinburgh under the tutelage of Henry Logan, former vice-president of Oscott. It was the fashion among young English gentlemen of this period, especially those with an interest in scholarship, to spend a year or two at one of the Scottish universities either before or after Oxford or Cambridge. In Acton's case, we may presume that he was taking his Scottish interlude in preparation for his entrance into Cambridge. He applied in 1849 and again in 1850 to Magdalene College, Cambridge, where both his father and uncle had been undergraduates. Magdalene, however, was probably worried about the rash of converts to Catholicism that had been unsettling its common room at the very time Acton applied; consequently, the future Regius Professor of Modern History was refused admission as a student. Two other colleges gave the same answer, and, in what for a Cambridge family must have been a last gamble, two Oxford colleges received Acton's application. The answer was everywhere the same.[7] It was hoped that at least he would learn Greek while at Edinburgh, but after two years he left, dissatisfied with his progress and knowing no more than five hundred words of the language.[8]

Yet it is apparent that the young Acton found the Scots intellectually inclined, if also remote. In a letter to his grandmother dated 29 January 1848, he described Edinburgh as a "polar exile" and "a town built for study." In a later letter to Lord Granville (5 February 1848), Acton wrote: "I find much less vivacity among the Scotch, also much more politeness, courtesy than at London. They are rarely in good humour but usually satisfied. I like them very much. There is nothing but books and lawyers and teachers in Edinburgh."[9] The home of the *Edinburgh Review* must have had some effect on his thought; since he later told a friend that he left Scotland stuffed with Macaulay and raw Whiggery, we may assume that that citadel of liberalism had done its work.

Acton's intellectual journey next took him to Munich, where in June 1850 he came to live at the house of Professor Johann Ignaz von Döllinger. Munich was chosen as the place for him to continue his studies for several reasons: not only was it a seat of Catholic learning at the time, it was also the home of his mother's relatives, the Arco-Valleys. Count Arco-Valley (whose daughter Acton later married) had known Döllinger for years; accordingly, arrangements were made for him to stay with the professor in Munich and to visit the Arco-Valley country house at Tegernsee on weekends.

As Professor Döllinger was to be important for Acton's intellectual life, the family that brought the two scholars together (the Arco-Valleys) was to be important in Acton's personal life. The Countess Arco-Valley became a second mother to Acton and indeed replaced, in large measure, Lady Acton (now Countess Granville) in his affections. (This relationship has recently come to light through the research of James Holland in the Woodruff papers.) Acton wrote to Countess Arco-Valley on 16 September 1857:

> I should like for you not to be anxious about my relationship with my mother. It is only you who think that way. The Professor knows and understands very well my position. If you compare her manner in general with her former intimacy with you, you will see how much she has changed. It's impossible for me to show affection which would be easily suspected and which she would certainly repel. Every difference between myself and Lord Granville will make her doubt my friendship or respect for him, the more so since he still has enough influence to destroy my credit with her. I should like you to understand truly this complicated state of affairs which has made me so unhappy and has always deprived me of the feeling of "home." This has played and does play such a great and painful role in my life that you ought to appreciate it and stop reproaching me about it. It is you who have given me all the consolation and compensations that I have had.[10]

Acton had revealed his strong emotional attachment to Munich in an earlier letter to Countess Arco-Valley. "Munich," he wrote, "is so completely associated in my mind with all that I love best, that I cannot leave it without some mournful sense of separation."[11]

Although a priest, Dr. Döllinger was primarily concerned with the life of the mind; he had refused the archbishopric of Salzburg because it would have interfered with his scholarship. Generally considered to be

one of the greatest historical scholars in Europe, he was to
be more influential than any other single individual on Acton's intellectual development. In the opinion of Miss Gertrude Himmelfarb, "The most decisive fact of Acton's life
was his apprenticeship under Döllinger."[12] The priest-
scholar was a humble man with the simple tastes and standards of the German bourgeoisie. He was himself the son
of a professor of anatomy at the University of Würzburg.
"His personal appearance," Acton wrote to his stepfather,
"is certainly not prepossessing. His forehead is not particularly large, and a somewhat malevolent grin seems
constantly to reside about his wide, low mouth."[13]

Despite the minimum of flattery in Acton's description
(which perhaps reflects the inevitable student-teacher
relationship on the first day of class), the young
Englishman had great respect for the scholar's enormous
capacity for work and his austere manner of life. He
seemed to be the personification of the cold, dispassionate
scholar, interested in nothing but the plain search for truth
for its own sake.

Catholic scholarship throughout most of the world in the
nineteenth century was in a lethargic condition. The
University of Munich, by contrast, was in the midst of intellectual ferment. At the beginning of the century Protestant scholarship had taken the lead in the German universities. Men such as Ferdinand Baur and David Strauss
broke new ground in biblical criticism, B. G. Niebuhr and
Leopold von Ranke were developing whole new schools of
history, and Friedrich von Schelling and Friedrich
Schleiermacher were attracting international attention for
their work in the philosophy of religion. The Catholic
scholars of Tübingen and Munich took it upon themselves
to explore such problems as the relationship of science and
religion or the historical analysis of the Old Testament.
Their goal was to make Catholicism intellectually respectable by the standards of the most rigorous secular

philosopher or historian. They succeeded so well in this task that for decades Munich was the intellectual center of world Catholicism.

Upon his arrival in Munich, Acton threw himself into a course of study as broad and as demanding as the professor's own schedule. During his first few enthusiastic weeks, Acton later recalled, he read the whole of the *Biographie Universelle*—a work of some fifty-tive volumes. "My day," he wrote to his stepfather, now Earl Granville,

> is portioned out something in this manner—I breakfast at 8—then two hours of German—an hour of Plutarch and an hour of Tacitus. This proportion was recommended by the professor. We dine a little before 2—I see him then for the first time in the day. At 3 my German master comes. From 4 till 7 I am out—I read modern history for an hour—having had an hour's ancient history just before dinner. I have some tea at 8 and study English literature and composition till 10—when the curtain falls.[14]

A few years later, Acton, as a more mature scholar, explained his personal philosophy of education to Lord Granville. He admitted that his studies at first glance seemed to be useless or unrelated. There was, however, definite unity in his method. He studied English history, the classics, the history of the Middle Ages and of the Church, theology, and the history of philosophy in order both to prepare himself for a role in public life and to lay the foundation for an academic career as a serious writer, not as a dilettante. The common theme that united all his studies, he said, was history; his academic goal was to become an original historian and to teach others of his countrymen to become the same.[15] His political goal was to promote in both Church and State the supremacy of principles over interests, of liberty over despotism (whether from above or below), and of plain truth over evasion and rationalization.

"He had no desire," two of his editors note, "to make of intellectual pursuits an end in themselves. His scholarship was to him as practical as his politics, and his politics as ethical as his faith."[16]

In the 1850s both Döllinger and his young student grew out of some of their intellectual shells, and both changed their minds on a number of important issues. Almost on his arrival Acton was told to read Burke in order to broaden his mind and as an antidote to Macaulay. Döllinger had an aversion to Macaulay but recommended Bacon, Newman, and especially Burke's *Letters on a Regicide Peace*, which the professor called "the literary starting point of Legitimism."[17] At the beginning of Acton's stay in Munich, Döllinger, like most of the Munich faculty, was an ultramontane and monarchist who saw little wrong with the status quo. He was comfortable in his life and derived satisfaction from being an industrious scholar, a loyal subject of the king, and a devoted servant of the pope.

Döllinger's first serious quarrel with Rome was in 1854 over the proclamation of the dogma of the Immaculate Conception of Mary. Although there was a long tradition in the Church that maintained that Mary was herself conceived without original sin, Döllinger opposed the intended proclamation on three main grounds. First, he asserted that historically it was not held to be a divinely revealed truth and that many leading Catholic scholars, including St. Thomas Aquinas, had demurred to it. Secondly, it was to be decreed by Pope Pius IX on his own authority without the confirmation of a council of the Church. Thirdly, he believed that unnecessary additions to the creed would serve only to make the Catholic Church more isolated and to widen further the split between it and the Protestants. After the new dogma was officially proclaimed, however, Döllinger accepted it and consoled himself with the thought that he had fought it as long as possible. Pius IX's early exercise of papal infallibility in this matter foreshadowed the more serious struggle that was to come in 1870 when papal infallibility in faith and morals was itself to be proclaimed by the same pope as binding on all Catholics.

The latter doctrine was to be ratified by a council of the Church, which presumably vitiated at least one of Döllinger's procedural objections. At that time, however, Döllinger was not to submit; he and a small minority left the Roman Catholic communion and, calling themselves Old Catholics, continued to venerate every dogma of the Catholic Church but the last.

The basic transformation in Döllinger's intellectual outlook, which ultimately led to his excommunication, took place in those years when he and Acton lived together in Munich. In Acton's case, there is little doubt that he acquired his lifelong distrust of ecclesiastical power largely as a result of his participation in these early battles in the 1850s.

The old Döllinger would have joined, in fact did join, in condemning any Catholic philosopher or theologian who inquired too deeply into matters that earned him the wrath of Rome. In 1835, a leading German theologian, Georg Hermes, was officially condemned by the Church for overemphasizing natural reason and rationalistic religion in the tradition of Kant. At that time Döllinger saw nothing improper in this proceeding. Two decades later, however, a similar controversy erupted over the theological works of Anton von Gunther and Jakob Frohschammer. The first philosopher maintained that science and religion were coequal in the area of scholarship and that science could assert its own truths independent of the teachings of religion. The second writer, Frohschammer, went further than this and claimed that science must take precedence over religion. In this case, Döllinger reversed his earlier position and came to the defense of the alleged heretics. If Rome were to silence every serious thinker who attempted to explore such problems as the relationship of religion and science, he insisted, Catholic scholarship would be reduced to sterile servility. There must be at least a reasonable amount of freedom of thought for Catholic intellectuals, he said, if the universities were not to become centers of stagnation. Döllinger's efforts met with a cold rebuff, however, and the two scholars were duly condemned.

Döllinger's work in the theory of development—that is, the notion that moral truths and religious dogmas were not fixed for eternity but instead changed and developed as man's civilization and understanding advanced—was to eventually lead him into irreconcilable conflict with the Church. Miss Gertrude Himmelfarb, writing in her masterly biography, *Lord Acton: A Study of Conscience in Politics*, asserts that it was from Döllinger and not from Newman that Acton adopted his own theory of development. "The theory . . .," Miss Himmelfarb notes, "is more popularly known in the form given it by Newman in his *Essay on the Development of Christian Doctrine* of 1845. . . . Newman was unfamiliar with German theology, with the work of Drey, Mohler or Döllinger, and it appears that he arrived at the theory independently."[18]

The fundamental idea, of course, was not new; its origins go back at least as far as the efforts of such men as Gottfried Leibniz, Jean Mabillon, John Robinson, and Petavius.[19] Inherent in this way of studying religion were implications that eventually took both Acton and Döllinger to the very limits of the orthodoxy of the nineteenth-century Church. Ironically enough, it was the influence of this same theory that led Döllinger to leave the Church after the Vatican Council and persuaded Acton to remain in it. Although Acton never in his life doubted a dogma of his religion,[20] he did not fear the most rigorous historical criticism of church history or doctrine.

He was convinced, for example, that the Resurrection was a historical fact in the same sense as the Battle of Waterloo was an event and could be documented by all the usual rules of historical evidence. He had little patience with historians who refused, for one reason or another, to deal with facts. Of F. C. Baur he once wrote:

> According to Baur, the business of history is not so much with facts as with ideas; and the idea, not the fact, of the Resurrection is the basis of the Christian faith. Doctrines are developed out of notions, not out of events. Whether or no the belief is true, he refuses to inquire. In the most characteristic passage ever written by a German historian, he declares that it is a question beyond the scope of history.[21]

In Acton's interpretation, the theory of development meant that "the action of Christ who is risen on mankind . . . fails not, but increases; that the wisdom of divine rule appears not in the perfection but in the improvement of the world; and that achieved liberty is the one ethical result that rests on the converging and combined conditions of advancing cilization. . . . History is the true demonstration of Religion."[22] This view, that God will ultimately make clear in his own good time what may appear to us now to be wrong or unjust, enabled Acton to reconcile his submission to the Vatican decrees with his conscience. As will be seen, Acton believed that God would not allow his Church to remain for long in a grossly imperfect state; that time would "perfect" the doctrine of papal infallibility. As we also know, Döllinger did not agree with his former student's interpretation and left the Catholic Church shortly after the Council.

In 1857, a journey to Rome confirmed the worst fears and suspicions of the now theologically liberal Döllinger and his twenty-three-year-old student. They went, not to indulge in disputations with the conservative Curia, but simply to read manuscripts in the Vatican library. Acton himself, probably because he lacked clerical status, was refused admission and had to rely on Döllinger's summaries of them. Döllinger's first and only impression of Rome left him, according to Acton, "despondent, without confidence and without respect." He was appalled not by any indications of self-interest or immorality but simply by the lethargy and inefficiency. He was convinced that few men in Rome cared deeply about any aspect of the Church and almost none had the slightest interest in scholarship. Acton himself thought that Pius IX was definitely the intellectual inferior of his predecessor. "Now nobody feels," Acton wrote, "that the Pope will think less of him because he knows nothing at all."[23]

Döllinger had, in particular, two unfortunate experiences that seriously affected his own, and Acton's, attitude toward the hierarchy. In a conversation with the secretary of the Inquisition, Modena, that gentleman admitted he knew no German and then went on to note that a German book could be placed on the Index of Prohibited Books if a critic translated just one heretical or otherwise unsound sentence from it. Modena's only reply to Döllinger's suggestion that such a sentence could easily have its whole meaning distorted by being torn out of context was the unruffled assertion: "It is our rule."[24] Döllinger's audience with the pope was an even worse experience for him. His puritan sensibilities were shocked by the elaborate ceremonials and by the sight of women prostrating themselves before the papal chair. He found the pope himself to be unbearably and indecently arrogant. Pius IX had assured his liberal priest-professor from Munich that "only when the world had learned to bow before the Apostolic Chair would the welfare of mankind be assured."[25]

The expedition to Rome was one of many undertaken by Döllinger and Acton together. Once a year during Acton's residence at the university from 1850 to 1858, they set off on a tour of Italy, England, Austria, Switzerland, or Germany, stopping to see old friends or to meet new ones or to attend scholarly conferences. They explored libraries and bookstores voraciously; they applied at first hand the modern historical techniques of manuscript research learned from von Ranke's lectures at Munich on the "new" history. These journeys revolutionized the attitudes of both Döllinger and Acton toward history as well as the Church. For Döllinger it meant that the work of decades was suddenly obsolete. For Acton, however, it meant that the young historian had found his purpose in life: to aid in that "full exposition of truth [that is] the great object for which the existence of man is prolonged on earth."[26]

Looking back on his Munich experiences after many years of independent scholarship, Acton was inclined to revise his original estimate of the university and even of Döllinger. The Munich faculty, he wrote, was "not remarkable for originality or freshness, or warmth, or play of mind." He thought the professors too committed to "defending a settled cause" to "start a voyage of discovery." Döllinger, Acton thought, was overly interested in the romantic school of historical writing and in criticizing Protestant versions of history.[27] Apparently Döllinger was successful in teaching Acton many important aspects of the historian's craft; he was not, however, able to impart to his student the attitudes and techniques needed for sustained work. Döllinger himself predicted that if Acton did not write a major book before he was forty, he never would.[28] As in his reminiscences of Oscott, Acton had the feeling in later life that Munich had somehow let him down.

Although he spent eight years attending lectures and studying at the University of Munich, he never took a degree. (This oversight was corrected in 1872, when the faculty of Munich awarded Acton an honorary doctorate.) It is doubtful, however, if this changed his attitude toward German universities. In 1867, almost ten years after leaving Munich, Acton wrote an essay on German education that might well have been written about one of the many "multiversities" of our own century. The function of the German universities, he said,

> was to prepare candidates for public employment and to teach things necessary to be known in order to obtain a salary under government or in the Church, as a doctor or a schoolmaster. They existed to promote certain public objects of society, not to promote the independent ends of literature and science. They suffer alike from the want of liberty and the want of discipline. They are subject to the patronage of the State and they exert no effective restraint over the lives of the students. The very theory to which they owe their fame and influence has done harm, by the utter sacrifice of educational to scientific purposes; for it supplies a more perfect machinery for the production of good books than of good men.[29]

Acton's many tours with his professor reinforced his taste for travel and his talent for observation. In 1853, he was offered an opportunity to go much farther afield than his usual book-hunting expedition. Lord Ellesmere, an older relative, had been appointed chief British commissioner to the New York Industrial Exhibition; Acton was invited to come as secretary and general aide-de-camp. In the diaries he kept of his American travels, Acton was able to add to his list of illustrious personages: he met, among others, Oliver Wendell Holmes, Henry Wadsworth Longfellow, Charles Dana, William Prescott, James Russell Lowell, the scientist Louis Agassiz, the English geologist Sir Charles Lyell, and the Catholic essayist and philosopher Orestes Brownson. Of this distinguished company, only Brownson made a good impression on the young and somewhat haughty Acton.* He kept up a correspondence

---

*During his years as Regius Professor at Cambridge, Acton was to say that he had an aversion to "bright young men"; this is probably because he was one himself, with all the faults and virtues of that class.

for many years with Brownson, and the American philosopher sent contributions from time to time to journals Acton was editing.

America was a disappointment to the young baronet. Even before he landed, he wrote of New York City that "the city cannot be seen for it is very flat and quite surrounded with shipping." He recorded that there was "great anxiety about the washing. It is said that there is but one laundress in the city." After landing, his worst fears were realized. "The typical Yankee face," he noted, "is not a very intelligent face . . . it is a selfish face." He was later to add, in a burst of fair-mindedness, that the people he met were "perhaps not the best specimens."[30]

Acton, Lord Ellesmere, and other members of their party were invited to the home of a social-climbing New York businessman who had "one of the largest houses on 5th avenue, the street where all the great people live." His name was Mr. Haight, and Acton's first impression was that he was a "dirty old fellow—looked rather like Lord Brougham."* Acton guessed that he had made his fortune either in "hat-bands or drugs." There was a large "library" that housed some half-dozen books. The granddaughters of his host, Acton found to be incredibly vulgar with "detestable twangs." He added, however, that "there was no shyness that I could see, they were rather free and easy, indeed, as I had an instance of." Acton says no more about the young ladies of the household, but he does describe the hostess as "vulgar, affected, pompous" and unimaginably "ignorant." Mr. Haight himself would have made "a good character in a novel"; in fact, Acton understood that he had been featured in some satirical articles in New York. All in all they were "the most vain, purse-proud and boorish" family Acton had ever met.[31]

Acton's visit to Harvard convinced him of the intellec-

---

*One of the leaders of the Whig party and a rather formidable gentleman, but one whom Acton quite obviously disliked.

tual superiority of Munich despite the many weaknesses of
that center of Bavarian culture.

> Surrounded with a few trees appears a couple of red
> brick buildings of rather tumbledown appearance,
> and two small edifices of stone. . . . This is Harvard
> College, the oldest and principal university in the
> United States. . . . It is supported entirely by private
> means. . . . The students number about 600. They pay
> about $80 a year . . . they pass for the most dissipated
> set of students in the Union. . . .
>
> Nothing is studied for its own sake, but only as it will
> be useful in making a practical man; thus rhetoric is
> cultivated, as each man may be called upon to speak in
> the course of his life, indeed he is very like to speak
> often without being called upon. Mathematics and cer-
> tain of the sciences are pursued because they cor-
> respond to the utilitarian character of the country.
> There is no demand for learning [for its own sake]. . . .
> Learning may become desirable sometime or other; I
> should not wonder if this was to happen out of vanity;
> more men may have leisure after a time, and will be
> able to devote themselves to occupations which are
> their own reward. This is seldom the case now, as
> money is the great object of life. These deficiencies
> are well-known to the members of the university,
> many of whom have studied in Germany. . . .[32]

From Harvard, Acton crossed the Charles River to attend
a Massachusetts State Constitutional Convention that was
being held at that time. Sitting with Charles Dana, Acton
was overwhelmed by raw democracy in action. The casual
language and manners of the legislators were in sharp contrast to the more elegant House of Commons, where Acton
was himself to sit a few years later. "A half-madman," he
notes, "made a speech suggesting equality in all things . . .
there was talk of votes for women and such-like."[33] Even
more than by the thought of votes for women, Acton was
shocked to hear that the state of Maine had passed a law

prohibiting the sale of liquor. "This specimen of bureaucratic interference," he wrote, "appears strange in such a free country."[34]

The remainder of his American journey only confirmed Acton's suspicions of the superficiality and materialism of American life. Six years later he was to write to a friend that a visit to America was a quick cure for an infatuation with democracy.[35] It should be said, however, that the mature Acton was in substantial agreement with Alexis de Tocqueville, who he said was "of all writers ... the hardest to find fault with. He is always wise, always right and as just as Aristides."[36] Russell Kirk's description of Tocqueville, that he was "the best friend democracy ever has had, and democracy's most candid and judicious critic,"[37] could properly be applied to Lord Acton, who in 1878 wrote that

> American independence was the beginning of a new era.... The greatest statesmen in England averred that it was just. It established a pure democracy; but it was democracy in its highest perfection, armed and vigilant, less against aristocracy and monarchy than against its own weaknesses and excess. Whilst England was admired for the safeguards with which, in the course of many centuries, it had fortified liberty against the power of the crown, America appeared still more worthy of admiration for the safeguards which in the deliberations of a single memorable year, it had set up against the power of its own sovereign people. It resembled no other known democracy, for it respected freedom, authority and law.... Ancient Europe opened its mind to two new ideas—that Revolution with very little provocation may be just; and that democracy in very large dimensions may be safe.[38]

In the last lines of the last lecture that Lord Acton delivered at Cambridge he said that federalism in America "has produced a community more powerful, more prosperous, more intelligent, and more free than any other which the world has seen."[39]

Although in the course of his development, Acton changed his mind about American democracy (as he did about many things), his first conclusions about absolutism in Russia (which he visited in 1856) were to remain essentially the same all of his life. It impressed him then, as it did in his last days as Regius Professor, as "an amalgam of power and servility."[40]

"Russia," he was to write a few years after his visit there with Lord Granville,

> has existed a thousand years; it is the most populous of the European nations, the most united and vastest state in the world. And yet it has accomplished nothing for mankind, and has not produced a monument or an idea that men will be unwilling to forget. The Russians have created nothing; but they have not assimilated the foreign elements which their rulers have introduced. They have preserved the national character unchanged, in spite of the elaborate efforts of the government; and under an incessant despotism they have retained the art of providing for themselves. They do not resist the interference of the State; but they do not require it.[41]

Acton's stepfather, who had recently succeeded his own father as the second Earl Granville, was sent as the representative of Queen Victoria to the coronation of Tsar Alexander II. The diplomatic earl and his scholar stepson worked well together at the embassy, but they were of essentially different temperaments. Granville was the Whig *milord* who could get on well with almost anyone; Acton could charm his high-born friends with his learning and his fellow scholars with his knowledge of high society, but the young baronet was fundamentally much more withdrawn and serious-minded than his guardian.

There was an air of levity about Granville, which doubtless made him a welcome member of the irrepressible Melbourne's cabinet, that was alien to the young and sensible Acton. Granville, who then held the ponderous title of Lord President of the Privy Council, never hesitated to mock himself or his position. In a letter to a friend, he once described a dinner party he had attended: "The house beautiful, the china of the softest paste, the wine excellent, the Lord President rather drunk."[42]

Although he was not without literary interests, it was *de rigueur* for a Whig earl to take nothing seriously. He wrote to his good friend Lord Canning (then governor-general of India) that he was working on a Life of Madame de Chevreuse in the *Revue des Deux Mondes*, adding the customary remark, "It seems very amusing." About the earnest, industrious young Gladstone, he commented in the same letter, "He is devoted to Homer. He is going to *rehabiliter* Helen, whom he has discovered to be a much injured woman."[43]

Still, the gentlemanly earl did have some influence on his brilliant stepson's way of looking at the world. For instance, in describing the Tsar's sister (the widow of the Empress Josephine's brother), Acton wrote: "The only [member of the imperial family] I thought really pleasant was the Grand Duchess Marie; so easy, so grande dame, so clever, so insolent, so civil."[44] *Insolence* is a quality the aristocratic Granville would have appreciated in a woman; it is difficult to imagine the bourgeois Döllinger sharing this taste.

The brief visit to the seat of autocracy lasted only from August to September, but it was long enough to convince Acton that he "would rather be a citizen of the humblest republic in the Alps than a subject of a superb autocracy which overshadowed half of Europe and of Asia."[45] Four decades later, Acton was to draw upon his brief experience with Caesarism to write with prophetic power that out of the Renaissance came the idea that

> the State alone governs, and all other things obey. Reformation and Counter-reformation had pushed religion to the front: but after two centuries the original theory, that government must be undivided and uncontrolled, began to prevail. It is a new type, not to be confounded with that of Henry VIII ... or Louis XIV, and better adapted to a more rational and economic age. Government so understood is the intellectual guide of the nation, the promoter of wealth, the teacher of knowledge, the guardian of morality, the mainspring of the ascending movement of man. That is the tremendous power, supported by millions of bayonets, which grew up in the days of which I have been speaking at Petersburg, and was developed, by much abler minds, chiefly at Berlin; and it is the greatest danger that remains to be encountered by the Anglo-Saxon race.[46]

When the young Acton returned to England from Petersburg, he was just past his twenty-first birthday. The years of preparation were almost over; it was almost time for him to decide what he was to do with his talents and privileges.

Notes

[1]Gertrude Himmelfarb, *Lord Acton: A Study in Conscience and Politics*, p. 15. Besides the very thorough chapter on Acton's education in Miss Himmelfarb's biography, the interested reader may consult a chapter by the Cambridge historian Herbert Butterfield, "Acton: His Training, Methods and Intellectual System," in *Studies in Diplomatic History and Historiography in Honour of G. P. Gooch*, ed. A. O. Sarkissian.

²Wilfrid Ward, *The Life and Times of Cardinal Wiseman,* 1:348.

³Ibid., p. 343.

⁴Ibid., p. 349.

⁵Ibid., p. 353.

⁶Lord Acton, *Selections from the Correspondence of the First Lord Acton,* ed. John N. Figgis and Reginald V. Laurence, pp. 1-2.

⁷Ibid., pp. 256-57. Acton, in 1890, thanked Gladstone for securing his appointment as a Fellow of All Souls. He added that King's College, Cambridge, and "a famous college at Oxford" had offered him fellowships at the same time. "All this has flattered me unduly," he noted, "as both universities refused me as an undergrad."

⁸Mountstuart Grant Duff, *Out of the Past,* 2:190.

⁹Woodruff MSS., quoted in James C. Holland, "The Education of Lord Acton" (Ph.D. thesis, Catholic University of America, 1968), p. 136.

¹⁰Ibid., p. 129.

¹¹Ibid., p. 138.

¹²Himmelfarb, *Lord Acton,* p. 19.

¹³Acton, *Correspondence,* p. 8.

¹⁴Ibid.

¹⁵Ibid., p. 24.

¹⁶Lord Acton, *The History of Freedom and Other Essays,* ed. John N. Figgis and Reginald V. Laurence, p. xviii.

¹⁷Himmelfarb, *Lord Acton,* p. 69.

¹⁸Ibid., p. 23. The reader interested in learning more about Döllinger may consult Acton's essay on his teacher, "Döllinger's Historical Work," in the *English Historical Review,* V (October 1890): 700-744.

¹⁹George E. Fasnacht, *Acton's Political Philosophy,* p. 48.

²⁰Grant Duff, *Out of the Past,* 2:195. Acton is quoted as saying, "I am not conscious that I ever in my life held the slightest shadow of a doubt about any dogma of the Catholic Church."

²¹Lord Acton, *Historical Essays and Studies,* ed. John N. Figgis and Reginald V. Laurence, p. 369.

[22]Lord Acton, "Inaugural Lecture on the Study of History," in *Lectures on Modern History*, ed. John N. Figgis and Reginald V. Laurence, p. 12.

[23]Add. MSS. 5751. (See n.14 to chap. 1.)

[24]Himmelfarb, *Lord Acton*, p. 28.

[25]Ibid.

[26]*Home and Foreign Review*, July 1863, p. 163.

[27]Himmelfarb, *Lord Acton*, p. 23.

[28]For more on Acton's early training, consult E. L. Woodward, "The Place of Lord Acton in the Liberal Movement of the Nineteenth Century," *Politica*, IV (September 1939): 248-65; and, Sarkissian, ed., *Studies in Diplomatic History*.

[29]*Chronicle*, 13 April 1867, p. 57.

[30]Lord Acton, "Lord Acton's American Diaries," *Fortnightly Review*, CX (1921): 728-33.

[31]Ibid., pp. 740-71.

[32]Ibid., pp. 929-31.

[33]Ibid., CXI (1922): 74.

[34]Ibid., CX (1921): 733.

[35]Lord Acton, *Lord Acton and His Circle*, ed. Abbot Francis A. Gasquet, p. 95. Acton described "several years' residence in the United States" as a "homoeopathic cure for democracy." This letter was written in 1859, when Acton was twenty-five years of age.

[36]Lord Acton, *Lectures on the French Revolution*, ed. John N. Figgis and Reginald V. Laurence, p. 357.

[37]Russell Kirk, *The Conservative Mind, from Burke to Eliot* (Chicago: Regnery, 1960), p. 226.

[38]Acton, *History of Freedom*, pp. 84-85.

[39]Acton, *Lectures on Modern History*, p. 314.

[40]Ibid., p. 285.

[41]*Home and Foreign Review*, January 1863, p. 285.

[42]Lord Edmond Fitzmaurice, *Life of . . . 2nd Earl Granville*, 1:128.

[43]Ibid., p. 129.

[44]Ibid., p. 205.

[45]Fasnacht, *Lord Acton's Political Philosophy, p. 206.*

[46]*Acton, Lectures on Modern History*, p. 289.

3. The Journalism of Church and State

Acton returned to England in 1858 after having spent the greater part of eight years studying in Germany and most of the other major countries of Europe. He immediately noticed the sharp contrast between the stirring intellectual life of Germany and the stagnant state of Catholic thought in his own country. His duty, he believed, was plain: he should employ his wealth and education as best he could in order to bring liberalism to his fellow Catholics, Catholicism to his fellow liberals, and the discoveries and techniques of German historical research to both. As Herbert Butterfield has put it, "He conceived it his mission to reproduce something like the Munich circle in England to educate his co-religionists, to raise the standards of their scholarship and to provide intellectual leadership and something like a programme for their politics."[1]

That English Catholicism badly needed intellectual and political leadership for a variety of reasons there can be no doubt. In the United Kingdom as a whole, it would appear, at first glance, that Catholics were a very respectable minority, about one-fifth of a population of twenty-five million. Almost all British Catholics, however, were Irish, and Ireland at that time, although nominally an equal partner in a tripartite kingdom, was scarcely the master of its own destiny. Most of her people were uneducated and many were near starvation. Catholics as well as Anglicans were forced to pay for the support of the established church. Despite Catholic emancipation, only one English M.P. was a Catholic (a younger son of the duke of Norfolk); the ancient universities no longer barred Catholics by statute (as they did Jews), but in practice continued to discriminate against them. Dogged at almost every turn by Protestant prejudice, Catholics were further weakened by the fact that they themselves were disunited. Many English and Irish Catholics regarded the ties of blood as stronger than the ties of religion and consequently failed to support each other politically and economically. The older English Catholics tended to be anti-Roman while the newer converts were often "more papist than the pope."

Acton saw, as one of his chief tasks, the gradual removal of anti-Catholic prejudice from the minds of intelligent Protestants. He knew that the primary reason for this conviction, held by most educated Englishmen, was a distrust of the freedom and sincerity of Catholic scholarship. In an age of discussion, freedom of the mind must be king. In 1858, Acton and Richard Simpson (who shared Acton's liberalism in both secular and clerical politics) took over the *Rambler*. Simpson put the matter well.* "I know," he wrote, "for I have experienced the thing, that the great prejudice against the Church among educated Englishmen is not a religious one against her dogmas, but an ethical and political one; they think that no Catholic can be truthful, honest or free, and that if he tries to be he is subjected to persecution."[2]

---

*Simpson was an Oxford convert.

From the start, it was clear that one of Acton's primary aims was to overcome by example the belief of English Protestants that Catholics could not be good and honest scholars. Although the *Rambler* was only a decade old, it was already regarded as a serious threat by the English ultramontanes, who had their own organ in the *Dublin Review*, founded by Wiseman.

> I have thought and read a good deal upon political subjects [Acton wrote to Simpson in 1858 at the age of twenty-four] and have read a great lot of the famous writers, to try to find out a clear view which I could rely on in public life. I will endeavour to turn these studies to account and to pursue them farther in the service of our common undertaking.
>
> Now the first point [Acton continued] . . . is that I am very far from agreeing with any of the more famous Catholic writers, or with any of the political parties in England. . . . There is a philosophy of politics to be derived from Catholicism . . . and from the principles of our constitution . . . as remote from the absolutism of one set of Catholics as from the doctrinaire Constitutionalism of another.* I conceive it possible to appeal at once to the example and interest of the Church and to the true notion of the English Constitution . . . that the true notion of a Christian State, and the true, latent, notion of the constitution, coincide and complete each other.[3]

True to his word, Acton threw himself with all his energies into his chosen career. He usually wrote one long article himself for each issue, collaborated closely on

*This is apparently a reference to *Le Correspondant*, a French liberal Catholic journal, one of whose contributors was Acton's first teacher, Bishop Dupanloup. Their motto was the words of Canning: "Civil and religious liberty for the whole world." At this time in his career, Acton thought such a goal to be doctrinaire, believing as he did that serfdom in Russia and slavery in the U. S. were justified by circumstances.

several others, and, in addition, would often review twenty or thirty books of several languages. He was no rich young dilettante supporting a little magazine with his family's money and occasionally writing an editorial or meeting a contributor for lunch at a fashionable club. The fact that he did work so hard is doubly remarkable since he could have easily spent his time in leisurely and genteel scholarship in between the rounds of weekends at the country houses of the great Catholic families.

Acton had also hoped to take part in the founding of a great Catholic university in England; when this was found to be impossible, he devoted his efforts to the further education of literate Catholics by means of the *Rambler*. Although the bimonthly's circulation was never more than three thousand (small even by nineteenth-century standards), under Acton's guidance it became recognized as one of the most learned and influential periodicals in Europe. According to the *Times*, "Its notices of the current literature . . . [were] most complete; some of its contributors were men of the highest distinction in various countries."[4]

There were well over forty contributors from a dozen countries; almost all were friends of the young editor that he had met on his travels. In keeping with the practice of the time, the articles were unsigned, but, besides Acton, Simpson, and Newman, other contributors are known to have included Lord Sherbrooke, Prof. Wilhelm Roscher from Leipzig, Orestes Brownson from Boston, Peter Renouf, Denis McCarthy, and William Palgrave. Although he was only twenty-four when he began his editorship, Acton impressed his personality on the *Rambler* from the very beginning. He assigned the various articles and indicated the sources he wished consulted, the questions that should be answered, the pitfalls that should be avoided, and the general form the articles should take. As Mr. F. E. Lally put it, "His mastery of detail was phenomenal." Due to his influence, the bimonthly "virtually lost its general character and became more and more a journal of political education."[5]

The intellectual success of the *Rambler* would not have been achieved, of course, without the contributions (both literary and financial) of Acton's good friend and coeditor Richard Simpson. He was fourteen years older than the young baronet but could date his Catholicism only from his twenty-fourth year, when he gave up his Anglican vicarship and joined the Roman communion. Simpson was a man of considerable private means who, like Acton, could have had a life of ease and luxury, or at least of peace and quiet, if he had wished. A graduate of Oriel College, Oxford, and a secure member of the English establishment, he chose to be a rebel throughout most of his life. Having left the Church of England because he was of independent mind, he did not adopt an attitude of meek submission within his new Church.

In one of his first articles for the *Rambler* in 1859, Simpson ventured to criticize the conduct of some Catholic bishops in regard to a Royal Commission. This was the opportunity that Cardinal Wiseman (who had been viewing the *Rambler* with increasing misgivings from the year of its founding) was waiting for. The encroachment upon episcopal prerogatives gave Wiseman the excuse he needed to threaten censure. Wishing to avoid a direct clash with the hierarchy, both Acton and Simpson agreed to resign as editors on condition that John Henry Newman took over direction of the offending journal. Dr. Newman, after some hesitation, agreed and made a sincere effort to preserve the principles of liberal Catholicism without incurring the displeasure of the hierarchy. His tactics of conciliation were to be of no avail, however.

One of his own articles, which appeared in his second issue, was sent by Wiseman to the Congregation of the Index in Rome for formal censure. The essay was entitled

"On Consulting the Faithful in Matters of Doctrine" and, according to Wiseman, it implied the fallibility of the Church. The result was that Newman also resigned and the *Rambler* was returned to its former owners, Acton and Simpson. For appearance' sake, Simpson remained a contributor, while Acton and John Moore Capes were responsible for the editing.

Acton was constantly in trouble with the hierarchy of the Church, not because he was a weak or indifferent Catholic, but precisely because he took his religion so seriously. He was always regarded with suspicion by the party leaders of the Whigs and Liberals for the exact same reason. To Acton, politics and religion were inextricably intertwined. "Have you not discovered," he once wrote to Mary Gladstone (daughter of the prime minister) ". . . what a narrow doctrinaire I am, under the disguise of levity? . . . Politics come nearer a religion with me, a party is more like a Church, error more like heresy, prejudice more like sin, than I find it to be with better men."[6] He insisted that the statesman, and the historian, must realize that men could "lose their souls by political, as they do by domestic error."[7] If both religion and politics were regarded by Acton in a serious vein as subject to the same ethical criteria, nonetheless they were looked on as distinct entities insofar as their institutional existence was concerned. A nation dominated by either church or state was the poorer, for, ultimately, it was liberty that was encumbered.

In 1862, Acton wrote to his collaborator Simpson a brief but brilliant analysis of the dangers inherent in a state dominated by a religious government.

> . . . a religious government depends for its existence on the belief of the people—Preservation of the faith is *ratio summa status*, to which everything else must yield. Therefore not only the civil power enforces the religious law, but the transgressions of the religious must be watched and denounced—therefore es-

pionage & religious detectives, and the use of the peculiar means of information religion provides to give warning to police. The domain of conscience [is] not distinct therefore from the domain of the state—sins = crimes, and sins against faith, even when private, without proselytism, are acts of treason. Seclusion from the rest of the world necessarily follows, if the rest of the world has not the same religion, or even if it is not governed on the same principles. For liberty is extremely contagious. Therefore travel and commerce, facilities of communication, &c., [are] necessarily proscribed; for they would be solvents of a state founded on religion only. But all these prohibitions restrain material as well as intellectual well-being. Poverty and stationary cultivation, that is to say, in comparison with the rest of the world, retrogression, [are] the price of such a [government]. Two things put an end to this. The economical dependence on other countries [which] needs ensues, ultimately break down the seclusion, as the determination of capital to exploit undeveloped resources is resistless in the long run—and the increase of communication gradually destroys barriers and brings the forbidden knowledge and desires into the sequestered community. All this is perfectly applicable to Tibet and Maroc. . . .[8]

Acton was almost as fearful, however, of the completely secular or unreligious state. Democracy without religion, he was convinced, would sooner or later lead to despotism or anarchy. Like Burke and Tocqueville, he stressed again and again that nations lacking the self-governing force of religion are unfit for freedom. Unless there are checks from within, he agreed, there must surely be checks from without. He always opposed those who ignored the moral nature and purpose of the state and simply treated it as "a police organization for the protection of property."[9]

He found as much to fault in religious quietism and secular liberalism as in ultramontanism. Both the radical secularists and the religious quietists, Acton maintained, shared a common error: they both believed that Christianity (or any religion) should have no effect on politics, that there was an absolute divergence between church and state. Acton firmly denied this. The essence of Christianity, he claimed, was its foundation upon the individual conscience; upon the idea that the soul was more sacred than the state.[10] "The essence of Whiggism," he once wrote, "is the acknowledgement of the supremacy of the higher law."[11]

Acton believed that the state has a divine origin and purpose; that church and state "have the same origin and the same ultimate objects."[12] The great object of the Christian statesman is, "by keeping the two spheres permanently distinct—by rendering to Caesar the things that are Caesar's, and to God the things that are God's—to make all absolutism, of whatever kind, impossible."[13] He once wrote to Simpson that "all liberty consists [ultimately] in the preservation of an inner sphere exempt from State power—That reverence for conscience is the germ of all civil freedom, and the way in [which Christianity] served it. That is, liberty has grown out of the distinction (separation is a bad word) of Church and State."[14]

Although church and state have many aims in common and are not fully separable, neither should they be united. "The State aims at the things of another life but indirectly," Acton wrote. "Its course runs parallel to that of the Church; they do not converge."[15] Acton regarded the admiration of the ultramontanes for the theocracies of the ancient Jews and Greeks as anti-Christian, not ultra-Christian. The union of church and state (with either subordinate to the other) was a pagan ideal, he maintained, not a Christian one. In the Middle Ages, the characteristic dualism of Christianity (at least of the Western branch) came to its highest fruition in the struggle between emperors and popes. Acton was convinced that the outcome of that balancing of forces was a great increase in liberty, which would not have come about if the bishop of Rome had followed the lead of his colleague at Constantinople and allowed his see to be subordinated to the state. Neither would it have come about if the contrary had happened.

In Acton's view, the truly Christian state *was* the truly liberal state; there could be no conflict between the principles of ethical Christianity (unencumbered by the tendencies toward corrupting power inherent in any institution) and the principles of disinterested liberalism. He thought, in fact, that the ideal liberal would be a Christian clergyman.[16] The ideal commonwealth he believed to be Pennsylvania in the eighteenth century, founded by the Quakers on a constitution that guaranteed liberty, equality, and toleration.[17]

He insisted that, by his standards, England was the most truly Catholic state in Europe, despite its break with the Holy See. This was because in most of the self-proclaimed Catholic nations of Europe, the Church had subordinated itself to absolute monarchies.[18] The secular liberals, however, were concerned with freedom for the state but not for the church; this path, according to Acton, also led to an unhealthy concentration of power. The emancipation of the individual became a sophisticated means of enslaving him, since the limited powers once enjoyed by the church and other independent institutions and corporations, as Tocqueville had also pointed out, were replaced by an absolute state. The French Revolution did not end the centralizing tendencies of the *ancien régime;* it accelerated them. For these reasons, the permanent answer must be a free church in a free state, the slogan of the liberal Catholics.[19]

For Acton, conscience was all. Though he did not believe that the conscience was infallible,[20] he held it to be the best moral guide given to us and the one to be most relied upon, even, if necessary, against the express commands of pope, king, council, or House of Commons. A man who acted against the persistent urgings of his own conscience, in Acton's eyes, would almost certainly lose his soul. Acton believed there was a greater moral risk, therefore, in membership in the Catholic Church than there was in attending Quaker meeting houses. This was because the Catholic Church had the strongest hierarchical structure and had at various times and places enforced opinions that were perhaps perilous to the soul.

"A Liberal," he once wrote,

> does not believe that Catholicism, Lutheranism, Calvinism . . . offer a sufficient security against moral error. They all have promoted persecution. Therefore, he gives higher value to Socinians, Independents, Baptists, and to systems of philosophy that do not persecute. He holds that a sound morality and escape from sin is more easy to find in philosophy than in religion. He checks his theology with philosophy. . . . He grounds himself, not indeed against the lower types of clergy, but against the priesthood of the great Churches.[21]

And yet Acton often said that communion with Rome was dearer to him than life. Many of his friends recalled that he had told them there was no doctrine of the Church which he had "the slightest difficulty in believing."[22] Acton recognized that the sacraments and dogmas were never the sufficient instrument of salvation or of earthly liberty and morality, but he was certain that, for himself at least, they were the necessary means of spiritual salvation.[23]

Acton believed that, "Principles make a strong man, maxims a wise man, doctrines a complete man."[24] He was sure that rigorously scientific men who studiously ignore the transcendent were in a very real sense incomplete. He was not one of those who, like his distant relative Edward Gibbon, valued religion as a utilitarian device for holding society together (although he knew, of course, that a moral creed had infinite social value). Nor did he share the attitude of those esthetes for whom religion, especially the Catholic Church, was a psychological escape from the barrenness of their own times. Acton believed in the Catholic Church, quite simply, as the means for his personal salvation.

In Acton's lifetime, England as a nation gradually abandoned certain religious norms (Anglican Protestantism), partly through his and his associates' efforts at the *Rambler* and other such journals. In place of the old structure, there gradually grew up a system of limited toleration for certain dissenters (not at first including Catholics, Jews, or atheists); this was eventually replaced by an almost secular establishment that tolerated all religions (as well as nonreligion) while granting certain unimportant favors to one (the Church of England by Law Established).* Thus the goal of Acton's first teacher, Bishop Dupanloup (civil and religious liberty for the whole world), was to come to fruition at least in the British Isles. Although the young Acton, as we have seen, did not entirely approve of this objective, the more mature Acton derived considerable satisfaction as the transition from intolerance to tolerance was gradually accomplished (with at times crucial help from Lord Acton in both houses of Parliament). The new era represented a change from less liberty to more, and from a time of less respect for the individual conscience to one of almost complete freedom in matters of thought and spirit. For Acton, *this* was the Christian state, insofar as it could be realized on earth: a state where every man has the right and the duty to obey his own conscience.

Acton's frequently professed loyalty to the doctrines and sacraments of the Church was not enough for the ul-

---

*Such as the right to crown the monarch.

tramontanes, however; these churchmen believed that Christianity was threatened most seriously by the increasing growth of science and secularism. Only unswerving obedience to the authority of the Church, they reasoned, could combat these increasing social evils. The liberal Catholics, they thought, were stabbing the Church in the back.

Science, to Acton, was no threat to his faith; he emphasized again and again that science could endanger the Catholic Church only if it rejected geology, anthropology, and all the other new studies, and permitted them to be used by enemies of the faith.[25] "We must not pursue science," he once wrote, "for ends independent of science. It must be pursued for its own sake, and must lead to its own results."[26]

From Acton's viewpoint, the real enemies of conscience and the Church were those overzealous clerics who knew and then taught that the end justifies the means; that because science sometimes disturbs the faith of partially educated persons, it is right to censor science or to limit education; or, in the extreme case, that assassination is moral if the victim is a Protestant. According to two of his colleagues at Cambridge University (writing after Acton's death),

> In Acton's view the supreme evil is the telling of lies and the shedding of blood in order to secure ecclesiastical power.... He wished to attack Ultramontanism ... in the root and stem.... The root and stem, are, in Acton's view, a certain corruption of the conscience. Christianity to Acton is primarily a system of ethics; whatever violates that on principle is anti-Christian. What Acton felt to be the root of evil was the notion that acts otherwise reprehensible could take on a different colour if they were done to promote religion, e.g., the notion that truth may be suppressed for the sake of edification. Out of this main root grows

the notion that the Church in self-defence, as an organization, may develop a machinery for putting assailants out of the way. Such machinery was developed ... in the Medieval Inquisition. This was what Acton meant when he spoke of the system of austere immorality established at Trent. Austere in the sense that it condemned sexual vice, and enjoined self-denial, the system of Trent was immoral in that it enjoined persecution and the suppression of inconvenient truth.[27]

The papacy as an institution, Acton once wrote to his good friend and fellow historian, Lady Blennerhassett, aims at power, and since power tends to corrupt, we must always keep the dangers inherent in Church authority in proper perspective.

> It is well that an enthusiast for monarchy be forced to bear in mind the story of Nero and Ivan, of Louis XIV and Napoleon; that an enthusiast for democracy be reminded of St. Just and Mazzini. It is more essential that an enthusiast of the papacy be made to contemplate its crimes, because its influence is nearer the Conscience; and the spiritual danger of perverted morals is greater than the evil of perverted politics. . . . The corruption which comes from revolutionary or absolutist sympathies is far less subtle and expansive. It reaches the lower regions of the mind and does not poison that which is noblest.[28]

Acton emphasized, in the same letter, that he did not "prefer the Sorbonne to the Congregations or the Councils to the Popes." He was not a proponent of national or conciliar Catholicism. He regarded those Catholics who wish to transfer supreme authority to a council of the church as no better than those, like De Maistre, who wanted to lodge all power in the pope. In this, his religious views reflected his secular politics; he was not so much interested in *who* was to rule (people, king, or aristocracy) as he was in limiting the power of any government and guaranteeing the supreme rights of conscience. "The essence of Whiggism," he had written (as noted above), "is the acknowledgment of the supremacy of the higher law," a law that must be respected by popes and councils as much as by kings and majorities.[29] His position within the Church, he told Lady Blennerhassett, was nothing but the "adjustment of religious history to the ethics of Whiggism."[30]

Although the *Rambler* devoted a good part of its efforts to criticizing the ultramontane view, it did not confine its unsolicited advice to Catholics. As Acton once remarked to Simpson, the *Rambler* was a double-barreled gun, one for shooting its friends and one for its enemies. The positivists, for instance—that scientistic school of thought that sought to explain the world without reference to the transcendent—were the recipients of a salvo every few months. Henry Thomas Buckle's monumental *History of Civilization*, for example, was reviewed by Acton. In outlining his plan of attack to Simpson, Acton wrote, "Setting aside the theory, the learning of the book is utterly superficial and obsolete. He is altogether a mere humbug and a very bad arguer. He has taken great pains to say things that have been said much better before in books he has not read. He has no knowledge of the classics and still less of theological literature. We can expose him completely."[31]

In "The Protestant Theory of Persecution," possibly the most important article that Acton ever wrote for the *Rambler*, the young historian took the surprising position (in the light of his later views) that Catholic religious persecution was somehow less objectionable than similar activities carried out by Protestants. Acton reasoned that while Catholics persecuted heretics for practical causes (in order to preserve the fabric of society, which rested on a special moral order), Protestants justified their intolerance on purely speculative grounds by punishing religious errors as errors and not as dangers to the social order. Acton admitted that Catholic persecutions were probably more bloody, but he maintained that Protestant persecution was a greater sin against conscience.

This was not an isolated essay on Acton's part. During most of his youth, as we have seen on other occasions, he held the view that freedom and intolerance are relative conditions, appropriate or inappropriate to different stages of civilization. On these grounds, he refused to condemn slavery in America and serfdom in Russia. "To say that persecution is wrong—nakedly," he once wrote to Simpson, "seems to me first of all untrue, but at the same time it is in contradiction with solemn decrees, with Leo X's Bull [against] Luther [and others]."[32]

"The theory of intolerance," he maintained in another essay of about the same time,

> is wrong only if founded absolutely upon religious motives; but even then the practice of it is not necessarily censurable. It is opposed to the Christian spirit, in the same manner as slavery is opposed to it. The Church prohibits neither intolerance nor slavery, though in proportion as her influence extends, and civilization advances, both gradually disappear. . . . The law naturally follows the condition of society, which does not suddenly change. . . . The exclusion of other religions—the system of Spain, of Sweden [and others]—is reasonable in principle, though practically untenable in the present state of European society.

Continuing in his Burkean vein, Acton wrote,

> The acquisition of real definite freedom is a very slow and tardy process. . . . These liberties are the product of a long conflict with absolutism, and of a gradual development, which by establishing definite rights revives in positive form the negative liberty of an unformed society. The object and the result of this

process is the organization of self-government, the
substitution of right for force, of authority for power,
of duty for necessity and of a moral for a physical relation between government and people. Until this point
is reached, religious liberty is an anomaly.[33]

For his own country and his own time, however, Acton
was certain that religious persecution was morally and
politically wrong. In fact, "The Protestant Theory of
Persecution" was meant to be an attack on intolerance in
general and was only in part a defense of Catholic as opposed to Protestant forms of persecution. The essay was
certainly in the Burkean tradition, and even John Stuart
Mill would have disagreed with little of it; it is in comparison with Acton's later writings, as he gradually
developed a more uncompromising and abstract liber-
tarianism, that the early essay seems illiberal and compla-
cent.

In the short time of two or three years, as it happened,
Acton almost completely reversed his earlier position. In a
review published in 1863 in the *Home and Foreign Review,*
he concluded that the Albigensians were almost certainly
destroyed, not because of their antisocial doctrines, but
primarily because of their theological heresies.[34] He
gradually became convinced that Catholics, as well as
Protestants, were more interested in eradicating those
errors which they believed were dangerous to souls than
those which threatened society.[35] In a notebook probably
dating from 1866 and 1867, he goes even further and asserts
that the Spanish Inquisition was dedicated primarily to
maintaining the authority of the church hierarchy and only
secondarily to protecting either society or the souls of men.

[The] object of the Inquisition [was] not to combat
sin—for the sin was not judged by it unless accompanied by [theological] error. Not even to put down
error. For it punished untimely or unseemly remarks

the same as blasphemy. The object was only unity. This became an outward, fictitious, hypocritical unity. The gravest sin was pardoned, but it was death to deny the donation of Constantine [a forged document that claimed that the first Christian emperor had "willed" the Western Empire to the pope]. So men learnt that outward submission must be given. All this [was] to promote authority more than faith. When ideas were punished more severely than actions—for all this time the Church was softening the criminal law . . . and the Donation was put on a level with God's own law—men understood that authority went before sincerity.[36]

Although it probably seemed to Acton and Simpson that they spent a good part of their time battling with the enemies of the Church, most outsiders saw the ultramontane *Dublin Review* and the *Rambler* mainly as the antagonists in fratricidal quarrels. The *Saturday Review*, for instance, a nonsectarian journal, noted with some amusement that "it is clear, from the extraordinary freedom with which names and persons are handled, and from the eagerness of bishops and dignitaries to enter into the lists, that an amount of pugnacity exists among Roman Catholics which by no means finds sufficient vent in its onslaught on Protestantism."[37]

Despite occasional lapses, Acton always tried to give an intellectual opponent the benefit of any doubts and to treat him with courtesy and scrupulous fairness. He once wrote to Gladstone that "it always seems to me a valid test of sincerity whether a man begins by appreciating, and even it may be, fortifying and strengthening the adversary's position, supplying the gaps and correcting the flaws of his argument before he declares it untenable. To set up [weak opponents], mere material for demolition, betrays the infancy of art."[38]

Even in writing short book reviews, Acton's conscience was always present, forcing him to put aside such considerations as friendship and kindness. "If books are to be noticed at all," he once reminded his coeditor,

> it must be done uprightly, on their merits, and with even scales. I sat down with the best resolution of speaking favourably of [James Burton] Robertson, who had begged for a notice, but I found so little good to say that I am afraid he will hardly be grateful and that we have not much assisted the sale of his book. However, I urged Wallis to notice it, who has an easier conscience, or a more shifting standard and he said, long ago, that he was doing it.[39]

On another occasion, he insisted to Simpson that the *Rambler* should set up a high and pure standard and not swerve from it. "You want things to be brought to bear," he wrote, "to have an effect. I think our studies ought to be all but purposeless. They want to be pursued with chastity, like mathematics."[40]

If the editors of the *Rambler* had been as chaste as vestal virgins were supposed to be, and had they been scholars as disinterested as hermit monks, the hierarchy of the Church still would not have been satisfied. To it, disagreement was rebellion. The English hierarchy contained the most devoted readers of each issue as they searched for some plausible excuse for having the irritating journal suppressed once and for all. Their opportunity came in 1861 when Acton gave a sympathetic hearing to his old professor's views in an article entitled "Döllinger on the Temporal Power."[41] Döllinger's suggestion that the pope should extricate himself from the conflicting forces of Italian nationalism and Roman democracy, which threatened to sweep away the Papal States, by voluntarily renouncing his temporal power and seeking refuge in Germany, was, to the ultramontanes, a proposal worse than heresy: it was treason—even ingratitude (the ultimate sin for all politicians). Cardinal Antonelli, Pope Pius's secretary of state, demanded that the *Rambler* unequivocally support the papacy when its very existence (as an independent state) was in immediate danger.

At this juncture, Newman tried to intervene to make peace between Acton and Rome. Acton, he tactfully suggested, should not waste his time on ephemeral topics but should instead retire to Aldenham and there write the great work he was entirely capable of producing. Acton replied that he considered the matter to be a political and not a theological issue and therefore not within the legitimate censoring power of the Church. "In political life," he insisted to his former collaborator, "we should not be deterred I suppose, by the threat or fear of even excommunication, from doing what we should deem our duty."[42]

Nevertheless, Acton chose to avoid papal censure by suspending publication of the Rambler. He and his friends immediately founded a new journal, the Home and Foreign Review, however, and soon were back at the same stand with exactly the same ideas but with a different cover. Although Acton worked as hard as or harder than before (in one issue he wrote thirty-one of the sixty-three reviews himself, the rest being divided among nine reviewers), the circulation of the new Review never rose above a thousand.[43] Still, as the hierarchy was only too well aware, the influence of the journal was great not only among leading Catholics but among important Anglicans and agnostics as well. According to the Dictionary of National Biography, the short-lived Home and Foreign Review was "the high-water mark of the Liberal Catholic movement" in the nineteenth century. "Probably no review of the reign of Queen Victoria maintained so high a standard of general excellence."

Excellence, of course, was not enough for Acton's enemies in the Curia; subservience was more to their taste. Almost upon the first appearance of the new Review, Cardinal Wiseman condemned it in a formal statement. He cited "the absence for years of all reserve or reverence in its treatment of persons or of things deemed sacred, its grazing over the very edges of the most perilous abysses of error, and its habitual preferences of uncatholic to catholic instincts, tendencies and motives."[44] Despite what a lawyer might call the vagueness of the indictment, it was clearly only a matter of time before the *Review* would be forced to stop printing. When the end finally came, it was to be Döllinger again who forced the issue.

At a Catholic Congress in Munich in 1863, Döllinger criticized the traditional scholastic philosophy and asked that the medieval analytic method be replaced by the principle of development to encounter scientific error with scientific weapons. When Acton published a laudatory account of this speech in the January 1864 issue of the *Home and Foreign Review,* the Curia's response was swift. In March 1864, Pope Pius published a brief that had been previously addressed to Döllinger's superior, the archbishop of Munich. The pope censured Döllinger's views and declared unequivocally that the opinions of all Catholic writers were subject to the authority of the Roman congregations.

In a letter to Newman shortly afterwards, Acton wrote:

> I have to give you the important news of the suppression of *The Home and Foreign Review. . . .* I have determined not to risk a censure, but to take the significant warning . . . and put an end to the *Review* after the appearance of the next number. In an article . . . I shall find means of giving a full and intelligible explanation of my motives, which will be as satisfactory as it can be made without renouncing any of our principles. I shall sign this paper in order to make the act and the declaration entirely my own.[45]

In the last issue of the *Home and Foreign Review* (April 1864), Acton's first signed article was published, under the title "Conflicts with Rome." He argued that the true interests of the Church would be best served by cherishing both political and intellectual liberty. The true interests of the Church, he maintained, are not always the same as those of the Church government. Both conscience and political wisdom may make it imperative to overthrow a Catholic king or obey a Protestant one. The apparent interests of religion, he noted, might have much to say against our accepting the fraudulence of the Donation of Constantine or the course of the earth around the sun. Still, he held that it was religion itself that prevented considerations of temporary expediency from prevailing.

"It would be wrong," he continued,

> to abandon principles which have been well considered and are sincerely held, and it would also be wrong to assail the authority which contradicts them. The principles have not ceased to be true, nor the authority to be legitimate because the two are in contradiction. To submit the intellect and conscience without examining the reasonableness and justice of this decree, or to reject the authority on the ground of its having been abused, would equally be a sin, on one side against morals, on the other against faith.

He would rely, he wrote, on books and more serious scientific studies to be the agent of eventual change.

If we understand the importance of the concept of development in Acton's thought, we will understand how he could reconcile his idea of the supremacy of conscience with submission to authority. He could do this because he was convinced that the present government of the Church would in time change and that his principles would one day be vindicated (as indeed, they have been in the twentieth century). He would no more leave the Church over a disagreement with the Curia than he would renounce his British nationality because he was deeply aggrieved by the Disraeli cabinet.

". . . I will not provoke ecclesiastical authority," he concluded,

> to a more explicit repudiation of doctrines which are necessary to secure its influence upon the advance of modern science. [Again, Acton was looking to the future.] I will not challenge a conflict which would only deceive the world into a belief that religion cannot be harmonized with all that is right and true in the progress of the present age. But I will sacrifice the existence of the *Review* to the defence of its principle, in order that I may combine the obedience which is due to legitimate ecclesiastical authority, with an equally conscientious maintenance of the rightful and necessary liberty of thought . . . the principles it has upheld will not die with it, but will find their destined advocates and triumph in the appointed time.

At the age of twenty-six Acton had written to Newman of his position as "editor in the midst of a hostile and illiterate episcopacy, an ignorant clergy, a prejudiced and divided laity."[46] Simpson, in a similar mood, had complained to Orestes Brownson that the aristocratic Catholic families use Catholic books only as decorations for their chapels, while the "lower orders" are interested only in sentimental novels or trash.[47] With all these obstacles, it is little wonder that the efforts of Acton and his small circle of friends to unite science and religion and Catholicism with liberalism were doomed to failure.

The end of Acton's brief journalistic career had not quite yet come, however. In the autumn of 1866, a new weekly to be called the *Chronicle* was founded. T. H. Wetherell was to be editor, Acton's close friend Sir Rowland Blennerhassett was to finance it, and former writers from the *Rambler* and the *Home and Foreign Review* were to staff it. This publication was to be a secular journal with no religious connections, although, of course, it would appeal mainly to· liberal Catholics. During most of 1867, Acton acted as its Roman correspondent, a fact that, it will be easily imagined, did not please the pope.

The *Chronicle*, while not as scholarly as Acton's previous journals, was very strong on foreign affairs and published good reviews of political and literary works. Its life was also short, however, and the last issue came out in February 1868. As Gladstone remarked, "It was too Catholic for the Liberals and too Liberal for the Catholics."

The last nonacademic journal with which Acton was to be regularly associated was the *North British Review*, which was taken over by Wetherell and other liberal Catholics in 1869. It was in some ways odd and in some ways fitting that this journal was originally founded by the antiestablishmentarian, evangelical Scottish Free Kirk group. Acton published two long historical essays in the first issue under the new editor; one concerned the coming Vatican Council, the other was on the Massacre of St. Bartholomew.[48]

E. L. Woodward, writing in *Politica*, considers Acton's journalistic years to be largely a wasted effort that ultimately hurt his effectiveness both as a historian and as a member of Parliament. Acton, according to Woodward, fell into

> the dangerous habit of writing history to persuade instead of writing it merely as history. It associated him with men of sharp wit and great talent but of little judgment. It brought him into conflict with the authorities of his church which was severe enough to use up much of Acton's energy, to chill his enthusiasm and to leave him in the isolation which had been dangerous enough in his first years.[49]

It is doubtless true that despite his announced intentions, most of Acton's historical articles were polemical. This, however, might just as well be a virtue as a detriment, a point of view that, it must be admitted, would seem to be preferable to bias concealed behind the thin veil of objectivity. The fact that Acton did divide his time between editing, historical scholarship, and his parliamentary duties necessarily meant that some of his activities had to suffer. As it happened, Acton usually chose to neglect his political obligations.

Notes

[1] Herbert Butterfield, *Lord Acton*, Pamphlets of the English Historical Association, no. G9, p. 4.

[2] Lord Acton, *Lord Acton and His Circle*, ed. Abbot Francis A. Gasquet, p. xlvii.

[3] Lord Acton, *The Correspondence of Lord Acton and Richard Simpson*, ed. Josef L. Altholz and Fr. Damian McElrath, 1:6 (hereafter cited as *Acton-Simpson Correspondence*).

[4] *Times* (London), 20 June 1902.

[5] Frank Edward Lally, *As Lord Acton Says*, p. 56.

[6] Lord Acton, *Letters of Lord Acton to Mary . . . Gladstone*, ed. Herbert Paul, p. 314.

[7] Ibid., p. 180.

[8] Acton, *Acton-Simpson Correspondence*, 2:252.

[9] *Home and Foreign Review*, April 1864, p. 723.

[10] Lord Acton, *Lectures on Modern History*, ed. John N. Figgis and Reginald V. Laurence, p. 33.

[11] *Home and Foreign Review*, January 1863, p. 253.

[12] Acton, *Acton-Simpson Correspondence*, 1:121.

[13] Lord Acton, *The History of Freedom and Other Essays*, ed. John N. Figgis and Reginald V. Laurence, p. 205.

[14] Acton, *Acton-Simpson Correspondence*, 2:251.

[15] Acton, *History of Freedom*, p. 251.

[16] Add. MSS. 4952. (See n.14 to chap. 1.)

[17] Acton, *History of Freedom*, p. 84. Despite the comment of Figgis and Laurence in their introduction to Acton's

Correspondence (page xx) [see n.27 below] that Acton had "no mind for Quakerism," it is clear that Acton admired the Quakers, probably as much for their lack of organization as for their liberalism and morality.

[18]Ibid., p. 210.

[19]Gertrude Himmelfarb, *Lord Acton: A Study in Conscience and Politics,* p. 44. For a more complete understanding of Acton's religious views, this is the best analysis available.

[20]Ibid.

[21]Add. MSS. 4973.

[22]Oscar Browning, *Memories of Sixty Years,* p. 16.

[23]Himmelfarb, *Lord Acton,* p. 229.

[24]Add. MSS. 5684.

[25]See the *Rambler,* XI (1859): 7390.

[26]Add. MSS. 5742.

[27]Lord Acton, *Selections from the Correspondence of the First Lord Acton,* ed. John N. Figgis and Reginald V. Laurence, p. xvii.

[28]Ibid., p. 56.

[29]*Home and Foreign Review,* January 1863, p. 253.

[30]Acton, *Correspondence,* p. 56.

[31]Acton, *Acton-Simpson Correspondence,* 2:21.

[32]Ibid., pp. 227-28.

[33]Lord Acton, "Mr. Goldwin Smith's Irish History," in *History of Freedom,* pp. 252-53.

[34]*Home and Foreign Review,* II (1863): 218.

[35]For further comment on this problem, see Himmelfarb, *Lord Acton,* p. 49.

[36]Add. MSS. 5536.

[37]*Saturday Review,* XIV (1862): 195.

[38]Acton, *Correspondence,* p. 214.

[39]Acton, *Acton-Simpson Correspondence,* 2:52.

[40]Ibid., 1:142.

[41]Acton, "Döllinger on the Temporal Power," reprinted in *History of Freedom,* pp. 301-374.

[42]Wilfrid Ward, *The Life of John Henry Cardinal Newman,* 1:527.

[43]William E. Gladstone, *The Political Correspondence of Mr. Gladstone and Lord Granville, 1868-1876*, ed. Agatha Ramm, 1:458.

[44]Himmelfarb, *Lord Acton*, p. 58.

[45]Lord Acton, *Essays on Church and State*, ed. Douglas Woodruff, p. 30.

[46]Ward, *Newman*, 1:510.

[47]Acton, *Lord Acton and His Circle*, p. lxiv.

[48]Published in *History of Freedom*, pp. 101-149.

[49]*See* E. L. Woodward, "The Place of Lord Acton in the Liberal Movement of the Nineteenth Century," *Politica*, IV (September 1939): 248-65.

4. The House of Commons

On 28 November 1857 at the age of twenty-three, Acton received a letter that was to launch him on his political career. "My dear Sir John, . . ." it began.

> It would give me the greatest pleasure to see you in Parliament. I am sure you would discharge your duties there with independence, and in a thorough Catholic spirit. If this expression of my high opinion of you can be of any service to you in your efforts to attain an honourable position, which I think you well deserve, you are at liberty to make use of what I write with any of our Bishops and Clergy. Should any of them wish for a more direct communication from me, I shall be most happy to give it.[1]

It was signed "N. Card. Wiseman," and was doubtless regretted by the author to the end of his days.

The endorsement was certainly important to Acton, however; in the House of Commons at the time, the only seats open to Catholics were from Ireland, and in these constituencies, the clergy was often decisive.* The Whig managers, who were given the task of locating an appropriate seat for the stepson of the lord president of the council, shopped around for several months. Dublin was considered, then County Clare and one or two others; finally Carlow was hit upon. The electorate was small (236), so the expenses would not be great; the population was about 85 percent Catholic, and the most influential local priest, Father James Maher, was all for the Shropshire baronet.

The candidate himself, however, was by no means eager to take to the hustings (and, in fact, never did). He expressed his doubts in a letter to his sponsor, Lord Granville.

> There is a sort of fastidiousness produced by long study which public life possibly tends to dissipate, but although the profession of anything like independence of party appears ridiculous, I am of the opinion that to a Catholic a certain sort of independence is indispensable. Reasons of religion must separate me occasionally from the Whigs, and political convictions from the Irish party. I am free, moreover, from the motives which generally make decided partisans, for I am conscious of no political ambition, and I have an aversion and an incapacity for official life. I must therefore most positively declare that I cannot undertake always to vote for Lord Palmerston's Government or with any other. . . . I could not of course promise the Catholics of Clare more than I have promised you. I hope, if I am Whig enough for the Government, that I shall be Catholic enough for them.[2]

Granville was apparently satisfied. After all, the partly reformed House of Commons was different from the

---

*In the 1860s, the only English seat held by a Catholic was a pocket borough of the duke of Norfolk's, represented by one of his younger sons. Disraeli, in his Reform Bill of 1868, allowed the senior English peer to retain his borough so that English Catholics might have at least one vote.

automatically ratifying assembly that it is today; no one then expected able men of independent means to follow orders slavishly. In the nineteenth-century House, it was even possible to change someone's vote by an especially well-reasoned speech; a modern M.P. who admitted to being so influenced would be thought weak-minded and probably lacking in character as well.

"I am trying to get Johnny Acton in for some place in Ireland," wrote Granville to Canning, then in India. "I am glad to find that, although he is only a moderate Whig, he is also a very moderate Catholic."[3] The optimistic earl, even forgetting about his stepson's obvious reluctance, wrote to Canning a few months later that "He has, I am glad to say, a yearning for public life."[4]

If Acton had indeed changed his mind about a political career, the change was short-lived. From the ease and solitude of Munich he wrote to Simpson in the spring of 1859 that ". . . I have heard of the dissolution, and Lord Granville wants me to come and try my chance in Ireland. I fear I shall be obliged to try it pour acquit de conscience, and because an election is cheaper than being Sheriff, but I do not feel sanguine."[5]

During the campaign, Acton confined himself to paying the expenses and writing one platitudinous letter to his chief local supporter, Father Maher. His first and last appearance in Carlow was not to be until after the polls closed. It is very doubtful, in fact, that the candidate himself would have made much of a difference. Then, as now, most elections were decided along party lines with some allowances for religious or ethnic biases one way or the other. Although the population of Carlow was over 9,000, only 236 were qualified to vote—a little over 2½ percent, or about 10 percent of the adult males. This was less than the average percentage for the United Kingdom as a whole, where about 15 percent of the adult males had the franchise. There was, of course, the £8 householder qualification, which kept away all but the most affluent gentlemen in the district, 98 of whom were Protestants, and 134 of whom were Catholics.

The year of Acton's debut in politics, 1859, was a bad year for the Liberals (as the Whigs were coming to be called) in Ireland. The Ecclesiastical Titles Bill, passed by the Russell administration, mortally offended all Catholics. The bill, which forbade the reestablishment of the Catholic hierarchy in England, was a dead letter from the start, but that made no difference to the bishops of Ireland. The bishops' suspicions that Lord John Russell was an enemy of the Church were strengthened when the Liberal leader declared himself in favor of Italian independence. Since Italian unity would be at the expense of the pope, almost every Catholic bishop in Ireland was supporting Lord Derby and the Conservatives at the 1859 election. As if those were not albatrosses enough for a Liberal candidate, it happened that the last Liberal M.P. for Carlow, Mr. John Sadleir, resigned in haste after some financial scandals came to light. These would have been heavy obstacles for an experienced politician; for a novice they were expected to be insurmountable.

One of the local Conservative newspapers commented: "That his [Acton's] chances of success are small is admitted by the Radicals themselves unless bribery to a large scale will be resorted to."[6]

Bribery, in fact, was fairly common at the time. In the aftermath of the 1859 election, no less than nine M.P.s were unseated as a result of proven charges of bribery made against them, their agents, or followers. Acton himself was to be unseated in 1866 on just these grounds, although he and his agents were declared innocent of any involvement. According to James J. Auchumuty in his most thorough essay "Acton's Election as an Irish Member of Parliament," some electors in previous Carlow elections had been offered and took £100 for their vote.[7] With the increasing democratization of the franchise, the market value of votes has, of course, dropped considerably.

Although only a select few were privileged to choose an M.P., it was the custom at most elections for the agents to buy drinks for "the boys" so as to whip up a show of popular enthusiasm for their candidate. Since "the boys" could not themselves vote, this practice was perfectly legal, although at times things would get out of hand and respectable members of the electorate would be "persuaded" to cast their vote for the candidate of the mob. When Acton's name was formally put in nomination (in his absence), crowds of supporters from both parties were on hand to express their views noisily. The *Saunders Newsletter* for 3 May 1859 reported that Acton was introduced as "a distinguished scholar who promised to be one of the first literary men in Europe." Although this was "greeted by tremendous cheers from the rabble," who were presumably admirers of men of learning, the newspaper (which did not hide its Tory leanings) added that the respectable citizens wanted to know where the candidate was.

Acton was politically fortunate in one respect only; his opponent, John Alexander, was one of the largest of the local landlords. Since landlords are rarely popular anywhere and since they ranked just above priest murderers in Ireland at the time, we may conclude that this was the principal reason why the final count showed 117 votes for Sir John Acton, and 103 for John Alexander, Esquire.

The new M.P. had the distinction of winning in one of the three Irish constituencies that switched from Conservative to Liberal; in Ireland as a whole, the Tories had a solid majority of seats for the first time in thirty years. To celebrate this unexpected victory, a dinner was held in Acton's honor at which he thanked his supporters and gave chief credit where it was due, to Father Maher. He also pronounced himself in favor of a new Reform Bill, of the secret ballot, of Irish tenant rights, and against jury-packing and involvement in continental affairs.

Father Maher responded by congratulating his new representative and predicting great honor and success for him at Westminster. He added, almost as an afterthought, that it would do him no harm if he took an Irish wife.

Although women, of course, could not vote (Acton, we noted, described an American radical democrat who suggested such an idea as "half-mad"), the canny priest had an eye for the source of political power. With considerable relish, he told the banquet that whenever he "found an elector hesitating to do his duty to his country, he was anxious to have a chat with his mistress. . . ." He was told by one Liberal lady that if her husband did not do his duty in the election (there were no secret ballots), she would go to America. The good father triumphantly concluded that only one of the votes promised to him had failed of delivery.[8]

On 10 June 1859 Acton cast his first vote in the House of Commons, joining the majority of thirteen that threw out Derby and the Conservatives and brought in Palmerston, Russell, and the Liberals. By this initial ballot he also helped to make the young Gladstone chancellor of the exchequer. He certainly owed his stepfather that much, but in his first years in Parliament, Acton was not especially happy with the Liberals; he was the weakest of partisans and sometimes the despair of his patrons. "Johnny Acton," Granville confided to Canning, "has thrown us over."[9] Acton once joined other Catholic Liberals in refusing to vote with the government to support Italian unity over the opposition of the pope. Since at that moment in history, the Liberal leaders were united only in their common support of Italian nationalism, this was an especially hard blow to Granville and his friends.

Of course, they had been warned. In his preelection statement to the electors of Carlow, Acton had said quite plainly, "I am no partisan but I had rather reckon on Liberal principles than on the fears of the Tories. I am sure we cannot make friends of the Tories, and I do not think it wise to make enemies of the Liberals."[10] Nor did Acton make any secret of his low opinion of most of the Liberal leaders. Lord Palmerston's "jaunty manner, the intense masculinity of the aged buck, the large sophisticated ignorance were all abhorrent"[11] to the young historian. Gladstone, later to become one of his closest friends, he condemned at the time for having left the Conservative party and come over to the Liberal.[12] The new chancellor, he wrote in the *Rambler*, was like the politician described by Edmund Burke as having "a disposition to hope something from the variety and inconstancy of villainy, rather than from the tiresome uniformity of fixed principles." His new radicalism, Acton added, had "neither the merit of sincerity nor the excuse of blindess."[13]

In his first years in politics he saw little to choose between the two parties. Both had their faults and both, no doubt, had their compensating virtues. Acton wrote to Simpson in 1858 that ". . . we [Catholics] need no longer humiliate ourselves and eat dirt to obtain the support of the liberal . . . party. We have got about as much as we shall get from them, and it would be well to see whether this alliance is a safe one."[14]

These were the years when Acton was Burkean to the core; he took for his own the great Irishman's empirical, antimetaphysical view of politics. He scorned the political economists and others who wanted to turn a great art into a mere science. "[Edmund] Burke," he wrote to Simpson, was a "teacher for Catholics. In the writings of his last years (1792–1797) whatever was protestant or partial or revolutionary of 1688 in his political views disappeared, and what remained was a purely Catholic view of political principles and of history."[15]

Like the older Burke, Acton at this time was distrustful of principles in politics; he preferred to proceed by a slow and gradual weighing of interests.[16] The ideologues who wanted to disengage principles from men and parties, he thought, wanted to reduce government from an art to a science. Such men looked upon Parliament as a machine for producing legislation; their only interest was to see the largest amount of laws produced by the quickest and most rational methods. Men impatient with tradition, who were usually Benthamites or socialists, regarded political parties as a nuisance because they obstruct this process. The ideal government of the rationalists, he believed, would be nonpolitical; it would be bureaucratic, with laws and regulations for every conceivable eventuality.

Political parties with all their imperfections and human failings were, Acton argued, all that stood between us and this awful fate. Each made up for the deficiencies of the other, and together they kept each other within reasonable limits. A radical idea had first to gain acceptance within the "miniature government" of the party organization, which was itself a coalition of diverse interests. Only after it had been tamed and put into a more moderate form was it offered for debate in the House of Commons as a whole. Then a further process of amendment and compromise took place before the new law would go forth into the country moderately certain of being acceptable to most and of giving offense to only a few. To the idealists who disdained the role of the "trimmers," Acton replied that to know the truth was not enough; it must be put into action, and to do that in a democracy, compromise was a necessity. Parties that wish to accomplish a program of reforms must deal with the elements of power in a society, and the constitution must reflect the existing distribution of power if stability and peaceful change are to be assured.

The Whigs and Tories, or Liberals and Conservatives as they were being called, were coalitions of varied interests who each agreed on a limited agenda but who disagreed about everything else. The Whigs, Acton thought, tended to be more concerned with politics, economics, and philosophy, while the Tories paid more attention to social values, to religion, patriotism, community, and tradition. They were the party of passion while the Whigs were men of philosophy. Acton knew, however, that all this was changing before his eyes and that both parties were becoming more and more spokesmen for definite economic interests. The Tories represented land and the Liberals manufacturing; the social and philosophic issues of English history were being forgotten in the mundane, day-to-day struggle over higher or lower tariffs. Since at the time Acton had practically no interest in business or economics (he thought the whole thing rather sordid), it is little wonder that he viewed both parties with almost equal detachment. The simple fact that most of his friends were Liberals probably tipped the balance.[17]

By 1863, however, Acton had arrived at a position on these questions almost entirely different from that previously held. In a review of T. E. May's *Constitutional History of England* published in the *Home and Foreign Review*, Acton relies on the younger Burke to refute the Burke of 1792-97 whom he had only recently extolled to Simpson.

> Burke, whom [Mr. May] quotes, does not admire, as he supposes, the balance and conflict of parties, but the concentration of the constitutional idea in a single party whose function it is to preserve the national institutions*. . . . "When bad men combine [the younger

---

*"In effect," Mr. Harvey Mansfield concludes about the younger Burke, "he demoted statesmanship to conservatism." Acton was about to do the same in favor of the Liberal party.

Burke noted in his *Thoughts on the Present Discontents,* 1770] the good must associate; else they will fall one by one an unpitied sacrifice in a contemptible struggle." . . . The constitution may be assailed on different sides [Acton continued], only that party which faces all attacks is constitutional. A party that defends only one breach, and resists only one form of encroachment or change, has its center of gravity beyond the limits of the constitution. . . . Every compromise marks an imperfect realization of principle—a surrender of right to interest or force. The constitution stands by its own strength, not by the equal strain of opposite forces.[18]

In this important essay, we see the beginnings of the great change in Acton's intellectual position. The elder Burke of the *Reflections on the French Revolution,* the unyielding opponent of ideology and abstraction, was losing his appeal to the mature Acton. Now he turned more and more to the younger Burke, the idealistic Whig, the upholder of principle, of the *Thoughts on the Present Discontents.*[19] As he grew older, Acton was to become still more devoted to moral principles without regard to practical consequences; he was, in fact, to turn completely against the philosophy of compromise that he had preached so often in his own first years in politics. Mr. James J. Auchumuty notes: "That [Acton's] private papers record judgements of Burke which conflict with his public statements and that in the last 25 years of his life he increasingly hardened against Burke's policy of balance and compromise, present problems still to be dealt with."[20]

With each passing year, Acton was to become more and more committed to the Liberal party and to its new leader, Gladstone. This was also a remarkable reversal on Acton's part. This same man—whom he had dismissed as made useless by ambition in domestic matters and unsafe in foreign affairs—he would soon be describing as "a wise and resolute leader, at whose call the nation has risen, for the first time in history, to the full height of its imperial vocation."[21] In later years, when Gladstone was considering resigning the leadership of the party, Acton begged him to stay on, saying that only he could hold the party together and safely lead the country in foreign affairs.[22] Oddly enough, it was not Gladstone's successes so much as his failures that attracted Acton. Above all, one commentator notes, it was Gladstone's "refusal to admit that nations, in their dealings with one another, are subject to no law but greed" that won Acton's admiration.

> Doubtless one who gave himself no credit for practical aptitude in public affairs, admired a man who had gifts that were not his own. But what Acton most admired was what many condemned. It was because he was not like Lord Palmerston, because Bismar[c]k disliked him, because he gave back the Transvaal to the Boers, and tried to restore Ireland to its people, because his love of liberty never weaned him from loyalty to the crown, and his politics were part of his religion, that Acton used of Gladstone language rarely used, and still more rarely applicable, to any statesman.[23]

The friendship, of course, became mutual. Even though Gladstone was fully aware of Acton's opinion of him in 1861, he sent the young editor a note praising his essay "The Political Causes of the American Revolution."[24] "I have read your valuable and remarkable paper," he wrote. "Its principles of politics I embrace; its research and wealth of knowledge I admire; and its whole atmosphere, if I may so speak, is that which I desire to breathe. It is a truly English paper." It is just possible, of course, that some political motivation may have been mixed with scholarly interest on the chancellor's part; the fact remains that this letter began a close friendship, which lasted until the death of the Grand Old Man of British politics in 1898.

As Acton became closer to Gladstone and to the Liberal party, he became more and more hostile toward the Tories and their leaders. In the same year that he began to turn against the older Burke, he denounced Toryism in unqualified terms as a party that

> subsisted by the deliberate suppression of political thought; made the denial of principle pass for a principle, and the repudiation of obligations for a duty; and carried, under pretext of expediency, measures which it declared to be wrong ... it was ready to question [the very existence of public right] if it appeared in antagonism with any cherished interest of some portion of society. [The interests of the Church and the landlord] did duty instead of a political idea.... Therefore the most illustrious chiefs of the party either were not reared in its arms, or deserted it in the maturity of their powers; and they are all reckoned by their party either converts or apostates.[25]

The full measure of Acton's contempt for what John Stuart Mill called "the stupid party" is revealed in a peroration he once directed at the Tory prime minister who served longer in that high office than any other. "Lord Liverpool," he began,

> governed England ... chosen not by the nation but by the owners of the land. The English gentry were well content.... Desiring no change they wished for no ideas. They sympathized with the complacent respectability of Lord Liverpool's character, and knew how to value the safe sterility of his mind. He distanced statesmen like Granville, Wellington and Canning, not in spite of his inferiority, but by reason of it. His mediocrity was his merit. The secret of his policy was that he had none. For six years his administration outdid the Holy Alliance. For five years it led the liberal movement throughout the world. The Prime Minister hardly knew the difference.... In the same spirit he wished his government to include men who were for

the Catholic claims and men who were opposed to them. His career exemplifies, not the accidental combination but the natural affinity, between the love of conservatism and the fear of ideas.[26]

His ideas on foreign affairs also began to change shortly after he entered the House of Commons. In this sphere as well he grew closer to the general Liberal position, outraging his Irish constituents in doing so. The *Carlow Sentinel* (on 7 January 1860) complained: "He is the stepson of the Lord President of the Council [who, of course, favored Italian unity even at the expense of the pope] and as blood runs thicker than water he naturally prefers the interests of his stepfather to those of the Holy Father." He was never an uncritical nationalist, however, and he often warned Gladstone that they must not admit "the priority of National Independence over individual liberty. . . . We do not find that Nationalists are always Liberals. . . ."[27]

In the House of Commons itself, the gentlemen's club that Acton once called "the noblest assembly in the world," the young M.P. did not take an active part. He spoke at question time on only three issues in his years there; out of forty-eight votes that were recorded during this period, Acton is listed for only twenty-seven.[28] In 1860, he voted to extend the franchise slightly, but was absent on the Secret Ballot Bill, which was of considerable interest to Irish voters. He also failed to vote on the Endowed Schools Bill, which would have aided Dissenters, and on an English Reform Bill. The next year he was absent for the vote on a Trustees of Charities Bill that would have permitted Catholics to serve as trustees. He also failed to vote for an Irish National Education Bill that would have provided education for all classes and was presumably of great interest to his constituents. In 1863, he failed to vote on the Affirmations Bill, which would have eased sensitive consciences other than those of Catholics. In his last year as M.P. for Carlow (an election year), he voted on ten of the thirteen recorded issues. One of his votes was for the abolition of religious tests at Oxford, a matter in which he held a personal interest.

Although Acton wrote some 475 pages of articles and 77 pages of current events for his two journals, while he was in the House he never once spoke in a debate, even one on foreign affairs (which was the concern of most of his writing). In addition to his retiring personality, his reasons might have been in part practical. The gentlemen of England who guided the House were not much interested in advice from experts, especially from young men who had acquired their education abroad.

Acton served on three committees, however, and it would be here, if anywhere, that one would expect him to make his influence felt. Acton did attend the meetings of the Poor Law Committee (where he was one of three Catholic members) fairly regularly, coming to twenty-one of thirty-four sessions in its first year. The problems dealt with by this committee are still, in great measure, with us today. Acton saw then what many are only beginning to see now: that poverty cannot be cured by make-work projects run by governments; that the only genuine solution is to erect a framework in which it is possible for the poor and unskilled to acquire skills and real jobs, earning wages for producing goods or services. He predicted with considerable accuracy that a welfare policy directed by the government only would have the effect of making the poor permanently dependent on that government and, of course, of increasing the power of the state and of decreasing the liberties of all citizens.

"The avoidance of a Poor Law," he wrote to Simpson in 1862,

> by means of public works not actually necessary is characteristic of centralized absolutism. It nurses artificially a proletariat, a classless community which, instead of being absorbed in its own places, is per-

manently relying on the State to provide for it ...
depriving it of the possibility of becoming independent and self-supporting. Thus a constant danger
menaces society, and the need of a strong hand
perpetually saving society and converting dictatorship
into a regular form of government is kept always
before it.[29]

Acton devoted most of his parliamentary efforts to "The
Select Committee to Enquire into the Constitution and Efficiency of the Present Diplomatic Service of this Country." This was an elite group chaired by R. M. Milnes, later
Baron Houghton; both Russell of the Liberals and Disraeli
of the Tories were members. Acton attended about half of
the sessions and usually took an active part in the questioning of witnesses. It was here that Acton's cosmopolitan
background and wide acquaintance with the courts of
Europe was most valuable.

The diplomatic service of the time was widely known as
a system of outdoor relief for the aristocracy, a source of
jobs for younger sons who were not virtuous enough for the
church nor yet quite stupid enough for the army. The key
to reforming this unabashed old-boy network lay in two
factors: an examination would at least weed out the most
incompetent and a restriction of the number of years
junior diplomats were required to serve without pay
would permit at least some of the upper-middle class to
apply. Acton was in favor of a stiff examination requiring a
knowledge of several languages coupled with a mandatory
provision that the first twelve qualifying candidates must
be appointed. This utopian idea was, of course, thrown
out—after all, one never knew *who* might show up at a
public examination. Nonetheless, an examination stressing
handwriting *was* instituted: the first halting step in the rise
of the meritocracy. Acton tried to have the period of unpaid service limited to no more than two years, which, at
least theoretically, would have allowed some of the

middle-middle class to compete. The committee decided to limit such service to four years. They also recommended an interchange of officers between the Diplomatic Service and the Foreign Office, which at the time were separate. Large salaries were also allocated to the major embassies so that a man need not be very rich to accept such a post. Although not all of Acton's attempts to democratize the service were accepted then, he had the satisfaction of seeing all of them come about within a few decades. "The most characteristic Liberal invention of the nineteenth century," he once noted, "was open competitive examination for the Civil Service."[30] Acton himself played a considerable part in putting the invention to work.

Acton's third committee was on the Births, Marriages, and Deaths (Ireland) Bill, but he took almost no part in its activities, probably considering it too impossibly boring. He paid very little attention to Irish affairs and to the economic interests of his constituents, a part of his character that was not popular back in Carlow. Acton generally spent his time on those matters that interested him, such as diplomacy and the extension of civil liberties, especially in matters of conscience. Although he missed some important votes on these issues, when he was there he always voted for the liberalizing measure. He also strongly opposed conscription. "Forced military service," he wrote, ". . . is entirely incompatible with what I call the Catholic notion of the State."[31] "A people," he warned, "that relies on a permanent system of compulsory military service resembles the statesman who declared himself ready to sacrifice not only a part, but the whole of the constitution, in order to preserve the remainder. It is a system by which one great liberty is surrendered and all are imperilled, and it is a surrender not of rights only, but also of power."[32] Acton's use of the qualifying word "permanent" would seem to imply that he would not oppose conscription in a genuine emergency, where all liberties really were endangered.

The good electors of Carlow, however, had very little interest in diplomacy and not much in civil liberties except possibly for Catholics. They expected their M.P. to look after their interests, which meant obtaining subsidies for their industries. The *Carlow Sentinel* for 25 May 1861 observed in a burst of fair-mindedness that "we will do him the justice of saying that no young gentleman ever entered the House of Commons who pays so little regard to the wishes, feelings or interests of a constituency whether Conservative or Liberal."

There is little doubt that Acton enjoyed neither politicians nor Parliament. Like most men who were born part of an inner circle, he vaguely resented others from the outside who were attempting to push their way in. As Archbishop Mathew remarks, "He early possessed a familiar intercourse with the great and a contemptuous knowledge of those who gained by devious paths the intimacy of politicians. The climber and the political middleman was a type distasteful to him; he was not a man who reined in his contempt."[33] Shortly after his election, the *Carlow Sentinel* for 7 January 1860 reported, some of Acton's Liberal supporters called on him in London. Presumably, these were the type of gentlemen immortalized as "Taper" and "Tadpole" in Disraeli's novels. Acton, who had only been in Carlow once in his life, failed to recognize them until they gave their names. After what must have been a desultory and awkward conversation, he politely bowed them out and bade them good morning.

There were constant complaints in the Carlow press (Liberal as well as Tory) that their M.P. paid almost no attention to his district. This, added to his independent voting policy, made it unlikely that the Carlow machine would want to renominate him. As it happened, in the election of 1865, the National Association of Ireland together with the Catholic hierarchy demanded that all candidates pledge themselves to support at least two parts of a three-point platform. Since Acton had always refused to give such assurances to his political associates, we may assume that this was the decisive reason why he chose to stand for an English constituency at the next election. He decided to enter his name at Bridgnorth, the nearest town to his family estate at Aldenham. The published accounts of the election campaign indicate that it was quite costly to Acton; he spent over 699 pounds, more than both his opponents combined. As in all elections, of course, no one knows how much was really spent.[34]

Acton was elected by one vote, but this victory does not seem to have been very welcome to him. He confided to Simpson that his greatest ambition was to get out of Parliament "in some honest way" and get back to his books. He obviously felt he would be disappointing his family and friends if he followed his inclinations and resigned from the House. In the following year his wish was at last granted, although perhaps not in just the way he would have preferred. As a result of a ballot scrutiny, Acton's one-vote margin vanished. Hansard for 22 March 1866 notes "that it was proved to the committee that the said Mark Philip Lee had been bribed with the payment of £4 by Charles Selby Bigge, under the pretext of travelling expenses; but that it was not proved that such bribery was committed with the knowledge and consent of the said Sir John E. D. Acton or his agents."

Although he stood again for Bridgnorth, he was defeated in 1868 and never again sat in the House of Commons. There is little doubt that he allowed himself to be pressured into a career that was not suited to his interests or talents. We must also conclude that both the mature Acton, with his rigorous standard of public morality and historical judgment, as well as the younger Acton, who so admired Burke, would never have condoned the half-hearted devotion to duty of the member for Carlow and Bridgnorth in the 1860s. The famous address of Edmund Burke to the electors of Bristol was certainly not unfamiliar to Acton: "It ought to be the happiness and the glory of a representative," he had said, "to live in the closest union, the closest correspondence, the most unreserved communication with his constituents."

The elevation of William Ewart Gladstone to the premiership in 1869, however, gave Acton the opportunity to keep one foot in public life without the disagreeable necessity of being concerned about constituents—a problem that has been the ruination of more than one otherwise brilliant statesman. In his first honors list in August 1869, Gladstone recommended Nathaniel Rothschild and two Roman Catholics for the peerage. One of these was a younger son of the duke of Norfolk, the other was Sir John Dalberg-Acton, eighth baronet, now to become Lord Acton, first Baron Acton. The queen refused to accept Rothschild* and only agreed to the two Catholics after much respectful persuasion on the part of the prime minister. Acton, he wrote to his sovereign, "is of the first order, and he is one of the most learned and accomplished, though one of the most modest and unassuming men of the day."[35] Granville also wrote to reassure the queen regarding this departure from the conventions of the constitution. Probably his most effective argument was the point that, if Archbishop Manning had any say in the matter, Acton would never receive any honor or

---

*Nathaniel Rothschild was the first Jew ever nominated for an English peerage (as Acton and Howard were the first Catholics proposed in centuries). Apparently merit will out, however, since Baron Rothschild took his seat in the House of Lords in 1885, with the public blessing of the queen and empress.

preferment.* In fact, Manning, writing to Gladstone in a rather injured tone in 1870, remarked, "I shall say no more about Lord Acton whose career has been a disappointment to his truest friends, not Catholics only. He might have done much in public life and among us."[36]

Acton's stepfather, Earl Granville, reluctantly agreed with the Archbishop's judgment. "I presume there is not Protestant or atheist whom Manning dislikes more than Acton," Granville wrote to Gladstone. "I am, however, afraid he may be right about the latter's public life. If anything will spur him into action it will be the knowledge of Manning triumphing in his not having done so."[37]

For a young man of thirty-five, a peerage in a premier's first honors list was a rare distinction. Gladstone's motives in recommending this early promotion were, as usual, mixed. Doubtless, personal friendship and genuine admiration for Acton's scholarly attainments played a large part as did party service and loyalty and the desire to keep the defeated M.P. in public life. A last factor might have been decisive in persuading Gladstone to nominate Acton some years before the usual time in such cases. The Vatican Council was to meet later in the year, and if Acton were to go to Rome with the title of Lord as a subtle indication of the favor in which he and his views (unofficially of course) were held by the British government, Gladstone had every reason to believe that his protégé's influence would be increased greatly.

*Manning and the queen were not on the closest of terms.

Notes

[1]Lord Acton, *Selections from the Correspondence of the First Lord Acton*, ed. John N. Figgis and Reginald V. Laurence, pp. 29-30.

[2]Ibid., pp. 28-29.

[3]Lord Edmond Fitzmaurice, *Life of . . . 2nd Earl Granville*, 1:227.

[4]Ibid., p. 262.

[5]Lord Acton, *The Correspondence of Lord Acton and Richard Simpson*, ed. Josef L. Altholz and Fr. Damian McElrath, 1:166 (hereafter cited as *Acton-Simpson Correspondence*).

[6]*Saunders Newsletter*, 3 May 1859.

[7]James J. Auchumuty, "Acton's Election as an Irish Member of Parliament," *English Historical Review*, LXI (1946): 394.

[8]*Carlow Post*, 11 June 1859.

[9]Fitzmaurice, *Life of Granville*, 1:387.

[10]Auchumuty, "Acton's Election," p. 401.

[11]David Mathew, *Lord Acton and His Times*, p. 20.

[12]Gertrude Himmelfarb, *Lord Acton: A Study in Conscience and Politics*, p. 90.

[13]*Rambler*, I (1859): 407. In a private note, Acton was even more damning: "He has not the instincts of a gentlemen . . . nothing handsome or chivalrous." Add. MSS. 5528. (See n.14 to chap. 1.)

[14]Acton, *Acton-Simpson Correspondence*, 1:6-7.

[15]Ibid., p. 7.

[16]Add. MSS. 5528.

[17]This analysis of Acton's ideas on political parties is derived from his own writings of the period and from an article by his coeditor Simpson on "The Theory of Party" in *Rambler*, I (1859): 332.

[18]John Acton, "T. E. May's *Constitutional History of England*," *Home and Foreign Review*, July 1863, p. 715.

[19]See Harvey C. Mansfield, Jr., *Statesmanship and Party Government: A Study of Burke and Bolingbroke* (Chicago: University of Chicago Press, 1965), p. 7.

[20]For his further excellent study of Acton in politics, see James J. Auchumuty, "Acton as a Member of the House of Commons," *Bulletin of the Faculty of Arts*, Farouk I University, Alexandria, vol. 5 (1950).

[21]*See* the editorial in the *North British Review*, 1 July 1869.

[22]Acton, *Correspondence*, pp. 198-99.

[23]Lord Acton, *The History of Freedom and Other Essays*, ed. John N. Figgis and Reginald V. Laurence, p. xxiii.

[24]Reprinted in Lord Acton, *Essays on Freedom and Power*, ed. Gertrude Himmelfarb, p. 196.

[25]*Home and Foreign Review*, April 1863, p. 635.

[26]Quoted in Acton, *History of Freedom*, p. xii.

[27]Acton, *Correspondence*, p. 185.

[28]Auchumuty, "Acton as a Member of the House of Commons," p. 8.

[29]Lord Acton, *Lord Acton and His Circle*, ed. Abbot Francis A. Gasquet, p. 291. (This letter will be published, presumably, in the third volume of the *Acton-Simpson Correspondence*.)

[30]Quoted in George E. Fasnacht, *Acton's Political Philosophy*, p. 184.

[31]Acton, *Acton-Simpson Correspondence*, 1:209.

[32]*Rambler*, September 1860, p. 295.

[33]David Mathew, *Acton: The Formative Years*, p. 4.

[34]Auchumuty, "Acton as a Member of the House of Commons," p. 5.

[35]John Morley, *The Life of William Ewart Gladstone*, 2:430.

[36]Fitzmaurice, *Life of Granville*, 2:17.

[37]Ibid., pp. 135-36.

5. The Vatican Council and Aftermath

Eighteen sixty-nine, the year in which Acton was raised to the peerage, marks the beginning of a five-year period of his life in which he unwillingly found himself constantly in the midst of passionate controversy. All the old quarrels with the hierarchy and the ultramontanes, which the young scholar wished to forget, were revived again in sharper and more bitter forms. These years, in fact, were to be a turning point in Acton's life; by 1875 he wearied of all politics, secular and sacred, and wished only to be left alone with his books, his family, and a few intimate friends.

Nine years previously, by 1860, it had become clear to Catholic and Protestant alike that the temporal power of the papacy, which had dominated central Italy and at times much more for over a thousand years, was in rapid decline. Italy was united except for the area around Rome guarded by French troops, and the new Kingdom of Italy under the House of Savoy was preparing to deprive Pius IX of the last remains of his worldly power. Acton, when a member of the House of Commons and an unofficial representative of British Catholics, made a half-hearted attempt to put the case for papal independence before the British public. (At that time he wrote to his collaborator Richard Simpson, "I am afraid I am a partisan of sinking ships, and I know none more ostensibly sinking just now than St. Peter's."[1]) Most Englishmen, however, preferred to see Rome the capital of a modern liberal monarchy than under the personal rule of a reactionary pope.

Pio Nono (as he was called) had once been described by Metternich as the one factor he had never contemplated—"a liberal Pope!" Ever since his maltreatment at the hands of Italian rebels in 1848, however, the reigning pontiff had become more and more ultramontane. In the *Syllabus Errorum,* published in 1864, the defiant Pius proclaimed that it was an error to assert that the Vicar of Christ can or should reconcile himself to "progress, liberalism, or modern civilization." As his earthly power waned, Pius IX stubbornly maintained his spiritual sovereignty. He canonized more saints during his reign than had all his predecessors for a century and a half. He proclaimed a new dogma in 1854: the Immaculate Conception of the Virgin Mary. Although there was a long tradition in the church that the Mother of God had herself been conceived without original sin, this pious belief had never been officially defined and was not regarded as an article of faith binding on all Catholics until the decree of 1854.

In 1867 it became known that an Ecumenical Council would be summoned to meet in the Vatican in December of 1869. It was well known that Pius IX was about to proclaim a second new dogma: that of papal infallibility. Acton reacted immediately; in the liberal Catholic journal *The Chronicle,* he expressed the view that the ultramontanes were once more attempting to concentrate power in Rome at the expense of the great body of the faithful.[2]

He also wrote, in October of 1869, a long review, entitled "The Pope and the Council," of a book of the same title published in Germany under the pen-name "Janus."[3] The author of this book was generally regarded to be Professor Döllinger. In this work, Janus-Döllinger presented (in full) the historical arguments in opposition to infallibility.

Not content with mere words, Acton set out for Rome and arrived in November of 1869. He immediately made contact with two influential opponents of infallibility. Lord Odo Russell was acting as unofficial representative of Her Majesty's Government at the council; he was, conveniently, the son-in-law of the foreign minister, Lord Clarendon, and the nephew of a recent prime minister, Lord John Russell. He was also, needless to say, a Protestant. His estimate of the key role his fellow Liberal peer was to play in the affairs of the council is given in a letter from Lord Clarendon to the British ambassador in Paris. "How right Odo has been throughout," the foreign minister wrote, "in declaring the Pope would end by having his way in all things. He has stood alone against all the representatives of the Catholic powers and all the opposition bishops plus Acton, who is worth them all put together."[4]

The second confidant of Acton in Rome was Johann Friedrich, theologian to the liberal Cardinal Prince Hohenlohe, brother of the prime minister of Bavaria. It was Acton and Friedrich who regularly sent on to Döllinger detailed information about the secret plans of the papal forces in the council. This maddeningly accurate stream of intelligence was published in the *Allgemeine Zeitung* under the pseudonym Quirinus and became known as the famous Quirinus Letters.

These letters revealed the internal politics of the council to the outside world. The wide varieties of pressures that were applied to the recalcitrant minority of bishops included threats of imprisonment, strict censorship of all documents pertaining to the work of the council, the banning of private meetings of more than twenty bishops, and the opening of letters by the ever-alert Roman Post Office.

In addition, the vast armory of papal privileges, titles, sees, and honors of all sorts was freely used by a pope determined to have his way.

Although the Quirinus Letters were sent to the publisher by Döllinger under that pseudonym, since they were based largely on information supplied by Acton, it is fair to say that they represent Acton's views and impressions while in Rome. The first letter will reveal how strongly Acton and his friends felt about the impending proclamation. (It should be remembered, however, that Acton strongly denied that he was Quirinus, and he stated several times that there were many things in the letters of which he did not approve.[5])

> Rome, December, 1869. The Council is opened. It is, we may say, in full swing, and the situation has to certain degree revealed itself. Two great questions are in every mind, and on every tongue—first: "Wherein will the freedom promised to the Council consist and how far will it extend?" and *secondly* "Will Papal Infallibility be erected into a dogma?" . . . The Spanish Prelates—men selected by Queen Isabella and the nuncio at Madrid, simply for their thorough-paced ultramontanism—pure absolutists in Church and State, would gladly see the new dogma ready-made at once, but they have to be restrained for a while. . . . That great ecclesiastical polypus, with its thousand feelers and arms, the Jesuit Order, works for it under the earth and on the earth. . . . And thus, if Papal Infallibility becomes a dogma, what inevitably awaits us is, that . . . the Jesuits will for the future be the regular stewards of this treasure, and the architects of the new dogmas we have to expect. It is enough to know the earlier history of the Society to know what this means, and what immense capital of power and influence it will place at their command. "Rulers and subjects"—that will henceforth be the relation between the Jesuits and the theologians of other Orders. . . .

Their Order is now really, and in the fullest sense, the
... breastplate of the High Priest—the Pope—who can
only then issue an oracular utterance when he has
consulted his breastplate, the Jesuit Order.[6]

On the first of January 1870 in a letter to Gladstone, Acton revealed his view that the coming proclamation of
papal infallibility was primarily a political and only secondarily a theological matter. In Acton's mind the essential problem was a growing centralization of power in the
Catholic Church, and Acton from principle opposed centralization wherever he found it—in a college, a nation, or
a religious institution. "We have to meet," he warned his
prime minister, "an organized conspiracy to establish a
power which would be the most formidable enemy of
liberty as well as science throughout the world. It can only
be met and defeated through the Episcopate, and the
Episcopate is exceedingly helpless."[7]

Several bishops of the United Kingdom, in what must
have seemed a response to Acton's letter to Gladstone,
presented a protest to the council on 15 March 1870.
English and Irish Catholics, they declared, were granted
the full privileges of citizenship in the United Kingdom
because of their solemn and repeated declaration that
their faith did not teach the dogma now being proposed for
adoption by the council. These declarations, they noted,
were made by the British bishops and were permitted by
the Holy See at that time, and these understandings were
the conditions under which British Catholics now held
seats in Parliament and other offices of the crown. The
bishops concluded that those promises could not be
forgotten or overlooked by themselves without dishonor.[8]

The French prelates, like their British colleagues, realized their essential helplessness in a council completely
controlled by their opponents. Archbishop Dubroy of Paris,
like most of the minority, saw that intervention by the

European Powers, especially the French and Austrian governments, was the only hope left. In the end, the Catholic nations declined to intervene, as did Protestant England. Much as Gladstone (who later wrote a pamphlet on this question) would have liked to have done something to assist the cause of the dissenters, he lacked support from the continental states and from his own cabinet and so was powerless. He had to let his friend Acton know that the minority bishops, like the Confederacy a decade previously, could expect no help from the British Empire.

The council dragged on through the long Roman summer, and more and more bishops, for various reasons, began to drift away. On 13 July, the preparatory vote was taken. Of the 764 bishops on hand at the height of the council, only about 680 remained; and of those, 88 voted *non-placet* (outright opposition), 62 voted *placet juxta modum* (acceptance with reservations), and about 80 or 90 more abstained despite their remaining in Rome. Thus barely half of the members of the council voted to give their unqualified assent to the new dogma.[9] As Acton was to point out, this was contrary to the historical practice of Ecumenical Councils, which normally required consensus or at least an overwhelming majority in order to define dogma. In the final session, on the eighteenth of July, only two dissenting bishops remained to hear the doctrine announced, record their *non-placets*, and then grant their obedience to the pope.

The important words that were promulgated that day are these:

> We teach and define that it is dogma divinely revealed: that the Roman Pontiff, when he speaks *ex cathedra*, that is, when in discharge of the office of Pastor and Doctor of all Christians, by virtue of his supreme apostolic authority he defines a doctrine regarding faith or morals to be held by the Universal Church, by divine assistance promised to him in

blessed Peter, is possessed of that infallibility with which the divine Redeemer willed His Church should be endowed for defining doctrine regarding faith or morals; and that therefore such definitions of the Roman Pontiff are irreformable in themselves, and not from the consent of the Church.[10]

It should not be forgotten that this great power was never employed by a pope in Acton's lifetime and has, in fact, been used only once: in 1950 Pope Pius XII solemnly proclaimed the doctrine of the bodily assumption of the Virgin Mary into Heaven. In the opinion of many theologians it was meant to be used and will only be used to define matters of speculative theology—such matters as the immaculate conception of Mary or the bodily assumption. In our own time (much as Acton predicted) the Second Vatican Council, called by Pope John, stressed the collegiality of all the bishops, including the bishop of Rome. In 1870, however, the new dogma was viewed very much in a political sense and sent repercussions throughout the Christian world. As someone observed, the bishops entered the council shepherds and came out of it sheep. Pope Pius had his spiritual supremacy, but many regarded it as a Pyrrhic victory; a few weeks after the proclamation, the French troops withdrew, and the army of the king of Italy marched into Rome.

Acton himself was now exhausted by the single most intense period of his long-standing struggle with the hierarchy of his church as well as by the oppressive heat of the Italian summer. He retired with relief to the coolness and tranquility of his beloved Tegernsee in the mountains of Bavaria. In England, Archbishop Manning rejoiced at the victory for ultramontanism, while Newman quietly deplored but submitted. His friend, Bishop Kenrick of St. Louis, wrote to Acton from America to offer what was a typical explanation for submission on the part of the minority. "I could not defend the Council or its action," declared the bishop of the western plains, "but I always professed that the acceptance of either by the Church would supply its deficiency."[11] This was a position substantially the same as Acton's own; the historian later told friends that his submission to the council's will was an act of pure obedience that he felt he owed the church and did not signify a change of heart.

Professor Döllinger was to be more intransigent. He wrote to his own archbishop in Munich stating that the decree offended him as a Christian because it went against Christ's warning against establishing a kingdom in this world; as a theologian, because it was opposed to the basic tradition of the church; as a historian, because it ignored the lessons of history on the dangers of universal sovereignty; and as a citizen, because it might well lead to a disrupting split between church and state. A few weeks after the letter was sent, Döllinger received his reply: he was excommunicated.

The following year, Döllinger and other recalcitrant priests and scholars met in Munich to issue their defiant "Declaration of Whitsuntide," which denounced the 1870 decree as illegal and affirmed once again their faith in the dogmas of the ancient church. This charter of the newly-founded Old Catholic Church carried Lord Acton's name as a signatory, but the English dissident stopped short of heresy and repudiated his "signature" as soon as he heard of it.

After this brush at the theological brink, Acton did his best to avoid further controversy and to settle down in his library to write relatively safe historical essays. In November of 1874, however, his hard-won peace was suddenly shattered by the publication of Gladstone's pamphlet, *The Vatican Decrees in their Bearing on Civil Allegiance.* During the council, when the *Schema de Ecclesia* was promulgated, Acton had unwittingly given a hostage to fortune when he wrote to the premier that "most assuredly no man accepting such a code could be a loyal subject or fit for the enjoyment of political privileges." This seed flourished in the Liberal leader's fertile mind and finally bore fruit in his pamphlet. The Vatican decrees, Gladstone argued in his usual persuasive manner, had altered the status of English Catholics, who had received emancipation in 1826 on the assumption that they were loyal citizens of the realm, but who were now obliged to transfer their primary allegiance to Rome.

Acton had tried to persuade his friend not to publish the pamphlet, but the day it reached the public, he wrote to the *Times* defending English Catholics while trying not to arouse the Curia too much. He was only partially successful in both these objectives.

Acton attempted to convince his fellow countrymen that Catholics had been as loyal historically as any other group of English subjects. He argued that some popes in the past, for various reasons, had sometimes promulgated canons that the average Catholic simply did not accept in practice. "I will explain my meaning by an example," he wrote.

> A Pope who lived in Catholic times . . . decided that it is no murder to kill excommunicated persons. This rule was incorporated in the Canon Law. . . . Again, the greatest legislator of the medieval Church laid down this proposition; that allegiance must not be kept with heretical princes. . . . This principle was adopted by a celebrated Council, and is confirmed by St. Thomas. . . . The *Syllabus* which you cite has assuredly not acquired greater authority in the Church than the Canon Law. . . . Yet these things were as well known when the oath was repealed as they are now. But it was felt that whatever might be the letter of the Canons, and the spirit of Ecclesiastical Laws, the Catholic People might be honourably trusted. . . . Whether there is more truth in your misgivings [Acton concluded] or in my confidence the event will show, I hope, at no distant time.[12]

The *Times* editorially described Acton as having treated the decrees as a "nullity." Archbishop Manning, realizing that this would be the general interpretation of Acton's letters, saw his long-awaited opportunity to humble the pride of a leader of the Catholic aristocracy that he, Manning, had always distrusted and to end what influence Acton had with the laity. The prelate demanded assurances from Acton that he had no heretical intent and asked him to explain clearly his exact position on the Vatican Decrees.

Acton's first letter (which is not now known to scholars) was apparently unsatisfactory since Manning immediately sent the following note.

> My dear Lord Acton, I have to thank you for your letter dated yesterday [15 November]: from which I gather, with much satisfaction, that your answer to my first question, whether in your letter to *The Times* you intended to repudiate the Vatican Decrees, is in the negative.
>
> I am not, however, able to gather what answer you desire to give to the second question, namely, whether you adhere to the doctrines defined in the Vatican Council: unless you intend to describe yourself as one of "those who adopt a less severe and more conciliatory construction" of those decrees.
>
> If I am right in this inference, I would still ask you to enable me to understand what that construction is.
>
> I see with great pleasure in your note that you had written an emphatic repudiation of the statements of *The Times*: and I regret much that any advice should have defeated your judgment of what is at this moment urgently needed for your own sake. Let me therefore ask you to enable me to reassure the minds of a multitude of those who at this time believe of you what *The Times* has sent all over the world.
>
> Believe me, my dear Lord, yours faithfully,
>   Henry E., Archbishop of Westminster[13]

Acton, of course, did not miss the meaning of the veiled threat in the silken line, "... what is at this moment urgently needed *for your own sake.*" He immediately consulted a few close friends and began to draft a reply. This first sketch has been published in Acton's *Correspondence* and is doubtless more revealing of the true state of the historian's mind than the letter he actually sent to Manning. (Lionel Kochan, in his *Acton on History*, maintains that the authentic Acton can be better comprehended from his not-for-publication notes than from his articles and public letters. Throughout most of his life, Acton was all too keenly aware that he was perpetually in a small minority no matter where he went and so tried to avoid controversy by constantly relying upon nuances or enigmatic subtleties. "His notes represent what he would like to have said, and his published works constitute what is blurred and incomplete."[14] Certainly in the case at hand, this assumption would seem to hold true.)

Acton's first draft is as follows (the words in brackets are alternative suggested phrases):

> My dear Lord, I gave no answer to the question, which did not seem to me to arise out of the terms or the spirit of my letter to Mr. Gladstone.
>
> But I must decline the inference which a passage of my letter of this last Sunday has suggested to you. I have no private gloss or special interpretation for the decrees of the Vatican Council [Trent].
>
> The acts of the Council are the law which I obey. I am not concerned [bound] to follow the comments of divines or to supply their place from [with] private judgements of my own. I am content to adhere implicitly with an absolute reliance on God's Government of his Church to the construction she herself shall adopt in her own time.
>
> *Command.* Submit accept.[15]

In the end, a more cautious, more conciliatory, and more

ambiguous letter was sent to the archepiscopal palace in
Westminster. Writing on 18 November from the Athenae-
um, Acton began once more with the familiar salutation,
"My dear Lord . . ." and continued,

> I could not answer your question without seeming to
> admit that which I was writing expressly to deny,
> namely that it could be founded on anything but a mis-
> construction of the terms of the spirit of my letter to
> Mr. Gladstone.
>
> In reply to the question which you put with
> reference to a passage in my letter of Sunday, I can
> only say that I have no private gloss or favourite inter-
> pretation for the Vatican Decrees. The acts of the
> Council alone constitute the law which I recognize. I
> have not felt it my duty as a layman to pursue the com-
> ments of divines, still less to attempt to supersede
> them by private judgements of my own. I am content to
> rest in absolute reliance on God's providence in His
> Government of the Church.
>
> I remain, my dear Lord, yours faithfully,
>
>   Acton.[16]

Acton's bland phrase that he did not feel it his duty as a
layman "to pursue the comments of divines" could not
have endeared him to a hierarchy that had been
fulminating against Acton's steady (and annoyingly
erudite) stream of comments on all manner of
ecclesiastical issues for the past two decades. Still, the
letter was not, on the face of it, evidence of heresy. On the
other hand, it was, to say the least, *restrained* in its submission to the authority of the Holy See.

Manning, as might be expected, was still not satisfied
and made clear his intention to refer the matter to Rome
for a final decision. Genuinely concerned that he might
suffer the blow of excommunication, Acton wrote a long
and earnest letter to his old friend Newman seeking his advice as a fellow devout Catholic who was also not an ul-

tramontane. This letter, which has only recently been published for the first time, was meant to be private, and Acton, as he often did in his notes to himself, explained his innermost thoughts on the decrees with a frankness that he did not dare permit himself in his public writings. For this reason, we have in this *private* statement convincing evidence that Acton did subscribe to the doctrine of development, that is, that the decrees, in God's own time, through the natural evolution of the church, would ultimately be interpreted in a more liberal spirit.

"I shall give myself a day or two to answer [the archbishop]," Acton wrote on 4 December from Aldenham.

> I will try to explain my position to you, if I may do so without presuming too much. The decrees have never been a difficulty to me not because I have ever examined them and found that they approved themselves to my judgement, but because, be they what they may, I am sure it will be all right, and if it is not evidently all right now, that is not my business. I take it that no interpretation holds that is inconsistent with tradition, and with former decrees. And if one does not see how the new and the old can be reconciled, time will show it, and the new will be digested and assimilated, and will be worked into what was there before. I feel no impulse to do this as well as I can for my own satisfaction, or to choose an interpreter. Indeed I have felt no more curiosity to read these decrees through than those of Trent, and know about them both only casually, imperfectly, and partly at second hand. Therefore, just as I have kept aloof from the Germans [Professor Döllinger and the others who signed the Declaration of Whitsuntide], who think that they ought to raise their voice and hand against the Council, I have gone through no process of study, comprehension and agreement with respect to the several propositions that it lays down. I take them in

the raw state, without the least resistance, subject to the process they have to go through, and to the law of interpretation which upholds the continuity and consistency of doctrine; but I do not guess what that process will effect, and do not attempt to apply the law myself. I am in the same condition with regard to hundreds of canons of former Councils; and I daresay you know how little most of us, native Catholics, care to master details. If therefore I am asked whether I accept the decrees with a definite understanding and inward conviction of their truth I cannot say either yes or no. But this is the question which the Archbishop—taking his letter and his pastoral together—wants an answer to. I certainly cannot satisfy him.

I hope you will understand that, in falling under his censures, I act from no spirit of revolt, from no indifference and from no false shame. But I cannot accept his tests and canons of dogmatic development and interpretation, and must decline to give him the only answer that will content him, as it would, in my lips be a lie. . . .

Acton then turned to his plan to circumvent Manning by making his peace with his own bishop.

Now the Archbishop is not my diocesan—I have neither house nor lodging in London—and my own bishop not only admits that I have said nothing contrary to Church or Council, but, when I thanked him for this recognition . . . he . . . acquiesced silently in the remark about my Catholicity. If I say this now, they may drive him into a corner. But it seems right to intimate that I have been in correspondence with my own bishop, and so decline the other jurisdiction. . . .[17]

Acton soon thereafter put into practice his proposal to Newman and wrote a much more friendly and natural letter to his own bishop, Brown of Shrewsbury, in which he

speaks more from the heart than from the head and substitutes Christian humility for noble pride.

"To your doubt whether I am a real or pretended
Catholic," he wrote,

> I must reply that, believing all the Catholic Church
> believes, and seeking to occupy myself with no studies
> that do not help religion, I am, in spite of sins and
> errors, a true Catholic, and I protest that I have given
> you no foundation for your doubt. If you speak of the
> Council because you supposed that I have separated
> myself in any degree from the Bishops whose
> friendship I enjoyed at Rome, who opposed the
> Decrees during the discussion, but accept them now
> that it is over, you have entirely misapprehended my
> position. I have yielded obedience to the Apostolic
> Constitution which embodied those decrees, and I
> have not transgressed, and certainly do not conscious-
> ly transgress, obligations imposed under the supreme
> sanction of the Church. I do not believe that there is a
> word in my public or private letters that contradicts
> any doctrine of the Council; but if there is it is not my
> meaning, and I wish to blot it out.[18]

Fortunately, Bishop Brown was content that his famous
parishioner was orthodox and a good Catholic in every
sense that mattered. Manning, however, was determined
that his old enemy should not slip through his fingers that
easily; on the recommendation of his theologians, he
referred the Acton correspondence to Rome.

In April of 1875, Acton was certain he would suffer the
same fate as his old professor, Döllinger. "It is simply at
the choice of authorities," he confided to Lady
Blennerhassett, "Pope, Cardinal, bishop or priest, when I
am excommunicated. . . . It can only be a question of
time."[19] He was convinced that the Curia and its supporters
had finally found the excuse they needed to rid themselves
of a longstanding thorn in their sides, and would take it,

after waiting long enough to put on a show of judicious and careful consideration.

Gladstone's attitude, however, was one of total unconcern; although for half a century a world symbol of liberalism, the premier was at heart an English country gentleman, and a remark about Acton's troubles with the hierarchy made a few years later illustrates his basic *sang-froid*. When someone suggested his old friend might be excommunicated, Gladstone reacted as though he were a young English captain staring down a thousand rebellious Afghans: "His work may be put on the *Index*; but that is all. They will never excommunicate an English peer."[20]

In the event, Gladstone was exactly right. Much as Manning and the pope would have liked to, they did not quite dare stir up a new storm when there was so little to be gained and so much in the way of world-wide good will to be lost. His own bishop was willing to vouch for his bare orthodoxy, and he was, after all, a layman. Better, thought the Curia, to let sleeping dogs lie.

Relieved that yet another unwanted controversy had quietly faded away, Acton resolved to return to Aldenham and take no more part in public life. That resolution, like many others, was easier to make than it was to keep.

Notes

[1]Acton to Simpson, 7 December 1859, Downside Abbey MSS., quoted in Fr. Damian McElrath et al., *Lord Acton: The Decisive Decade, 1864-74*, p. 30.

[2]Lord Acton, "The Next General Council," *Chronicle*, I (13 July 1867): 368-70.

[3]Lord Acton, "The Pope and the Council," *North British Review*, October 1869, pp. 127-35.

[4]Lord Clarendon to the British ambassador in Paris, 15 June 1870, quoted in *The Roman Question*, ed. Noel Blakiston, p. 445.

[5]Acton to Wetherell, 25 July 1970, Woodruff MSS., quoted in McElrath et al., *Acton: The Decisive Decade*, p. 24.

[6]Quirinus [Döllinger et al. (?)], "First Letter," *Letters from Rome on the Council*, pp. 59, 66, 74, 78-79.

[7]Lord Acton, *Selections from the Correspondence of the First Lord Acton*, ed. John N. Figgis and Reginald V. Laurence, p. 91.

[8]Lord Acton, *Letters of Lord Acton to Mary . . . Gladstone*, ed. Herbert Paul, pp. 54-55.

[9]Gertrude Himmelfarb, *Lord Acton: A Study in Conscience and Politics*, p. 106.

[10]Pastoral letter of Bishop Ullathorne of Birmingham, *The Council and Papal Infallibility: . . .* , October 1870 (London), quoted in David Mathew, *Lord Acton and His Times*, pp. 202-203.

[11]Frank Edward Lally, *As Lord Acton Says*, p. 108.

[12]Lord Acton, *Letter to the Times*, 9 November 1874.

[13]Acton, *Correspondence*, pp. 151-52.

[14]Lionel Kochan, *Acton on History*, p. 36.

[15]Acton, *Correspondence*, p. 153.

[16]Ibid.

[17]Acton to Newman, 4 December 1874, Birmingham Oratory MSS., quoted in McElrath et al., *Acton: The Decisive Decade*, pp. 113-14.

[18]Shane Leslie, *Henry Edward Manning*, p. 233.

[19]Acton to Lady Blennerhassett, 13 April 1875, Woodruff MSS., quoted in McElrath et al., *Acton: The Decisive Decade*, p. 118.

[20]Lionel Tollemache, *Talks With Mr. Gladstone* (London: Longmans, Green, 1903), p. 103.

6. Aldenham
and the History of Liberty

After his literally soul-rending experiences in Rome, Acton wanted nothing more than to settle down with his family and books (and a few close friends) in his country home at Aldenham Park. His most recent flare-up with the haughty Manning (after 15 March 1875, Cardinal Manning), culminating with the sword of excommunication hanging over his head for months, reinforced the historian in this decision.

Aldenham in Shropshire became his principal refuge, and he visited London only briefly while en route to his winter hideaway at Cannes. His wife's family home in Tegernsee, high in the Bavarian mountains, became his favorite resting-place in the fall. In these years Acton avoided controversy with the same determination that most students bring to avoiding study; for Acton at this time, the calmness of nature, his books, and his growing family were world enough.

Acton had married his younger cousin, the Countess Marie Anna Ludomilla Euphrosyne Arco-Valley, in the summer of 1865. Acton, who was then thirty-one, had known his bride of twenty-four since she was nine years old; they had grown up together when Acton was in Bavaria to study with Professor Döllinger. It was Marie's father, the Count Johann Maximilian Arco-Valley, who first brought Dr. Döllinger and the young Acton together.

As is often the case with the marriage of cousins, the match had been planned at least six years before by Acton's mother. When Lady Granville lay dying, Acton granted her last wish that he marry "little Marie." There is a note in Acton's handwriting that tells us of this deathbed promise. "Then she said," Acton recalls,

> —*Et la petite Marie*—partly as a question. I made them leave me alone with her, and asked: "*Si j'avais l'espoir d'épouser Marie, est-ce-que vous l'aimeriez?*" These words seemed to give my poor mother more pleasure than anything which happened during her illness. This was when she had asked most eagerly— *Est-ce vraisemblable?* and I answered: *Je l'ai désiré beaucoup depuis des années.* She was extremely agitated with the pleasure this gave her and seemed to have waited for it long.[1]

The marriage did not actually take place until six years later, which might have been because there was some hesitation on the part of one or both of the principals involved. It is more likely, however, that both families simply thought it best to wait until Marie reached a more suitable age. During this period, Acton was also traveling a good deal, working furiously editing journals, and standing for and sitting in Parliament. The delay, therefore, does not seem to be very important.

Until recently, none of the correspondence between Acton and his wife had been published, and previous biographies of Acton passed over with little comment his relationship with Lady Acton and their children.[2] At least one Acton student, in fact, has speculated that their marriage might not have been particularly happy. Lionel Kochan, in his *Acton on History*, writes that

> ... it does not seem to have been a happy alliance. Acton was by character far too interested in ideas and the outside world to be much given to introspection. The very rare passages of this sort amongst his notes are thereby of enhanced significance. In a confused way, one such note speaks perhaps of an unhappy family and married life. Acton asks: "May one resist the state? Or cashier a king? Or be husband of two wives? Or deceive a questioner? Or keep a slave? Or torture a prisoner? Or burn a witch? Or go to King Lear? Or back one's opinion?"[3] It is apparent that his family life was not able to console him for the isolation of his later years.[4]

There seems, however, little evidence to support this conclusion and considerable reason for believing that Acton was indeed happy in his family life, despite his troubles with the outside world. Acton made it a practice to write to his wife almost every day when they were separated and to send a telegram on those days when he could not manage his usual, fairly long letter.

During his engagement, for instance, Acton made a visit to Italy and sent his fiancée a letter from Naples beginning, "My own dear Love." He went on to say that "I sent off an imperfect letter to you this evening in order to save tomorrow's post. I had set down my conversation with the Cardinal because I should like, if possible, to make my correspondence with you a tolerably complete journal of all I see and hear and do." The letter was signed, "Your affectionate, J. Emerich."[5]

The next day, Thursday, 2 February 1865, he wrote, "My dearest Marie, ... When I came home from Mass this morning they brought me your dear despatch. It was very sweet to know that you were thinking of me, and I thanked you, Darling, a thousand times. Only two more days now, and my Love will be in my arms."[6] Another time, when he was uncertain as to her itinerary, he wrote to apologize for having "left you for several days without any news of myself, or one word of love."[7]

Acton did not, like so many husbands, become less attentive as courtship and the first years of marriage gradually faded into a more settled existence. Five years after their wedding he was still writing almost every day to "My own sweet Love" and sending a telegram when the press of work did not allow for a full letter.[8]

Nor would it be accurate to conclude that their relationship was a limited one; it is doubtless true that Marie Acton was not a scholar in her own right, but she seems to have shared her husband's interests and friendships as much as any wife and probably more than most. Two months before his wedding, Acton wrote to "My own dearest Marie" assuring her that she was

> the one joy, the supreme blessing, of my life, and that the sweetest occupation of each day is to look back upon the past times spent with you, and forward to the happy future which you will fill. Your admirable soul becomes continually better known to me; and the more clearly I see, the more confident and rejoiced I am in thinking of a life whose welfare will be part of your own, and so much your work.[9]

All in all, Acton and his young bride seem to have been well matched; they both came from deeply religious and cosmopolitan backgrounds. Although her father was Bavarian, Marie's mother, the Countess Anna Margareta Maria Pelina Marescalchi, came from one of the leading Italian families. More important than that, Marie's mother (as we have seen) was a second mother to the young Acton; he said many times that his happiest moments were spent with the Arco-Valley family and friends at Tegernsee.*

---

*Acton's relationship with Countess Anna Arco is indicated in Chapter Two, "Education and Travel." *See* pages 24-25.

Of Acton's six children, two unfortunately did not survive childhood. His eldest daughter, Mary Elizabeth, was born in August of 1866 and married, relatively late in life, Edward Herbert of an old Monmouthshire family connected to the earls of Pembroke. Mary Elizabeth died in 1955—the longest-lived of Acton's immediate family.

A second daughter, Annie Mary, was born in the fall of 1868.

Richard Maximilian was the third child (born in Bavaria in 1870) and the eldest son and heir to the title. He took up a career his eminent father had often considered but never actually entered, diplomacy. After serving with distinction in the First German War (as old-fashioned Englishmen still call it), he represented the king in several European nations, turning to advantage his unusual background.*

Acton's second son and namesake, John, was born in May 1872 and died in infancy ten months later.

A fifth child, Elizabeth Mary, suffered the same unhappy fate at the age of seven in 1881. Acton's deep faith sustained him at her bedside; he comforted her with the words, "Be glad, my child, you will soon be with Jesus Christ."[10] Afterwards, he wrote to his friend Mary Gladstone that "She has taken with her one of the strongest links that attached me to this world. . . ."[11]

The youngest daughter, Jeanne Marie, was born in 1876;

---

*Having been born in Bavaria (a fact of little consequence in a time now lost to the world forever), Richard Maximilian was officially declared a British subject by Act of Parliament in 1911. He had, of course, entered the House of Lords as the Second Baron Acton in 1902. Unlike his father, he was not turned away by Cambridge and studied at Magdalene College before entering the diplomatic service. In the war he was decorated with the French Legion of Honor and received a knighthood, the KCVO. He followed in his father's footsteps in one other respect: he was a Lord-in-Waiting to King Edward VII and to King George V. Richard Maximilian's eldest son, the Third Lord Acton, eventually moved his family to Rhodesia. The Hon. Richard Acton (great-grandson of the historian) studied at Trinity College, Oxford, where he and the author met when they were both members of the Oxford Carlton Dining Club.

her life also was destined to be cut short at the relatively young age of forty-three.

Besides his own family, Acton was fortunate to enjoy the friendship of at least two remarkable women. Charlotte von Leyden, who came from the same circle of aristocratic German Catholic families as did the Arco-Valleys, has been described as "perhaps Acton's closest friend."[12] He often spoke of her as one of the cleverest women he knew[13] and referred to her in a letter to Marie Acton as "the beautiful Charlotte."[14] Herself a historian of some note, she also shared Acton's interest in the liberalization of the Catholic Church. In 1870 she married one of Acton's parliamentary colleagues, Sir Rowland Blennerhassett, Liberal M.P. for Galway City.*

At one time he chided her for being too verbose in her writing (a fault some would lay at his own door!). "You observe the golden rule [in your biography of de Staël]," he wrote, "to state no fact without stating the evidence. But there is a silver rule, to give no unnecessary evidence."[15]

The letters of "his Egeria"[16] to Acton, sometimes in French, sometimes in English, were written in a more personal style than was most of his correspondence. It is clear that they had a warm and sympathetic relationship. Upon his death, she wrote three detailed and laudatory obituaries.

Mary Gladstone, another young woman with wide interests in religion, literature, and politics, was close to Acton from the time they first met at her father's country home in 1878 until her relatively late marriage to the Rev. Henry Drew in 1886. Acton was forty-six and Miss Gladstone thirty when they began to correspond regularly;

---

*Lady Blennerhassett was the author of studies of Madame de Staël, George Sand, Cardinal Newman, and Talleyrand. She also contributed two chapters to Volume X of *The Cambridge Modern History*: Chapter II, "The Doctrinaires" (a school of early nineteenth-century French liberals) and Chapter V, "The Papacy and the Catholic Church."

the prime minister's daughter was a reserved young woman, generally preferring the company of books to young men.[17] She had had one of those romantic flirtations with dashing young men that Victorian ladies liked to reminisce about in the sunset of their lives. In Mary Gladstone's case, it happened in Rome when she was visiting that city with her father, Lord Acton, and other friends. The young man was the handsome marquis of Lorne, eldest son of the duke of Argyll, who was not content with a premier's daughter but went on to marry a princess of Great Britain.[18]

Acton, as is well known, became a great admirer of Gladstone and saw in him almost the ideal statesman; it was quite natural, therefore, for him to become a good friend of the Liberal leader's unmarried and intellectually minded daughter. Doubtless, Acton took the opportunity in some of his correspondence to subtly pass on an idea or a proposal to the head of the government, but there seems little doubt that their friendship was long-lasting and sincere. David Mathew in his *Lord Acton and His Times* explains Acton's friendships with a few women by implying he liked sometimes to have someone he could talk down to (one would think enough men were available for that purpose, especially in Parliament and the Church). "It was part of Lord Acton's social gifts," Mathew writes, "that he could easily gain the interest of women. He had a didactic turn and therefore did not need the conversation of equals. He loved to *teach*, whether it was Mary Gladstone or his own daughters."[19]

Anyone who reads Acton's lengthy correspondence with his wife, his mother-in-law, and women relatives and friends (in which he frequently solicits their advice on a variety of subjects) may judge for himself whether Acton found as many equals in one sex as in the other.

On the other hand, it would be decidedly premature to enroll Acton among the pioneers of the movement for women's liberation. In a letter to Gladstone written from Cannes in 1891, Acton showed himself no more enthusiastic about women's suffrage than he was almost forty years before in Boston when he reported hearing someone "half-mad" call for votes for women.* Although in most respects Acton gradually shed his Burkean garments to walk in the unencumbered purity of liberalism as he grew older, he insisted on retaining one last conservative fig leaf: the exclusively male suffrage. His excuse for this exception to his general policy, ironically enough, was that women were mostly Tories!

He did concede that male-dominated society has often denied equal opportunity to women; he refers to them as "the perpetual victim of man." All things considered, however, he did not see female suffrage as a liberal principle. "It now seems to me," he told Gladstone,

> that there is no higher law deciding the question and that it falls within the computations of expediency. As I believe that the votes of women will be mainly Tory, I do not feel bound, by any superior consideration, to sacrifice the great interest of party.
>
> If it can be shown that the majority of women will probably be Liberal, or that they will divide equally, I should say that the balance is, very slightly, in favour of giving them votes.

Acton hastily added that liberalism's Grand Old Man must think his motives sordid. He was concerned, he said, about recent setbacks of the Liberal party (the coming loss of Irish seats, the inevitable retirement of its leader, etc.); these, he thought, must be counterbalanced if the Tories were not to become the permanent government. "A few years ago," he wrote, "[party advantage] would not have weighed with me against the necessity I thought I saw of

*See Chapter Two, "Education and Travel," page 36.

redressing the balance of power in favour of the perpetual victim of man."[20]

If Acton thought that he had earlier in his life favored women's suffrage, his memory must have been at fault. Obviously, he opposed it in his youth. On 30 March 1884, he wrote to Mary Gladstone that "I think women's suffrage an evil in many ways. Girls and widows are Tories, and channels of clerical influence, and it is not for them so much as for married women that your argument tells. If we ever have manhood suffrage—dissociating power from property altogether, it will be difficult to keep out wives. The objections to voting wives are overwhelming."[21]

If Acton's normal defense of minorities, of the weak against the strong, of Catholics, Jews, the poor, and others lacking in power to protect themselves, lapsed when it came to women, it is only fair to recall that few men of prominence (with the exception of John Stuart Mill) were arguing for women's rights until after the turn of the century. Indeed, the fact that in 1891 he was willing to consider seriously giving them the vote probably put him ahead of his time even among liberals.

In any event, Acton certainly did not view women (as did many men of that time or other times) as inherently inferior to his own sex. He corresponded with many women on all sorts of serious subjects, discussed his (and their) articles with them, and shared his extensive collections of books with them as well as with his male friends. Lady Blennerhassett remarked, in fact, that her greatest joy in visiting Tegernsee or Aldenham was to visit Acton's books —next to Lord Acton himself, of course.

The three country houses to which Acton retreated all were well stocked with books: Tegernsee had about 4,000,[22] Cannes somewhat less, and Aldenham held about 60,000 though some estimates went as high as 80,000 volumes or more.[23]

Acton had begun collecting books from an early age. His schoolboy letters are full of requests for money for books and more books. His stepfather, Lord Granville, half-complained in 1859 that Johnny Acton was filling the house with books. "I can hardly open a book," he wrote, "without finding marks or notes of his."[24]

Acton continued to scribble notes in the margins of his books and papers throughout his life. One of his librarians later wrote that

> seen among his books, so familiar to him that they appeared to be not mere bundles of paper and leather, but sentient realities, he was a never-to-be-forgotten figure. His knowledge of books ... was so complete that he never seemed to be speaking of dead and forgotten writers but of living persons. . . . His industry was colossal, and equalled by the rapidity with which he read. Knowing so much, he had the art of only look-ing for that which was new to him. Nearly every volume of his collection bore his special marks—a pencil tick to indicate a salient fact, and a thin slip of paper for a point of more importance.[25]

A large papal and Italian library was acquired at the Libri sale in 1860; in the same year, the death of Lady Granville brought Acton the ancient and valuable Dalberg collection; a year later, one of his favorite professors at the University of Munich, Ernst von Lasaulx, bequeathed his library of ancient literature and philosophy to the student who was sure to care for it. Over the years, the library at Aldenham grew steadily. When he was in the House of Commons, Acton told a fellow M.P. that he already had 30,000 volumes.[26]

Acton's books, as Gibbon said of the scrolls of one of his Romans, were decidedly for use, not ornament. He said himself that there were no fine copies, unless by accident. One friend said of the rooms in which they were housed that they had none of the charms of a library. "It was rather a gigantic bookstore, in which its owner could always find what he wanted, but which would never have suggested to the ordinary man the idea of a studious leisure."[27] Acton always urged students to beware of being seduced by the merely aesthetic; most of his books were in the cheapest paper editions available. At one time, he had many of them bound at eighteenpence a volume.[28]

They were not arranged in any imposing manner in some grand ballroom, such as the duke of Marlborough's leather-bound, gold-stamped library at Blenheim Palace. A visitor would receive the impression he was entering a jumble of shabby rooms overcrowded with the books of thirty or forty professors. On the left of the entrance hall was Acton's study—his desk, library catalogue, bibliographical works, indexes of manuscripts from a dozen countries—his working tools. Next was a kind of inner hall, a billiard room, in which on the left side were English, Scottish, Irish, and Colonial history, and that of the United States. On the right were arranged histories of the various kingdoms and dukedoms of the German Empire. Above was a gallery. Two drawing rooms, one large and one small, were on the right of the entrance hall; on their shelves were English, French, Italian, and German belles-lettres. Acton estimated that only about one in a hundred of his books could be called "light literature." Most of them were in ecclesiastical history, philosophy, theology, and modern European history, especially French, German, and Italian. Although probably more than half of Acton's books bore some relation to the church, not all of them would have gladdened the eye of a parish priest. Acton's own chaplain, Father David Williams, wrote to his bishop in 1883 that "I could say a great deal about the library here, which I prefer not to write. It is easy to trace a particular line of reading. The marks left are very numerous—Against the Jesuits—The Temporal Power—*Crimen Sacerdotium* etc. etc."[29] Less than a tenth of his books were in the English language, since Acton was concerned with accumulating books that were not readily available elsewhere in England.

Manuscripts and copies of original documents filled the next anteroom—many from the Vatican and Venetian diplomatic archives. After this, a visitor finally entered the library proper, a vast room with tall French windows opening onto a formal garden. It was in this room, which included an iron gallery, that the bulk of the collection was kept. On the left side were Greek and Latin classics, and on the right, the Fathers of the Church. There was a large alcove assigned to the many Italian states. French history dominated the end of the room directly across from the entrance.[30]

A single example may give an idea of the extent and thoroughness of this "scholar's monument" as it has been called. When this vast array of scholarship was catalogued for the Cambridge University Library (where it now forms a proud part), one section alone, political philosophy, was found to consist of 286 pages of titles. At least forty-five of these works refer to one author alone, Machiavelli. Editions of *The Prince* in several languages from every century from the sixteenth to the end of the nineteenth are included.[31] Nor was this a particularly favorite book of Acton's; this complete collection of almost all major works of a leading political thinker as well as important studies of his thought was representative and by no means exceptional in the Acton Library.

Seeing the extent of the raw materials brought together by Acton has compelled more than one observer to ask why the historian did not publish more of his own work. A friend of John Morley, for instance, left Aldenham feeling not elated but depressed. ". . . He beheld the most pathetic sight of wasted labour that ever met human eyes," Morley reports, the most impressive of all testimony to the vanity of human life. There were shelves on every subject [the friend noted]—Renaissance Sorcery—the Fueros of Aragon—Scholastic Philosophy—the growth of the French Navy—American Exploration—Church Councils—and many books were full of hundreds of cross-references in pencil, noting passages bearing on some particular development or evolution of modern life or thought. There were pigeonholes, cabinets, with literally thousands of compartments, into each of which were sorted scores of little white papers with references to some particular topic. . . . It is better to have produced one solid monograph on the minutest point—better to have edited a single Pipe Roll or annotated a single short Chronicle—than to have accumulated for forty years unwritten learning that goes down to the grave and is lost.[32]

Although this is by no means an uncommon criticism, even a cursory review of Acton's work would lead one to conclude it is unfounded. It is perfectly true that Acton never published a book in his own lifetime. Indeed, he published only a few articles under his own name; most appeared anonymously or signed with initials.* By the age of forty, however, he had published over four hundred reviews and short articles in serious journals with a high standard. In addition, his substantial scholarly essays filled over a thousand pages of print. Most of these essays, in fact, were fare more pregnant with insight than were most of the leading historical works of the day; Acton was to receive four honorary doctorates on the strength

---

*Acton's entry in Who's Who (based on information supplied by him) curiously mentions only one lecture in print. The unusually brief biography (only seventeen lines compared to fifty-two for the almost forgotten novelist Arthur William A'Beckett) reads, in part: "Publication: Lecture on the Study of History, 1895. Owned about 7,000 acres." For the full entry see note 33.

of these specialized articles. At the end of his life, the bibliography of his published works came to 32 closely printed pages. About four hundred and fifty titles comprise his "Complete Works." About eighty of these are major essays or lectures, the rest short reviews covering a wide range of subjects. Exclusive of correspondence, these published works would come to over five thousand pages and, if in book form, would easily equal ten volumes. Acton's letters, many of which are minor essays on historical or political problems, already comprise six published volumes, with more to come at this writing. The rich supply of papers in the Woodruff archives alone will in due time account for at least a dozen volumes. In short, there will someday be a "Complete Works of the First Lord Acton" consisting of upwards of fifty volumes of some four hundred pages each.

One of the first of a series of grand projects conceived by the young Acton was a "History of the Popes." After his return from his studies in Europe in the late 1850s, Acton devoted a considerable amount of his time to research on what was planned to be a definitive work on the medieval and early modern papacy. An extensive article entitled "The Political System of the Popes" was published in three installments in the *Rambler* in 1860-61. The great work was never finished; Acton's attention instead turned to America, and he resolved to write a history of the origins of the American Constitution, comparing it with the democracies of the ancient world. The result of this research was an article, "The Political Causes of the American Revolution," which appeared in the *Rambler* in 1861 and which favorably attracted the attention of Gladstone. Acton's interest in America continued throughout his life. In 1866 he delivered a lecture on the meaning of the American Civil War to his neighbors in Bridgnorth, and over the years he wrote reviews of books on the Great Republic of the West, including a study in

1889 of Bryce's *The American Commonwealth.* The *magnum opus* on the American Constitution, however, never appeared. An enterprising scholar someday may collect Acton's writings on the United States (which come to about two hundred pages and which have mostly not been published in book form) in one volume with some such title as *Lord Acton on Democracy in America.*

In 1863, Acton returned to German history and published an edition of some recently discovered manuscripts thought to have been written by Frederick the Great of Prussia as advice on the art of ruling. In an essay for the *Home and Foreign Review* (January 1863), he defended the authenticity of *Les Matinées Royales, ou l'Art de Régner,* which had aroused a storm of controversy in Prussia. The Crown Princess of Prussia wrote to her mother, Queen Victoria, to complain of this libel on the great king's reputation. As it turned out, Acton was almost certainly mistaken. In a private letter to Douglas Woodruff, G. P. Gooch (one of Acton's former colleagues and a biographer of Frederick) wrote that the king ". . . only wrote the two *Testaments* described in my book. The *Matinées* are ignored by biographers because they are a fake—one of many such concoctions in the eighteenth and early nineteenth centuries. . . . We must remember that Acton was writing before the vast (and still unfinished) *Politische Korrespondence* began to appear."[34] One might add that Leopold von Ranke, perhaps the greatest of German historians, was also taken in.

Acton also considered attempting a major study of James II and VII, the last Catholic king of England and Scotland. In 1862, he wrote for the *Home and Foreign Review* a fascinating (and incomplete) investigation of the eldest son of Charles II—a mysterious man who was apparently a bastard fathered by Charles with an unknown high-born lady while he was in exile in Jersey. Ten years later, Acton published an edition of *The Letters of James II to the Abbot of La Trappe*. Again, however, the major work was never finished.

One of Acton's favorite interests was federalism. On several occasions he contemplated devoting a number of years of his life to exploring in depth this solution to a perennial political problem. "Nationality," perhaps his most important political essay, was published in 1862 and periodically a review or short essay on this subject was written. But Acton never did for federalism what Tocqueville did for democracy.

A series of volumes on the Reformation—telling the whole truth based on original manuscripts—suggested itself. Acton was admirably, almost uniquely, equipped to complete this task. A brilliant and thought-provoking essay, "The Protestant Theory of Persecution," duly appeared in the *Rambler* (March 1862). Seven years later, "The Massacre of St. Bartholomew" was published in the *North British Review* (October 1869), and in 1877, "Wolsey and the Divorce of Henry VIII" was written for the *Quarterly*. Dozens of reviews touching on the Protestant Revolt also were written over this thirty-year period. Manuscripts were collected, copied, read, annotated, and edited, including Nicholas Harpsfield's *Narrative of the Divorce of Henry VIII* (1887). Although the above-mentioned work would have been enough to secure a reputation for most historians, and probably a chair and an LL.D., it was still, when all is said and done, not the grand panorama of the Reformation that Acton was fully capable of creating.

At least three other significant challenges attracted Acton's attention. He had always been fascinated by the use of power, and Machiavelli (even more than Frederick the Great and his spurious testaments) was a man from whom much could be learned. As noted above, Acton collected no less than forty-five editions of *Il Principe* as well as dozens of books and countless manuscript materials related to sixteenth-century Italy. This would have been a study worthy of his talents; in the end, however, Acton contented himself with writing a twenty-one-page introduction to L. A. Burd's edition of *Il Principe* (1891).

A massive study of Döllinger's life and work also beckoned Acton for years. In the end, he wrote a forty-four-page article (as always, filled with ideas others could pursue) for the *English Historical Review*.[35]

It will become apparent, from the recital of all these "great works" seriously planned by Acton at one time or another, that the famous *History of Liberty*—the "greatest book never written"—was simply one (although the most famous) of a series of aborted enterprises. Mary Gladstone, after hearing Acton discuss his *History* in fascinating language, wrote, with some exasperation, "It is extraordinary the way he tingles with it to his fingers [sic] ends and yet can sit patient and quiet over wife and children and wait and wait another year before writing it. What an extraordinary man."[36] A few years later, Acton began to call his unfinished work the "Madonna of the Future"—after the artist in the Henry James story who devoted his life to a single painting: after his death, the canvas was found to be blank.

Historians and biographers since the 1880s have speculated about why Acton who "loved liberty with all the ardour of Milton, and investigated it with all the science of Locke"[37] never completed the work to which, directly or indirectly, he had devoted most of his life. A wide number of explanations have been offered, most of which do not stand up under examination.

Miss Himmelfarb has suggested that Acton was hesitant to be as morally strict in his *History* as he believed he ought to be. She advances the theory that Acton was reluctant to step upon as many cherished values as he would have to in such a work.[38] Mr. Kochan agrees with this thesis: "In a word," he writes, "the reason why Acton did not write his 'History of Liberty' lay in his lack of courage to affront a hostile world unaided."[39]

If Acton's inability to finish projected designs was due to his dislike for controversy, then how are we to explain his many articles and short reviews that certainly aroused the antagonism of large numbers of churchmen and politicians? It can hardly be maintained that Acton avoided controversial subjects; on the contrary, despite his professed dislike of argument, almost all of his writings are polemical. On the other hand, we have to ask how this theory would explain his putting aside a major history of the American Constitution. Surely, that would not have aroused much animosity toward Acton in nineteenth-century England. Or the great work on "Federalism" that never appeared—this was hardly a subject that would lead men to walk out of clubs when Acton entered. When he first came to the *Rambler*, he told Simpson, "I have much to say about Burke," and it is well known that the ideas of Burke dominated his thought at that time. One might reasonably have expected this to mean a series of important articles. In fact, Acton eventually wrote a five-page book review of Thomas Macknight's *History of the Life and Times of Edmund Burke*.[40]

Other historians have speculated that Acton never finished the *History* because he could never definitely decide what were the causes of the French Revolution—or more generally, that he could never complete what he regarded as sufficient research to enable him to write with authority. As it happens, his lectures on the French Revolution at Cambridge University do provide definite views on its origins. It is true that Acton read more widely and in more languages than most historians before beginning to write, but the plain fact that he *did* write a large amount of presumably adequately researched material would seem to weaken this theory.

Other students of Acton have suggested that his break with Döllinger so shattered his life that he could not concentrate on historical work. The quarrel with Döllinger, however, reached its height in 1883, some time after Acton cheerfully acknowledged that he would never write a book about liberty. Another possibility is that personal tragedy (the loss of his son in 1873 and of his daughter in 1881) not unnaturally interfered with his research. While all of the factors mentioned doubtless *affected* his writing of the great history, none of these theories account for the half dozen or so *other* grand designs begun at *other* times and similarly never completed.

The simple answer that Acton was lazy or was incapable of putting his thoughts on paper will hardly do either; we have seen that his published writings (not counting his voluminous correspondence) came to 5,000 printed pages in his lifetime. If he had concentrated this great effort into one ten-volume work, he clearly could have finished it.

Can we not solve the Riddle of Acton by concluding that he was one of those brilliant and insightful scholars whose multitude of interests were insufficiently disciplined by an orderly sense of priorities? Most of our best scientists and scholars have asked themselves what it is that they can do well; preferably, what they can do best; ideally, what *only* they can do—and then have devoted most of their energies to that one isolated task. The result, of course, has been new knowledge and, perhaps, progress. Acton's talents and interests were by no means limitless. By his own admission, Acton knew little of science, practically nothing of economics, surprisingly little of philosophy, and not very much of the non-European world. His interest in art, music, and literature was minimal to say the least. The extensive bibliography of his own works reveals that he had passionate interests to which he turned again and again. These were modern French, German, Italian, English, and, to a lesser extent, American history. He was well versed in medieval history, but less so in the classical era. Throughout all his historical work, he sought to throw light on the relation of the individual to God; at least half of his published work directly concerns the place of religion in society.

Acton was far more cosmopolitan and more wide-ranging than his peers in the historical profession. If he had devoted as much of his energies to any one subject (even a broad one) as Edward Gibbon did to the Roman Empire, as John Motley did to the Dutch Republic, or as Henry Adams did to the early United States, we could have confidently expected a work in the first rank of histories.

I myself believe that Acton never seriously planned to write a *History of Liberty.* He surely knew himself well enough by his fortieth year to realize that he was a man who seized upon a passionate interest for several months or a year, wrote an incisive essay on the subject, and then went on to another problem to be approached for an equally short time with an equal amount of enthusiasm. Were it true that he was serious about finishing the *History,* he would have felt too guilty about his lack of progress to joke about it as openly as he did: "The Madonna of the Future." At one time he referred Mary Gladstone to page 50,000 of his great work . . . wherein would be discussed the Revolution of 1688.[41]

Moreover, if Acton were serious about writing a multi-volume *History,* there would certainly be among his papers or in his letters some plan of the work. No such plan has been found. The nearest approach to such an outline is a curious notebook with lines numbered up to 11,000 and with a title entered here and there.[42]

There is little use in lamenting that Acton never wrote the *History of Liberty* or another major work. What he *did* do was to provide his contemporaries and all future readers of his works with a rich vein of ideas from which they may extract nuggets at their leisure. As was often said of Tocqueville and Burke, books can be and have been written from one of his paragraphs. Acton was above all a great teacher, and the greatest teachers are those who can inspire their students to go beyond what they themselves have learned.

Anyone who reads Acton's two essays "The History of Freedom in Antiquity" and "The History of Freedom in Christianity" will immediately see that the grandness of the language is equaled by the pregnancy of the thought. How many volumes could be written as commentaries on the opening paragraph of the former?

> Liberty, next to religion, has been the motive of good deeds and the common pretext of crime, from the sowing of the seed at Athens, two thousand four hundred and sixty years ago, until the ripened harvest was gathered by men of our own race. It is the delicate fruit of a mature civilization; and scarcely a century has passed since nations, that knew the meaning of the term, resolved to be free. In every age its progress has been beset by its natural enemies, by ignorance and superstition, by lust of conquest and by love of ease, by the strong man's craving for power, and the poor man's craving for food. During long intervals it has been utterly arrested, when nations were being rescued from barbarism and from the grasp of strangers, and when the perpetual struggle for existence, depriving men of all interest and understanding in politics, has made them eager to sell their birthright for a pottage, and ignorant of the treasure they resigned. At all times, sincere friends of freedom have been rare, and its triumphs have been due to minorities, that have prevailed by associating themselves with auxiliaries whose objects often differed from their own; and this association, which is always dangerous, has been sometimes disastrous, by giving to opponents just grounds of opposition, and by kindling dispute over the spoils in the hour of success.

No obstacle has been so constant, or so difficult to overcome, as uncertainty and confusion touching the nature of true liberty. If hostile interests have wrought much injury, false ideas have wrought still more; and its advance is recorded in the increase of knowledge, as much as in the improvement of laws. The history of institutions is often a history of deception and illusions; for their virtue depends on the ideas that produce and the spirit which preserves them, and the form may remain unaltered when the substance has passed away.[43]

Acton has been accused by some scholars of using a simplistic definition of liberty, or using "freedom" as a meaningless "hurrah-word," or making an idolatrous god out of liberty—that is, worshiping liberty as the highest of all values.[44]

Anyone who reads Acton carefully will have difficulty coming to this conclusion. In the first place, he defines liberty very precisely:

By liberty I mean the assurance that every man shall be protected in doing what he believes his duty against the influence of authority and majorities, custom and opinion. The State is competent to assign duties and draw the line between good and evil only in its immediate sphere. Beyond the limits of things necessary for its well-being, it can only give indirect help to fight the battle of life by promoting the influences which prevail against temptation—religion, education and the distribution of wealth.[45]

Acton makes it quite clear that, by liberty, he does not mean the power to do whatever one chooses, regardless of God, of one's own conscience, or of society. His use of the phrase "every man shall be protected" presupposes an organized, indeed mature, society that encourages right actions and discourages wrong deeds—and that protects persons in their rights from malefactors. He is equally concerned to protect individuals who are honestly following an *informed* conscience (which he thought was "the audible voice of God, that never misleads or fails"[46]) from both tyrannical rulers or mob rule. He recognizes explicitly that the state's role is *protection* of the person in his rights and, in an advanced society, the state should remove obstacles to the full development of each citizen's potentialities. That is, the role of the state is to encourage the school and church and other private institutions in helping individuals to *realize* their liberty in the full sense of the word.

"Liberty," Acton went on to write, "is not a means to a higher political end. It is itself the highest political end. It is not for the sake of a good public administration that it is required, but for security in the pursuit of the highest objects of civil society, and of private life."[47]

Acton, of course, was choosing his words carefully. He said liberty was the highest *political* end, but he goes on to stress that only through liberty, through individuals exercising their free will, can one expect to have a virtuous and just and enlightened society. It is liberty that makes the full development of humanity possible. Politics—the state—is the means to an end. On reading "The History of Liberty in Antiquity" and his other writings, it becomes reasonably clear that Acton knew precisely what he meant when he spoke of liberty. Far from making a god of "liberty," Acton was certain in his own mind that "the rights of man on earth are the consequences of the rights of God in heaven."

In a larger sense, of course, all of Acton's writings can be read as forming a large and continuous "History of Liberty"; this was the goal and the passion that informed most of his work, and this profound concern for the freedom of the individual conscience is above all what Acton has to teach us today.

Notes

¹Add. MSS. 4862. (See n.14 to chap. 1.)

²A number of valuable letters of Acton to his wife have recently been published by Fr. Damian McElrath, O.F.M., in collaboration with James Holland, Ward White, and Sue Katzman, *Lord Acton: The Decisive Decade, 1864-1874* (Louvain: Publications, Universitaivas de Louvain, 1970).

³Add. MSS. 5645.

⁴Lionel Kochan, *Acton on History*, pp. 24-25.

⁵Acton to Marie Arco-Valley, Woodruff MSS., quoted in McElrath et al., *Acton: The Decisive Decade*, pp. 57-58.

⁶Ibid., p. 58.

⁷Ibid., p. 60.

⁸Ibid., p. 91.

⁹Ibid., p. 65. A photograph of Lady Acton appears opposite page 572 in the first volume of Johann Ignaz von Döllinger, *Briefwechsel mit Lord Acton, 1869-1870*, ed. Victor Conzemius.

¹⁰Lord Acton, *Letters of Lord Acton to Mary . . . Gladstone*, ed. Herbert Paul, p. lxxv.

¹¹Ibid., p. 209.

¹²Kochan, *Acton on History*, p. 28.

¹³Acton, *Letters to Mary Gladstone*, p. 141.

¹⁴Acton to Marie Acton, Woodruff MSS., quoted in McElrath et al., *Acton: The Decisive Decade*, p. 93.

¹⁵Lord Acton, *Selections from the Correspondence of the First Lord Acton*, ed. John N. Figgis and Reginald V. Laurence, p. 270.

¹⁶Egeria was a nymph, one of the four Camenae, who was the intellectual companion of the Roman king Numa Pompilius.

¹⁷Mary Gladstone once asked Acton to write out for her a list of the one hundred most significant books. This list is given in one of her own works, *Some Hawarden Letters*, published in 1917. Lord Acton's letters to Mrs. Drew (as she became) were published in 1904 after being edited by their mutual friend Herbert Paul. This volume was dedicated by "M.D." to Lady Acton. Mrs. Drew's *Diaries and Letters* appeared in 1930, and her book *Acton, Gladstone and Others* was published in 1930. After Acton's death, she wrote an admiring essay on his contributions to liberalism,

entitled "Lord Acton's Legacy to Liberals," for the *Optimist* (III [1908]: 34-39).

[18]David Mathew, *Lord Acton and His Times*, p. 172.

[19]Ibid., p. 250.

[20]Acton, *Correspondence*, p. 235.

[21]Acton, *Letters to Mary Gladstone*, p. 294.

[22]Acton, in an undated letter to Viscount Bryce, once invited him to visit Tegernsee. It is "by the side of a beautiful lake," he wrote, "with splendid mountains of six or seven thousand feet to scale, and endless walks in the forest. There is a villa there belonging to my kinsfolk, in which I have three or four thousand volumes at your service. It is only two hours from Munich." Bryce MSS., Acton Papers in the Bodleian Library, Oxford.

[23]Mountstuart Grant Duff, *Out of the Past*, 2:192.

[24]Lord Edmond Fitzmaurice, *Life of . . . 2nd Earl Granville*, 1:358.

[25]H. L. Tedder, "Lord Acton as a Book Collector," Bibliographical Tracts, 1894-1905, British Museum (no pagination), published in *Proceedings of the British Academy*, I (1903-4): 285-88.

[26]Duff, *Out of the Past*, 2:193.

[27]Ibid., p. 192.

[28]Ibid., p. 193.

[29]Father David Williams, 10 February 1883, Shrewsbury Diocese MSS., quoted in Mathew, *Lord Acton and His Times*, pp. 240-41.

[30]Tedder; see n.25 above. The description of the Aldenham library is based also on a letter from Acton to "Mr. Gladstone" (as Acton always addressed him) outlining the library's contents. The letter, dated 23 May 1890, is published in Acton, *Correspondence*, pp. 232-33.

[31]Frank Edward Lally, *As Lord Acton Says*, p. 188.

[32]John Morley, *Recollections of Viscount Morley*, 2:234.

[33]The *Who's Who* entry for Acton (from *Who Was Who*, 1897-1916) reads as follows.

Acton, 1st Baron (cr. 1869), Sir John Emerich Edward Dalberg-Acton, Bt.; cr., 1643; K.C.V.O.; cr. 1897; D.C.L., LL.D.; Professor of Modern History, Cambridge, from 1895; Royal Commissioner on Historical MSS,.; Trustee, British Museum;

b. Naples, 1834; *S.* father, 7th Bt., 1837; *m.* Countess Marie Arco-Valley, 1865. *Educ.* Oscott, under Cardinal Wiseman; Munich, under Dr. Döllinger, Lord-in-Waiting to Queen Victoria till 1895; M.P. Carlow, 1859-65; Bridgnorth, 1865-66; Romanes Lecturer, Oxford, 1901. *Publication:* Lecture on the Study of History, 1895. Owned about 7000 acres. *Heir:* s. Richard Maximilian Dalberg-Acton. *Address:* Aldenham Park, Bridgnorth. *Club:* Athenaeum. (*Died 19 June 1902*).

[34]G. P. Gooch to Douglas Woodruff, published in Lord Acton, *Essays on Church and State,* ed. Douglas Woodruff, p. 474.

[35]Lord Acton, "Döllinger's Historical Work," *English Historical Review,* V (October 1890): 700-744.

[36]Diary of Mary Gladstone Drew, 8 October 1879, in *Mary Gladstone (Mrs. Drew) Her Diaries and Letters,* ed. Lucy Masterman, p. 173.

[37]Acton, *Letters to Mary Gladstone,* p. 64.

[38]Gertrude Himmelfarb, *Lord Acton: A Study in Conscience and Politics,* pp. 145-46.

[39]Kochan, *Acton on History,* p. 33.

[40]Lord Acton, "Thomas Macknight, *History of the Life and Times of Edmund Burke,*" in *Rambler,* IX (April 1858): 268-73.

[41]Acton, *Letters to Mary Gladstone,* p. 101.

[42]Add. MSS. 4867.

[43]Lord Acton, "The History of Freedom in Antiquity," *Essays in the Liberal Interpretation of History,* ed. William H. McNeill, pp. 243-44.

[44]E. D. Watt, "Freedom as an Incantation: The Example of Lord Acton," *Journal of Politics,* 25 (August 1963): 461-71.

[45]Acton, "Freedom in Antiquity," p. 245. Acton offered many definitions of liberty in many of his works, but all are essentially the same, and none (I believe) contradicts the definitions I have quoted. When he was younger, for instance, he wrote to Simpson, "All liberty consists in . . . the preservation of an inner sphere exempt from state power—That reverence for conscience is the germ of all civil freedom. . . ." (5 January 1862, published in Lord Acton, *The Correspondence of Lord Acton and Richard Simpson,* ed. Josef Altholz and Fr. Damian McElrath, 2:251.) In his later years, while a professor at Cambridge University at the end of the century, he declared that a free government must be "so exer-

cised that the individual shall not feel the pressure of public authority, and may direct his life by the influences which are within him and not around him." (Lord Acton, *Lectures on the French Revolution*, ed. John N. Figgis and Reginald V. Laurence, p. 33.)

[46]Lord Acton, *Lectures on Modern History*, ed. John N. Figgis and Reginald V. Laurence, p. 31. Acton also said, it must be noted, that the idea the conscience was *infallible* was "indefensible." The questions under discussion here are not, of course, those that can be answered with a pat phrase or a neat system.

[47]Acton, "Freedom in Antiquity," p. 263.

7. Politics and Morality

The years between 1870 and 1895 were for Acton a time of self-doubt, unhappiness, and even failure. His hopes, so long nourished, of a diplomatic career or cabinet post were, in the end rewarded with little or nothing. His intermittent dream of a great work of history was never to be more than that. From 1878 to 1885 he published nothing at all, save for one review. He quarreled more and more with his friends; his ties to Döllinger and Newman almost (but not quite) reached the breaking point. He suffered the death of two of his children. He was forced to sell much of his property and even his great library. We have seen that from 1870 to 1875 his very salvation (in his own view) was at stake; he only narrowly escaped excommunication at the hands of the hierarchy of his own church. His political party, which he came more and more to regard as not merely a party but a means to *earthly* salvation, regarded him as a well-meaning but rather exotic Germanic scholar.

The happy days that were to come at Cambridge near the end of his life were unimaginable to the bewildered and besieged Acton of the 1870s and 1880s. His goal in life, of course, had never been to become a professor. Given his political interests and his family connections, he always assumed he would one day sit in the cabinet or at least fill a major diplomatic post.*

His own father, Sir Ferdinand Acton, had been in the diplomatic service of Naples, and his stepfather, Lord Granville, had been foreign minister of Great Britain. A close friend was prime minister of his own country; another friend and relative was prime minister of Italy (Marco Minghetti). He was on close terms with the crown princess of Prussia and with the royal families of Bavaria and Württemberg. It seemed *natural* that he should represent Her Majesty at one of the German or Italian courts.

Besides a natural desire to make a name in the political field, Acton was doubtless somewhat anxious for a dignified position that carried a salary. If we recall that he had not yet in his life earned any money (the appointment to Cambridge would be accompanied by a small stipend)—he gave more money to the publications he was associated with than he received—it will explain his necessity to rent out Aldenham and to sell his family estate, Schloss Herrnsheim, in 1879. Later he was unable to continue to retain his family chaplain, and in 1890 he was so hard-pressed that he even had to put up his library for sale. Fortunately, Gladstone secretly arranged for Andrew Carnegie to buy Acton's collection with the proviso that Acton would keep it for his lifetime. Acton never knew who his benefactor was, and after his death, the books were given to the Cambridge University library where they now remain. A major cause of Acton's financial troubles was his refusal to touch any money from his

---

*Assumed is the proper word. Born as he was into the ruling class, he neglected to notice the rising tide of meritocracy that made it almost impossible for a Liberal government especially to give high political positions to persons without the requisite political service if not qualifications.

grandfather, the prime minister of Naples. He believed these gains to have been ill-gotten through bribery and corruption.

Acton was, in fact, seriously considered for a number of embassies and legations. In 1871, after the struggle in Rome was finished, Odo Russell wrote to Lord Granville saying that Acton ought to be appointed to the vacancy in Berlin, an embassy "for which he is more admirably qualified than any man living."[1] As it turned out, however, Russell himself was appointed the ambassador to the new German Empire.

With Russell's death in 1884, Lord Acton was again considered for the post. He had been somewhat instrumental in easing Franco-German relations after the war and had, on other occasions, used his wide-ranging contacts throughout Europe to help the cause of peace. Lord Granville wrote to Gladstone on 26 August 1884 that

> the Crown Princess [eldest daughter of Queen Victoria who had married the future Kaiser Frederick III] ... would prefer Acton but I told her that it would be impossible and [I] believed almost equally for a person unconnected with him to put him over the heads of the whole Corps Diplomatique.
>
> That it was quite on the cards that he might be as good as Ampthill [Odo Russell was created Lord Ampthill]—but that he had never done any official business and that he had neglected to distinguish himself in Parliament.[2]

Gladstone replied a few days later that "I am sorry you should be precluded from considering Acton."[3]

This appointment, as before, was kept within the circle of experienced diplomats, and Sir Edward Malet was translated from Brussels to Berlin. At the beginning of Gladstone's last premiership, Acton essayed one final attempt at a foreign mission. He suggested himself for the legation at either Munich or Stuttgart (the capital of

neighboring Württemberg). He wrote to his friend in a dif-
fident, half-humorous manner: "I may of course fairly say
that there are no complications between this country and
Bavaria [although part of the German Empire, the
Kingdom of Bavaria proudly maintained a Foreign Office
until 1918] that would give me any opportunity for mis-
management; and I not only know Germany pretty well,
but I enjoy a measure of favor with the Royal Family. You
will laugh, but it is a fact due to family and social connex-
ions."[4]

Acton must have been disappointed that the man he
always called "Mr. Gladstone" did not feel able to reward
his friend with a political post. He never allowed this fact
to diminish one iota the almost unlimited admiration he
felt for the Grand Old Man of British politics.

In a letter to Mary Gladstone in 1880, Acton was un-
stinting in praise of her father:

> [Future generations of Englishmen will] say that Chat-
> ham knew how to inspire a nation with his energy,
> but was poorly furnished with knowledge and ideas;
> that the capacity of Fox was never proved in office,
> though he was the first of debaters; that Pitt, the
> strongest of ministers, was among the weakest of
> legislators; that no Foreign Secretary has equalled
> Canning, but that he showed no other administrative
> ability; that Peel, who excelled as an administrator, a
> debater and a tactician, fell everywhere short of
> genius: and that the highest merits of the five without
> their drawbacks were united in Mr. Gladstone.[5]

Warming to his theme, Acton went on to write that
Gladstone's only fault was that he was too virtuous and
honest himself to understand or deal with the sordid
motives of lesser men. He admitted that there were other
men who could equal or surpass Gladstone in particular
talents. Hamilton and Cavour, he thought, accomplished
work as great; Turgot and Roon were unsurpassed in ad-

ministrative skill; Clay and Thiers were as able parliamentarians; Berryer and Webster could equal his oratory; and Guizot and Radowitz came close to him in fullness of thought. But Acton believed that "in the three elements of greatness combined, the man, the power and the result—character, genius and success—none reached his level."[6] In other letters, Acton asserted that Gladstone had no peer among modern statesmen with the possible exception of Edmund Burke. "I admit of no comparison [of Mr. Gladstone]," he wrote, "except with the Burke of 1770-80."[7] And later, "It is impossible not to be struck by the many points of resemblance between Burke and your father—the only two men of that stature in our political history—but I have no idea whether they would have been friends or bitter enemies."[8]

Acton in the 1880s had thus come almost to reverse his opinion of Gladstone and Burke. In his youth, Acton had been uncritically enthusiastic about Burke and restrained, to say the least, in his estimate of Gladstone. He had told Pope Pius IX on a visit in 1857, for instance, that Gladstone's ambition had made him useless and that he was unsafe in foreign affairs.[9] Acton changed many of his important ideas as he grew older. He used to be tolerant of the social and economic conditions that led to slavery in certain countries: in 1863 he even published a pamphlet entitled *Human Sacrifice* in which he argued that we ought not to condemn people of other places and other times who practiced, in good faith, ceremonies that we could not fully understand.[10]

Perhaps partly because of a feeling of guilt about his earlier lack of unyielding moral principles and his past willingness to consider extenuating circumstances, Acton became, in his later years, a unbending moralist. He became, as he himself put it, a "hanging judge." He could no longer tolerate the least compromise, the least allowance for human weakness, the least concession to differences of time or place. He reversed the usual process of idealistic, puritanical youth gradually giving way to moderation and tolerance with the onset of maturity and responsibility. Whatever the reasons for his sharp change of attitude, Acton's conversion to rigorous standards of judgment was certainly hard on his friends.

His intellectual mentor, the man to whom he once confessed he owed everything—Professor Döllinger—wrote a preface for an article commemorating the recent death of Bishop Dupanloup (11 October 1878). The article, published in the February 1879 issue of *Nineteenth Century*, itself was written by another of Acton's closest friends, Lady Blennerhassett, and the subject of the obituary was Acton's old teacher from his schooldays in France. Acton was shocked and angry that Döllinger could praise Dupanloup who, although regarded as among the more liberal bishops, nevertheless defended the Syllabus of Errors and submitted to the infallibility decree. Acton's reaction in this manner is the more difficult to understand since Döllinger had been excommunicated for his failure to submit, while Acton himself had satisfied his bishop as to his orthodoxy.

In a mood of complete pessimism, Acton wrote, "Men are always divided on more points than they know of. Time brings on occasions that bring out their differences. Every colleague of to-day is a future opponent, if he only lives a few years."[11] Acton concluded that his old master preferred to ascribe wrongdoing to ignorance rather than to evilness. "It suited his way to distribute blame so that nobody suffered. . . . Folly, stupidity, ignorance, moral cowardice, the deceived conscience, did duty as long as possible. . . . [He preferred] to trace the gradual growth of things, so that no one was really responsible."[12]

After a continuous argument over this issue for five years, Döllinger finally concluded that he and Acton would simply have to agree to disagree. As Acton himself put it, in 1883 Döllinger "made it very clear that it was time for our conversations to cease, for this world."[13] Acton may well have been indulging in a weakness for over-dramatization here, however. It is more likely—in fact probable—that Döllinger simply meant there was little point in further discussing an issue they had both explored fully. Döllinger and Acton continued to meet every summer in Tegernsee from 1884 to 1889, the year before Döllinger's death.

It does seem to be true, nonetheless, that Acton took their disagreement very seriously and regarded it at least as a kind of intellectual break. Acton wrote to Lady Blennerhassett in 1886 that "I have lost the key to his [Döllinger's] mind, and find myself in outer and increasing darkness. And I often ask myself the question whether with your penetration, you have not got beyond the difficulty which is disabling me for all useful and definite work. . . ."[14]

Although it seems clear that Acton was plagued by self-doubt—he was by no means certain that his quest for certainty was the right course—his (unreasonable) argument with Döllinger was hardly an isolated incident. He excoriated other friends of many years' standing who had written something he held to be deliberately false. He wrote to Döllinger in 1882 calling Cardinal Newman a "brutal liar" and an "artful deceiver" who was doing "the devil's work."[15] The previous year, Newman had made an obviously joking reference to an article of Richard Simpson's in which Simpson had attacked Pius V. "I don't wonder at a saying which I heard reported of a Dominican," he wrote to Acton, "that he would like to have the burning of the author."[16] Several years later, Acton recorded a number of times in his notes that Newman had told him a Dominican wanted to burn Simpson and he, Newman, approved of the idea.[17]

There seems little doubt that Acton had a weakness for hyperbole and was inclined to make dramatic statements that he would not, upon reflection, have stood by. He was reconciled to Newman before the Cardinal's death in 1890, for instance, and often spoke movingly of him. Five years later, he gave his favorite daughter a Christmas present of Newman's complete works—which he would not have done if he *really* believed him to be doing the devil's work.[18]

At about the same time he was writing to Lady Blennerhassett describing the papacy as "the fiend skulking behind the Crucifix,"[19] he could also write to his daughter (on 14 August 1880) enjoining her against thinking ill of others—"not only wishing them well, but judging them favourably, making out the best case for them one can, understanding that others are wiser and better than ourselves, and have reasons for what they do beyond what strangers discover, who see only the outside."[20]

Twenty-two years later in his last days, Acton was to give the same advice to his son. Fifteen years earlier he had written to his fiancée along similar lines: ". . . you must learn that men who think seriously for themselves, and earnestly study great questions, never entirely agree with each other and know how to make allowances for such differences."[21]

It may well be that at least on the question of how rigorously moral standards should be applied to the holders of *ideas* (such as Döllinger or Newman, as opposed to men of action, such as Napoleon or Alexander VI), Acton was always of two minds throughout his life; that there were never two Actons (early and late), but rather one Acton who was forever torn within himself.

It was this very agonizing indecision and complexity of personality that made him an insightful historian, but that, on the other hand, disqualified him for a serious role in practical politics. One of his closest friends once wrote to Arthur Russell, a Liberal leader, about Acton's potential role in a Liberal government. Lady Blennerhassett began by saying that no one admired his intellect more than she did and no one had more reason to be grateful to him. "But as for politics," she went on,

> I believe in nobody who in regard to them has not assumed an open, direct and personal responsibility. There is no such thing as politics in an armchair and the most wonderful knowledge of books is no help toward the knowledge of men. In that way, and with due sense of his superiority in other ways, I think that Lord Acton is at the beginning of his experiences in life and not in a position favourable to the experiment. There is perhaps nothing more dangerous than being fenced in morally by a hedge of superior specimens of the race, as for example, the Athenaeum Club, and then proceeding to judge or legislate for mankind standing behind the hedge.[22]

This estimate of Acton's character (from a most friendly source) doubtless explains why he was always the politician *manqué* and never the ambassador or cabinet minister. Acton himself once wrote that "the best political thinkers, often very poor politicians." He appended to this line several names, including Turgot, Burke, and Webster. He might have added Tocqueville, John Stuart Mill, and, of course, one other.

Acton's last attempt to secure political office occurred during the forming of the last Gladstone administration in August 1892. It appears that Gladstone was inclined to have Acton in the cabinet but on reflection did not think the possible gain was worth the certain risk. The chancellorship of the Duchy of Lancaster (which carried almost no responsibilities) was mentioned for Acton, but opposition within the Liberal leadership immediately arose. Sir William Harcourt, Lord Spencer, and Lord Rosebery were opposed on the grounds that Acton lacked prior experience and would simply be a certain vote for Gladstone. John Morley, who was a good friend of both Gladstone and Acton, was also opposed, probably because he saw himself as the chief intellectual and personal friend of the premier in the cabinet and was not anxious for a rival.

At this point Gladstone may well have come to the conclusion that in view of his position in the Liberal Party he could have insisted upon the appointment of one personal friend to the cabinet (assuming he had some qualifications); but if Gladstone were to use up some of his political "capital" to do so, there was no guarantee that the highly moral Acton would support his premier even most of the time. To any reasonable politician the difficulties clearly outweighed any possible gains.* And Sir Algernon West was delegated to explain to Acton that there was no room for him in the new cabinet.[23]

There was, however, to be a consolation prize. Acton was offered the post of Lord-in-Waiting to Queen Victoria. The position was not as trivial as it might sound at first; Acton would spend a month at the court attending to ceremonial duties, but his principal task would be to represent the government in the House of Lords on Irish matters. He was what would be termed today a minister of state for Ireland, directly under the secretary of state for Ireland, who at that time was John Morley. So he was in reality a member of the subcabinet. In addition, Ireland at that time was a major problem in British politics—a situation that seems to be a constant factor in the British

---

*In private letter to the author, Professor M. R. D. Foot, who is currently editing the *Gladstone Diaries*, was kind enough to share his views on this point. "My own opinion," he writes, "is that Mr. G. was very fond of Acton as a man—far fonder than of any other Catholic, save his own sister Helen—and a great admirer of him as an historian. But, given the current difficulties with Rosebery, it was clearly impossible to force an outsider on the diplomatic service at head-of-legation level; and what reason other than personal friendship had Gladstone for giving high office to a man of no tact, slight political experience, and no administrative ability?" (Letter to author, 27 January 1969). The same arguments, of course, would hold for the cabinet post.

political equation. From all accounts, Acton fulfilled his duties, if not with zeal, at least with competence and genuine concern for an island with which he had many ties. He was, of course, a strong supporter of Home Rule and an opponent of imperialism in general. He quickly let it be known that he was a "Little Englander" and wished that his own nation would withdraw as soon as possible from both Ireland and the Afrikaner republics in South Africa.

Although the Queen-Empress did not agree with Acton on political questions, she seems to have liked him well enough personally. She described him in one of her journals as "a charming person with such pleasant manners (rather foreign) very like his mother the late Lady Granville (a widow, daughter of the last Duke of Dalberg) who was so agreeable and clever. . . ."[24]

The Queen prided herself on her minute knowledge of the genealogies of the multitude of small German courts where many of her relatives had come from or many of her descendants now were. Since Lord Acton was one of the few persons at Windsor who shared in this interest to any degree, the Queen quickly became rather fond of her learned but undeniably aristocratic courtier. She bestowed upon him her highest praise when she told a friend that she wished "Prince Albert could have known him."

As might be expected, Acton spent most of his time in the library at Windsor Castle where he said there was much "literature" (which he regarded as mere amusement) but on the whole a poor selection: ". . . this is not," he wrote to his friend Viscount Bryce, "an intellectual place."[25]

After three years of answering questions on Ireland and greeting visitors to Victoria's court, Acton was finally to be relieved of his political duties. In 1895 he was to leave Windsor for another Crown appointment, but this time to "an intellectual place."

The Queen did not forget him, however. In 1897 on the

occasion of her Diamond Jubilee, his sovereign, with a more personal interest than usual, created Lord Acton a Knight Commander of the Royal Victorian Order.

Notes

[1]Paul Knaplund, "Letters from the Berlin Embassy, 1871-4, 1880-5" (*Annual Report of the American Historical Association,* II, Washington, D.C., 1947), p. 47.

[2]William E. Gladstone, *The Political Correspondence of Mr. Gladstone and Lord Granville, 1876-86,* ed. Agatha Ramm, 2:236.

[3]Ibid., p. 244.

[4]Acton to Gladstone, 1 October 1892, Additional Manuscripts 44094, British Museum, London.

[5]Lord Acton, *Letters of Lord Acton to Mary . . . Gladstone,* ed. Herbert Paul, pp. 141-42.

[6]Ibid., p. 147.

[7]Ibid., p. 182.

[8]Ibid., p. 97.

[9]Herbert Butterfield, "Journal of Lord Acton: Rome 1857," *Cambridge Historical Journal,* III (1946): 199.

[10]For Acton's views on slavery, see the *Home and Foreign Review,* October 1863, p. 719. The pamphlet *Human Sacrifice* was published by Robson, Levey, and Franklyn in London, probably in 1863. A copy is in the British Museum. An excerpt is quoted in Frank Edward Lally, *As Lord Acton Says,* p. 221.

[11]Add. MSS. 4939. (*See* n.14 to chap. 1.)

[12]Ibid., 4908.

[13]Ibid., 5403.

[14]Lord Acton, *Selections from the Correspondence of the First Lord Acton,* ed. John N. Figgis and Reginald V. Laurence, p. 269.

[15]Acton to Newman, 16 June 1882, Woodruff MSS., cited in Hugh MacDougall, *The Acton-Newman Relations: The Dilemma of Christian Liberalism,* p. 149.

[16]Newman to Acton, 7 June 1861, Woodruff MSS., cited in MacDougall, *Acton-Newman Relations*, p. 149.

[17]Add. MSS. 4988, 4989.

[18]Acton to Gladstone, 28 January 1895, Additional Manuscripts 44094, British Museum, London.

[19]Acton, *Correspondence*, p. 56.

[20]Acton to his daughter Mary, 4 August 1880, Add. MSS. 4863 (19).

[21]Acton to Marie Arco-Valley, June 1865, Woodruff MSS., cited in Fr. Damian McElrath et al., *Lord Acton: The Decisive Decade, 1864-74*, p. 66.

[22]Lady Blennerhassett to Russell, 3 September 1886, Blennerhassett Papers, item 52, envelope 1, Cambridge University Library, Cambridge, England.

[23]Sir Algernon West, *Private Diaries* (London), pp. 38-43.

[24]Queen Victoria, *Letters of Queen Victoria*, ed. G. E. Buckle, 3rd series, vol. II (London: John Murray, 1931), p. 188.

[25]Acton to Bryce, Viscount Bryce Papers, Acton Letter Book, no. 74, Oxford University Library, Oxford, England.

8. Lord Acton at Cambridge

Lord Acton reached the height of his career as a historian when, in 1895, he was inaugurated as Regius Professor of Modern History in the University of Cambridge, one of the two most distinguished chairs in Acton's principal field of scholarship.

Almost all of his life was spent as an amateur historian; his first academic post did not come to him until the relatively advanced age of fifty-six. In 1890, Acton was appointed one of two honorary fellows of All Souls; the other honorary fellow was Acton's sponsor and old friend, William Ewart Gladstone.

(An invitation to dine at All Souls then, as now, was highly prized. Some of the most brilliant men and best conversationalists in the country were among its fellows, and cabinet ministers, generals, bishops, ambassadors, dukes, and the editor of the *Times* were frequent guests at its high table. Part of its distinction was due to the fact that it had somehow managed to achieve Platonic perfection as a college . . . it had no students. Its complement of dons was a bit inbred, however; as late as the 1850s, two-thirds were descendants of the family of the founder, Archbishop Chichile.)

When the Regius Professorship, which as a crown appointment is in the gift of the prime minister, fell vacant in 1892, Gladstone did not take the opportunity to nominate Acton; instead, he recommended a "safe" appointment, Sir John Seeley, known as a defender of straightforward "political" (kings and battles) history. The precise reason why Gladstone was reluctant to elevate the respected but unorthodox Acton is not known; we may guess that he was sensitive to the charge of personal favoritism and that he had sincere scruples about appointing a Roman Catholic, however close a friend, to what was meant to be an Anglican chair.

When the professorship was next vacant, upon the death of Sir John Seeley in 1895, there was a new prime minister, Lord Rosebery, who was known to be considering Acton. "My first thought," one of the Cambridge dons wrote, "was, if they are good to us they will send us Acton."[1] Although not widely known to the general educated public (Acton had written almost nothing for publication under his own name), he was regarded almost with awe among professional historians.

Among men whose learning would stagger the average scholar, Acton was looked upon as an oracle, a living encyclopedia. More than once, Gladstone would table a particularly abstruse point in theology or history with the remark, "We must ask Lord Acton." Viscount Bryce, himself the author of a dozen works in history, philosophy, and jurisprudence, once invited Mandell Creighton (the historian-bishop, author of a history of the popes), Robertson Smith (probably the leading Semitic scholar in Britain), and Lord Acton to a dinner party. "The conversation," Bryce later wrote, "turned first upon the times of Pope Leo the Tenth, and then upon recent controversies regarding the dates of the books of the Old Testament, and it soon appeared that Lord Acton knew as much about the former as Dr. Creighton, and as much about the latter as Robertson Smith."[2]

Another friend, H. A. L. Fisher (who was to sit with Bryce in the cabinet), once wrote that Acton "probably read and annotated more printed matter than anyone who has ever lived."[3] For all his vast erudition, however, it remained true that Acton had no earned degrees, not even a B.A. He had never published a book, and only a few essays had appeared under his name. In addition, he was both a Roman Catholic with many continental connections and an outspoken English liberal. His approach to history, emphasizing ideas rather than politics, was unorthodox; his scholarly style and methods were decidedly Germanic. Besides all of these negative factors, Acton himself was reluctant not only to push himself forward but even to accept the chair if it were to be offered.

The new prime minister had in fact written to Gladstone on 20 October of that year in secrecy. In that letter, Rosebery explained in a straightforward fashion the problems that would arise if Acton were to be appointed.

> One if not both of the Regius Professorships of History will soon be vacant. The name of Acton smiles upon me for one of them. I have, as you know, long had his position at heart. His learning is great and unquestionable, but
>
> 1. He is a Roman Catholic.
>
> 2. I do not feel sure from his writings that he would find it easy to impart his knowledge to others—to be in short a good lecturer.
>
> 3. I do not think that he was at Oxford or Cambridge.
>
> No. 1 is the crucial objection. Acton is eminently antipapal, but Great Britain on these points is eminently suspicious. . . . I do not the least know if Acton would entertain the idea. But I like to write and ask your guidance.[4]

Gladstone's reply gives us some insight into his earlier hesitancy to appoint his friend when he had the opportunity himself. "You do not underrate the difficulties," he wrote to Rosebery.

> As to the point of communicating knowledge, I think his lecturing would be more effective than his writing. But as to attacks I am afraid the case would be full of difficulty. He would be attacked as R.C. for party reasons: and the R.C.s might be found very shy of defending him . . . the storm would be from without. . . . My general feeling is against my wishes: it is that difficulty preponderates; but the matter is worth a very thorough probing.[5]

Rosebery did persist and found that there was strong support among leading historians for the unorthodox appointment; the Anglican Bishop Creighton, himself one of the most eminent scholars of the time, recommended Acton in the strongest terms, calling him "the most learned Englishman."[6] After being assured by her prime minister that there would be no significant objection to Acton on religious grounds from either the Church or the universities, Queen Victoria approved the appointment in February 1895.

His good friend Lord Bryce was the only person Acton consulted about the professorship, and he enjoined his fellow historian and Liberal politician to the strictest confidence in the matter. Bryce enthusiastically urged him to accept, and Acton finally agreed that there would be advantages to an academic post. Bryce also explained the meaning of "full term," which Acton had difficulty in comprehending, and discreetly found out the exact stipend that accompanied the honor.

"What he would do at Cambridge, and how he would do it," H. A. L. Fisher noted, "excited the liveliest interest."[7] As Mandell Creighton remarked, Acton was very much a "dark horse," almost unknown to university men. Modern history, in fact, was a relatively new subject at Oxford and Cambridge; there were few students enrolled in the field and fewer academic historians.

When Acton arrived at Cambridge in the fall of 1895, Trinity College paid him the singular honor of electing him an honorary fellow and providing him with the rooms in Neville Court, where, in the words of George Macaulay Trevelyan, he sat "amid his strange foreign books . . . with a brow and beard like Plato, ready all day long to welcome any visitor seeking historical knowledge, whether it was Maitland or the humblest undergraduate."[8] (The first Fellow in History of Trinity was not to be elected until 1898, when the college welcomed George Macaulay Trevelyan, its future master and the great-nephew of his illustrious namesake. G. M. Trevelyan was also, of course, one of Acton's former students.)

Another student of Acton's who also went on to become an eminent historian in his own right, G. P. Gooch,* described the college, which he entered in 1891, quite unabashedly as "the greatest college in the world. Christ's is proud of Milton, St. John's of Wordsworth, Jesus of Coleridge, Peterhouse and Pembroke of Gray, Sidney of Cromwell; but Trinity College alone could proudly boast of such a galaxy as Bacon and Newton, Byron and Macaulay, Thackeray and Tennyson, to say nothing of the innumerable statesmen who had dreamed dreams and seen visions within its ancient walls."[9] Trinity, in fact, had (when Gooch wrote his panegyric) educated six prime

*The late G. P. Gooch, to whom I am indebted for a personal account of Acton at Cambridge, was born in 1873 and educated at Eton and Trinity. An Honorary Fellow of Trinity, he authored innumerable books, including *History and Historians of the Nineteenth Century, Studies in Diplomacy and Statecraft,* and his autobiography, *Under Six Reigns.* Like his mentor Acton, he sat in the House of Commons as a Liberal M.P. For fifty years he was editor of the *Contemporary Review.*

ministers, more than any other college: Perceval, Grey, Melbourne, Balfour, Campbell-Bannerman, and Baldwin —as well as several kings and princes.

No less than five students who were at Cambridge during the years Acton held his chair were later to receive the Order of Merit. Four of these were from Trinity alone: the historians G. P. Gooch and George Macaulay Trevelyan, the philosopher G. E. Moore, and the earl's son who had perhaps the greatest mind of our century, Bertrand Russell. The fifth, Jan Christian Smuts, later field marshal and prime minister of South Africa, was at neighboring Christ's College. Acton's fellow dons were no less distinguished than the students. His colleagues included the master of Trinity, Henry Montague Butler (father of the present master and former deputy prime minister, Lord Butler), who was reputed to be the most polished after-dinner speaker in England next to Lord Rosebery. Sir Frederick Pollock and Sir Frederick Maitland, following in the tradition of an earlier Trinity man, Lord Chief Justice Coke, were engaged in creating a new science and philosophy of English law. At the same time, Sir James Frazer, author of *The Golden Bough*, was laying the groundwork of the new discipline of anthropology. In the realm of philosophy, Acton doubtless had the frequent pleasure of hearing the respective merits of utilitarianism and Hegelianism argued by their two arch-proponents in England, Henry Sidgwick and Ellis M'Taggart respectively. Outside the walls of Trinity, Alfred Marshall, whom Keynes once described as the greatest economist since Adam Smith, lectured to crowded halls on the principles of political economy.

This was the atmosphere that Acton entered when he first took his place at the Trinity high table in 1895; it is very probable that the happiest days of his life were to be spent along the banks of the Cam. "He loved Cambridge from his soul," Lady Blennerhassett averred, "loved the grounds and the trees, the buildings and the romance of the old colleges, the treasures of the libraries, the intercourse with scholars. Above all he loved the younger generation, the future as it were, entrusted to his care."[10]

With an entirely understandable trace of irony, Acton expressed well his feelings for Cambridge in the opening lines of his inaugural lecture: "I look back today to a time before the middle of the century, when I was reading at Edinburgh, and fervently wishing to come to this university. At three colleges I applied for admission, and as things then were, I was refused by all. Here, from the first, I vainly fixed my hopes, and here, in a happier hour, after five-and-forty years, they are at last fulfilled."[11]

A large and expectant audience was gathered in the Cambridge hall to hear the first strictly academic work of the stranger who had brought learning from afar.[12] Acton did not disappoint them—he offered two controversial pronouncements for their consideration. His first principal assertion was that ideas, not politics, were the proper stuff of history, that intellectual movements were of more enduring significance than political struggles. As one of his listeners later noted, history was to Acton "not literature, but political philosophy; not an interesting narrative but a scientific study of cause and effect."[13]

Secondly, Acton stressed the role of the historian as judge rather than as objective observer. He exhorted his students and colleagues "never to debase the moral currency but to try others by the final maxim that governs your own lives, and to suffer no man and no cause to escape the undying penalty which history has the power to inflict on wrong."[14]

Acton's emphasis on the history of ideas rather than the history of politics that had so preoccupied his distinguished predecessor as Regius Professor, Sir John Seeley, was in essence a plea for the supremacy of the spiritual over the material. "If we are to account mind, not matter," he declared,

> ideas, not force, the spiritual property that gives dignity and grace and intellectual value to history . . . then we shall not be prone to explain the universal by the national, and civilization by custom. A speech of Antigone, a single sentence of Socrates . . . the footsteps of a silent yet prophetic people who dwelt by the Dead Sea, and perished in the fall of Jerusalem, come nearer to our lives than the ancestral wisdom of barbarians who fed their swine on the Hercynian acorns.[15]

Modern history, according to Acton, began at the end of the fifteenth century when half a dozen great ideas so revolutionized the world that a new civilization emerged.

> Columbus subverted the notions of the world. . . . Machiavelli released government from the restraint of law. . . . Erasmus diverted the current of ancient learning from profane into Christian channels. . . . Luther broke the chain of authority and tradition at the strongest link. . . . Copernicus erected an invincible power that set forever the mark of progress upon the time that was to come. . . . The law of stability was overcome by the power of ideas . . . ideas . . . that take wing and traverse seas and frontiers . . . they compel us to share the existence of societies wider than our own . . . to live in the company of heroes, and saints, and men of genius, that no single country could produce.[16]

If Acton's description of the study of history as the study of the causes and effects of ideas was a mild rebuke to the philosophy of history of his predecessor, his conception of the historian as a "hanging judge" placed him in sharp conflict with a much greater master of the craft, Leopold von Ranke. In his youth, Acton had studied with the great professor, who could fairly claim to be the founder of modern historical science. Again and again Ranke impressed upon his students the importance of strict and unyielding impartiality; their task was only to tell what had happened, not to comment, evaluate, or make judgments of any kind.

For Acton, however, the ideal of an objective historical science was an abdication of the scholar's responsibility. With his pessimistic view of human nature, he wrote that "great men are almost always bad men" and described history as the "disclosure of guilt and shame." It was natural for him to hold that the fear of historical condemnation (as well as of eternal damnation) must be one of the checks that serve to deter men from giving free rein to their vices. Not only was it morally incumbent upon the historian to disassociate himself from corruption, it was also of great utilitarian importance.

The upholders of Ranke's point of view often argued that it was unfair to judge the past by the standards of the present. What is immoral in one time or place may be condoned in another. Acton severely opposed this variety of moral relativism. "History ... does teach that right and wrong are real distinctions. Opinions alter, manners change, creeds rise and fall, but the moral law is written on the tablets of eternity."[17] He held that anyone who failed to protest against a political murder done for "reasons of state" was morally as guilty as the statesman who ordered the murder himself.

He looked to his old master, Burke, for support in asserting that there not only *need* not, there *must* not, be a difference between the moral standards of private and public life. "The doctrine that ... morality is not ambulatory," he declared,

> is expressed as follows by Burke, who, when true to himself, is the most intelligent of our instructors: "My principles enable me to form my judgement upon men and actions in history, just as they do in common life;

and are not formed out of events and characters,
either present or past. History is a preceptor of
prudence, not of principles. The principles of true
politics are those of morality enlarged; and I neither
now do, nor ever will admit of any other."[18]

It might be thought that Acton was rigid in his opinions,
even arrogant, and that he was swift to condemn to the outer darkness men with whom he disagreed. Those who
knew him were quick to deny this. One of his Cambridge
colleagues, the professor of Greek, Dr. Henry Jackson,
later wrote that "on the one hand he was observant of
everything, and he made up his mind about everything. On
the other hand, except where supreme principles—Truth,
Right, Toleration, Freedom—were in question, he was
cautious and reserved in the expression of opinion, and he
always preferred to leave action to others."[19]

In his inaugural lecture, Acton himself had stressed that
historians "should not rest until we have made out for our
opponents a stronger and more impressive case than they
present themselves." The spirit in which Acton approached moral problems is revealed in a letter he wrote
to Mary Gladstone: "So complex are [moral problems] that
almost every act can be honestly seen in different lights,
and I can imagine so strong a case against our policy in
Africa as to drive from his moorings any man not anchored
in justice. . . . Be true to your own beliefs and gracious
toward those who dispute them."[20]

One of the most enduring contributions of Lord Acton to
political thought was his careful avoidance of the pitfalls
of both the absolutist and the relativist position in ethics.
While he was certain that there was a right standard of
conduct and that morality was not merely a matter of
custom or taste, he was not sure that he or anyone else
could always know what the right course of action in any
given case was. While it was doubtless true that only God
could know some things with certainty, it was also true that
this did not free men from their obligation to search their

consciences and use their intelligence to determine as best they could what was right. If certainty in morals must be left to God alone, the conscience and mind of man, while not infallible, were nevertheless powerful sources of light.

Acton concluded his lecture by urging his audience to use to the utmost the wisdom accumulated from their ancestors and their own intelligence in order to build a new science of history that would both illuminate and evaluate the past and so be a guide to the present and future.

> The historians of former ages, unapproachable for us in knowledge and talent [he warned] cannot be our limit. We have the power to be more rigidly impersonal, disinterested and just than they; and to learn from undisguised and genuine records to look with remorse upon the past, and to the future with assured hope of better things; bearing this in mind, that if we lower our standard in History, we cannot uphold it in Church or State.[21]

The reaction to Acton's first address as a professor was, of course, varied. Among his colleagues at Cambridge and among historians generally, the almost universal view was that the lecture was one of the great contributions to scholarship of the century. "The new professor," wrote H. A. L. Fisher, "proved to be a brilliant success."[22] The future master of Trinity, G. M. Trevelyan, later recalled that "under Acton's leadership we did not care how proud we were, for he had excited the imagination of the whole university and indeed of the country at large."[23]

Sir George Trevelyan, relying upon the firsthand information of his undergraduate source, George Macaulay Trevelyan, wrote to inform the prime minister in November:

> You may care to know, what perhaps you may have heard from other quarters, what an immense success Acton is at Cambridge. At least 200 people came to his

first lecture, and quite as many attend every one of
them since: whereas I am told that even a famous
Regius Professor thinks himself happy if he can draw
one freshman, and three or four young women. It is not
only undergraduates of both sexes: but the cleverest
and most fastidious of the young historical specialists,
who themselves are lecturing and writing, are always
there. He is regarded distinctly as a *great* man, and the
young people pay him the unusual compliment of
thinking him a great deal younger than he is. The feeling is that the lectures which he is delivering are
literature of a very high order. Altogether, it has been
a tremendous hit.[24]

Most of the adverse criticism came from laymen, if the
"journals of opinion" may be said to reflect the thinking of
the generally educated man. The *Saturday Review,* a
favorite journal among the more literate Tory squires, attacked Acton for his "overpowering deluge of verbiage."
The lecture, it complained, was weighed down with unnecessary erudition (there was some truth in this) and was
hopelessly confused and obscure (there was no truth in
this). This "review" ended on what might be taken as a
partisan note; it urged the Liberal junior minister to resign
his new crown appointment for which he was obviously
unqualified.[25]

The *Spectator* took a similar line. "It is possible for a historian to know too much," it asserted, "and, if we wished
to be bitter, we might say that Lord Acton was himself a
living example of the new trouble."[26] Most critics, both lay
and professional, confined their comments to Acton's
style; very few came to grips with the substance of his
ideas. Those who did generally focused their attention on
Acton's belief that the historian should be a moral judge.
J. L. Hammond, writing in the more scholarly *Independent
Review,* defended Acton's principal thesis.

Few men give justice the first place in politics, though almost everyone gives it the second. Most men think vaguely or certainly that the maintenance of established interests in some category is the sovereign end, and as far as morality is friendly or neutral they are glad enough to patronize it; or they think that morality is not meant for slippery times, though it does well enough for tranquil and comfortable days. Lord Acton gave morality itself the preeminence; and he allowed no boisterous storm of temptation or disorder to excuse men for reclining on some other standard.[27]

The American medievalist, Henry C. Lea, held to the opposite view. "The historian," he wrote, "who becomes an advocate or a prosecutor instead of a judge forfeits his title to confidence, and, if he aspires to be a judge, he should not try a case by a code unknown to the defendant."[28] Acton's premise, of course, was that the moral code *was* universal and not dependent upon time or place.

Having accomplished his first duty as Regius Professor, Acton settled down to the daily tasks of his chair, which, while undefined, were by no means light. The professor in any discipline was expected to lecture, to organize his department, and to do research. As John Stuart Mill said of the House of Commons, his function was not so much to do things as to get things done. Acton had come to Cambridge with some misgivings; before he had arrived, he wrote in confidence to a friend that "there is, I think, no great school of history there and not much studious curiosity about it. And as my predecessor did not awaken it, there is no chance of my doing much."[29]

Nevertheless, his lectures, from the first, were always well attended, and students and great scholars came from the corners of the civilized world to hear him. Not all of his auditors were serious, of course: many were fashionable middle-aged ladies attracted by Acton's social position and what they considered his good looks. But it is likely that even the most casual visitor derived something from an hour with Acton. As one of his younger colleagues noted,

> No one could fail to see how the speaker's mind was possessed with the greatness of human affairs, with the moral (or immoral) aspects of political and ecclesiastical dexterity; above all, with the final supremacy of the soul over circumstance, as the real ground for asserting the sacredness of truth and the inalienable glory of Liberty. It was this sense of the fundamentally spiritual nature of his work which formed the distinction, the difficulty and the triumph of Acton. . . . No hearer . . . could fail to find in Acton's austere judgments, in the dignity of his language, in the tones of his voice, a warning against any treatment of history that was mean or utilitarian, and any view of human nature that demands of it less than may become a man.[30]

It was generally expected that, while Acton would doubtless advance historical scholarship with his lecturing and writing, he would probably prefer to lead the life of a solitary scholar and would pay little attention to the affairs of the university. The opposite proved to be the case, which should not have been so surprising. After all, although Acton could not properly be called both a man of letters and a man of action, as his friends Gladstone, Bryce, and Morley could, he was still (as one don put it) "the ally of statesmen and a trusted leader in one of the greatest fights in the cause of liberty seen by the last century [the struggle for home rule for Ireland]."[31]

Few, if any, professors were more accessible than Acton was, whether to undergraduates, candidates for fellowships, or eminent scholars. Students who went to him for information often found upon arriving home that Acton's servant had already left a half-dozen books in as many languages with a message apologizing for the poor selection but adding that more would follow tomorrow.

While he was invariably kind to undergraduates, he could not resist an occasional touch of irony. One of his brighter students, who was given to monopolizing most discussions, once delivered, in a rather self-satisfied tone, a paper that rivaled Acton in erudition. After reading his work, which upset a widely held historical thesis, the student sat back to await his due. Acton, as everyone expected, praised the elegant style of the paper and then added in an undertone, "You are aware, of course, that the manuscript upon which your essay is based is a forgery?"

On the other hand, Acton could and did go to some lengths to avoid giving pain. One of his friends at Cambridge at one time presented Acton with a copy of his latest book—which unfortunately was totally inept and unreadable. Rather than hurt his friend's feelings, Acton carefully cut all of the pages and then inserted slips of paper at intervals. When the author next called on Acton, he was naturally gratified to see his book prominently displayed and apparently thoroughly studied.[32]

The combination room of Trinity College, centuries old and decorated with the paintings of noblemen and magnates of another era, was reserved for the fellows of the College. Here Acton would often hold forth on some misunderstood subject to the delight and edification of his peers. Acton was often deferential and reluctant to speak out, but as another Cambridge historian was to later recall,

> if he could be caught at the right time, and in the right mood, he would expand like the universe, and let loose a copious flood of illuminating facts, generally of a kind to refute some popular theory, or upset established tradition. He seemed to take a special interest in what has been termed the "backstairs" aspect of history and would trace to some obscure and

generally discreditable incident what historians have very differently explained.[33]

The Trinity Historical Society, where dons and undergraduates meet regularly to read and discuss their research, owes its founding to Lord Acton, who became its first president in the Michaelmas term of 1896. By this means, the professor came into contact with many students and younger dons he otherwise might never have met. The example of Trinity was imitated in other colleges in the university, and interest in history, which at that time was considered a rather new subject in the curriculum, was much increased.

Those who met with Acton to discuss one aspect or another of the past could not fail to note his passion for making precise judgments. Someone once suggested that so-and-so's book was very good. "Yes," was Acton's ready answer, "perhaps five percent less good than the public thinks it is." Someone else asked vaguely "When was London in the greatest danger?" "In 1803," came the immediate answer, "when Fulton proposed to put the French army across the Channel in steamboats, and Napoleon rejected the scheme."[34] He could also at times be severe as well as swift in his appraisals. "Are you aware," he was once asked, "that Borromeo was a party to a scheme of assassinations?" Another don intervened by asking, "Must we not make allowances for the morality of the time?" Acton's emphatic response, according to a participant, was instantaneous: "I make no allowance for that sort of thing." "The contrast," an observer noted, "with the measured and sedate tones of Acton's ordinary utterance made the explosion all the more impressive."[35]

To the somewhat isolated English scholars of *fin de siècle* Cambridge, smug in the knowledge that their widow at Windsor owned "'alf of creation," Acton seemed a "traveller from antique lands of European statecraft, religion and learning."[36] "To be with Acton," a friend who knew him then recalled

> was like being with the cultivated mind of Europe incarnate in its finest characteristics.* In the deep tones of his voice there seemed to sound the accents of history. In those unflinching phrases we heard the impersonal estimate of posterity weighing in unerring balance the thoughts and deeds of the actors of the present or past, with a knowledge that knew no gap. We do not of course mean that Acton knew everything, but that he thoroughly understood the operation of forces—religious, political, social, economic—which create from what without them would be the sandheap of individual caprice and personal interest, the enduring bonds of secular and religious society."[37]

Acton was welcome in the Trinity combination room for all these reasons and more; almost everyone he met learned something important from him that he did not know before. As the distinguished philosopher and political economist Henry Sidgwick remarked, a trifle ruefully, Acton was certain to know more about your subject than you did yourself.[38] While he was inclined not to speak until spoken to, he was generous with his ideas and knowledge; many a don received the substance of an important book, freely given in an hour's conversation. He would often pour out in answer to one modest question a whole new theme of historical intrepretation, or on another occasion, a small store of the spiciest gossip—about European courts, the House of Commons, or of hypocritical prelates—depending on what happened to be the commodity in demand. As one of his Cambridge friends later wrote, he was far from being a "mere Dryasdust; he was a watchful observer of men and affairs. If he studied the

---

*Apart from Guizot, Acton was personally acquainted with every historian of renown in Europe and frequently corresponded with them.

detail of history, it was in order that he might the better elicit its significance and its teaching. He was slow to express an opinion; but in his judgments there was never any indecision. In the advocacy of intellectual freedom he was eager: in the denunciation of tyranny and persecution he was at a white heat."[39]

In addition to directly assisting fellows and students in their historical work, Acton delivered two series of lectures, which were collected after his death and published by two of his younger colleagues.* Although his lectures were attended by many undergraduates, the university thought it advisable to ask Oscar Browning to deliver another series of lectures on the same topics, but more specifically designed to help undergraduates in passing the final examinations.

Acton promised to publish his lectures after two or three years, but somehow never did; nor did he ever finish a collection of his essays that Macmillan was anxious to publish. His inability to complete any major work has already been noted (see Chapter Six). Acton's extreme conscientiousness, which prevented him from writing until he had exhausted every possible source of information, is well known. This would not account for Acton's failure to publish his lectures and essays, however, except insofar as he regarded them as imperfect. There can be no doubt that, for whatever reason, Acton had an aversion to publishing. The essays published under his own name in his lifetime, mostly in the *English Historical Review*, may be counted on the fingers of one hand. It was common knowledge, of course, that Acton wrote most of the reviews in the *Rambler* and the *Home and Foreign Review*; that

*See Acton's *Lectures on the French Revolution* and *Lectures on Modern History*, both edited by John N. Figgis and Reginald V. Laurence, listed in the Bibliography of Lord Acton's Works under "Books of Collected Essays and Correspondence" (section I) at the back of this book.

they were unsigned apparently made a difference to Acton.

As a result, the only volumes that bear his name are collections of lectures, essays, or letters, all published posthumously. The work for which he is most widely known is the massive twelve volume *Cambridge Modern History;* and here he appears not as writer but as editor and even then but for the first two volumes. The title page of the series bears the proud but somewhat sad legend "Planned by the Late Lord Acton."

When he was asked by the syndics of the university to coordinate this ambitious enterprise, he readily accepted because he believed his office made it a duty not to be declined and because (as he wrote in a letter to one of his first contributors, G. P. Gooch) "such an opportunity of promoting his own ideas for the treatment of history has seldom been given to any man. We shall avoid the needless utterance of opinion or service of a cause. Contributors will understand that our Waterloo must satisfy French and English, Germans and Dutch alike."[40]

Acton set to work with his usual thoroughness and enthusiasm. He first wrote to all of his friends asking them for suggestions; the authors that Acton sought were to be the best available in each field. For this purpose he combed bibliographies and libraries, hoping to find in some out-of-the-way place just the right man for a minor but important chapter. Some historians had to make their excuses because of previous commitments, some could not be asked (such as the free-thinking Morley) because their presence would offend other contributors (the bishop of Oxford, for example). His old friend, the former ambassador to the United States, James Bryce, suggested numerous writers from across the Atlantic; his chief assistants, Bishop Creighton and R. L. Poole, shared the burden of the heavy correspondence between editors, writers, and publishers.

The object and guiding principles of the series are set out in the letter that Acton sent to all prospective authors.

> Our purpose [he began] is to obtain the best history of modern times that the published or unpublished sources of information admit.... By dividing our matter among more than one hundred writers we hope to make the enlarged opportunities for research avail for the main range of modern history.... Our scheme requires that nothing shall reveal the country, the religion, or the party to which the writers belong. It is essential not only on the ground that impartiality is the character of legitimate history, but because the work is carried on by men acting together for no other object than the increase of accurate knowledge. The disclosure of personal views would lead to such confusion that all unity of design would disappear.
>
> By the judicious division of labour, we should be able to do it, and to bring home to every man the last document, and the ripest conclusions of international research.... All this does not apply to our own time and the last volumes will be concerned with secrets that cannot be learned from books, but from men.... The recent past contains the key to the present time. All forms of thought that influence it come before us in their turn, and we have to describe the ruling currents, to interpret the sovereign forces, that still govern and divide the world....
>
> By Universal History [he concluded] I understand that which is distinct from the combined history of all countries, which is not a rope of sand, but a continuous development, and is not a burden on the memory, but an illumination of the soul. It moves in a succession to which the nations are subsidiary. Their story will be told, not for their own sake, but in reference and subordination to a higher series, according to the time and the degree in which they contribute to the common fortunes of mankind.[41]

The plan of this great effort, which Acton once described as "the nineteenth-century historian's bequest to the twentieth century,"[42] clearly reflects three of Acton's chief goals: a universal history, a history of ideas, and an impartial and objective history. It might be thought at first glance that the goal of an impartial, nonpartisan history contradicted Acton's well-known belief in the duty of the historian to make moral judgments. In fact, however, Acton held that his moral judgments *were* objective since they were derived from an objective, universal moral law common to all men, nations, and times. Secondly, Acton believed in the primacy of conscience above all; this required him to respect other men's moral beliefs, which might differ from his own. Since both his professional and moral ethics taught him to tolerate the sincere and well-founded convictions of other historians, it was only natural that he did not attempt to dictate a particular policy to his writers. In addition, as he noted in his circular letter, he could not have imposed his personal views on the project even if he had wished to because it would have reduced the overall unity of the project to chaos.

This does not mean that Acton did not leave his personal stamp upon the *Cambridge History*. It is safe to say that the final product would have been substantially different had he not guided its birth; it would almost certainly have been much more conventional, both in contributors and design. The syndics, in fact, had complained that Acton had invited too many "eminent outsiders" (their polite phrase for foreigners and nonacademic historians); without Acton to argue the case for cosmopolitanism, it is a good bet that the publishers would never have looked outside the walls of Oxford and Cambridge. After much effort, Acton managed to secure the services of some of the most original and interesting historians of the time, including Lady Blennerhassett, James Bryce, J. B. Bury (Acton's successor as Regius Professor), Bishop Creighton, G. P. Gooch, F. W. Maitland, C. W. Oman, W. A. Phillips, A. F. Pollard, G. W. Prothero, J. H. Rose, and H. W. V. Temperley.

The general design of the series was unmistakably Acton's. Instead of the usual division by countries, or centuries, the volumes consisted of general topics, usually based on some overriding idea that united the histories of several countries. Some of his divisions, for instance, were: the Renaissance, the Reformation, the religious wars, absolute monarchy, and revolution. Acton was convinced that there were "some twenty or thirty predominate currents of thought or attitudes of mind" that provided the structure of modern history and held the key to explaining it. The majority of these ideas, he thought, were "either religions or substitutes for religion."[43] Acton saw to it that his contributors did not neglect to deal (in their own way, of course) with such influential ideas as Puritanism, ultramontanism, Lutheranism, Anglicanism, rationalism, utilitarianism, positivism, materialism, Whiggism, communism, and so on. This approach to history seems second nature to us now, but in Acton's own time it represented a new departure, and many were fearful of where it would end.

In the words of a recent Regius Professor of Modern History, G. N. Clark, Acton's last great self-imposed task "weighed him down."[44] Acton wrote hundreds of letters in his own hand regarding the *History;* in trying to direct such a large enterprise personally, he attempted the impossible. Acton unfortunately had almost no capacity for organization, for employing limited resources in the most effective manner. In particular, he could not or would not delegate the many duties he took for himself. In addition to his basic role of editor, Acton planned to write several of the articles himself (the introduction to the series, the opening chapter, and the final chapter on contemporary England). He also acted as fund-raiser (he persuaded his old friend

Baron Rothschild to send a substantial check) and public relations officer. In the end, however, none of his scheduled articles were completed. In April 1901, when the first volume was in type, Acton suffered the paralytic stroke that brought his effective work at Cambridge to a sudden conclusion.

It is ironical, for this reason, that the chief criticism directed at the *Cambridge Modern History* has been that it was a product of "the new industrial age" with all the "depersonalizing" effects of the "division of labor." Arnold Toynbee, a long-standing critic of industrialization, took Acton to task in his own monumental work of universal history for allowing himself to be sacrificed to the modern idols of efficiency and progress. If only Acton (whom he terms "one of the greatest minds among modern Western historians"[45]) had lived in an age before the division of labor was heard of, the eighteenth century say, then, Toynbee thinks, he would have written the great work to rank himself with Gibbon.

One can imagine Acton's reaction to the charge that he was a victim of superorganization and modern efficiency. *Had* he made use of only a few of the modern techniques that Toynbee deplores, he would have given to the world a *History of Liberty* and much more besides. Acton, of course, had much the same opinion of the "division of labor" as Toynbee does; he also regarded it as a second-best device. Acton's ideal historian was a man who not only was a master of detail, of languages, monographs, bibliographies, and manuscripts in huge quantities but who also possessed a high imagination, a sympathy for everything human, a philosophy of history, and an instinct for elegance. All these qualities, as all who knew him attested, Acton did possess; what he lacked was the crucial ability to organize and marshal them for a given goal. His great contemporary, Professor Frederick W. Maitland, was convinced that "if the worst came to the worst, or perhaps the best to the best, Lord Acton could write the twelve volumes (given sufficient time, of course) and never turn a hair."[46]

As it is, the *Cambridge Modern History*, completed by other hands, stands as a monument to Acton's vision and power of imagination alongside of his library, in which rest thousands of pages of notes for books that, most unfortunately, were never given to the world.

Notes

[1]The don was Dr. Henry Jackson, professor of Greek, quoted by Herbert Paul in his introductory memoir to the second revised edition (1913) of Lord Acton, *Letters of Lord Acton to Mary . . . Gladstone*, ed. Herbert Paul, p. lxii.

[2]James Bryce, *Studies in Contemporary Biography*, p. 387.

[3]H. A. L. Fisher, "Lord Acton's Lectures," *Independent Review*, XI (1906): 224.

[4]Alan Bell, "Lord Acton Gets His Chair," *Times Literary Supplement*, 8 February 1974, p. 137.

[5]Ibid.

[6]Ibid.

[7]Fisher, "Acton's Lectures," p. 225.

[8]G. M. Trevelyan, *Trinity College* (Cambridge: At the University Press, 1946), p. 112.

[9]G. P. Gooch, *Under Six Reigns*, p. 15.

[10]Lady Blennerhassett, "The Late Lord Acton," *Edinburgh Review*, CXCVII (1903): 532.

[11]Lord Acton, "Inaugural Lecture on the Study of History," in *Lectures on Modern History*, ed. John N. Figgis and Reginald V. Laurence, p. 1.

[12]G. M. Trevelyan, *The Present Position of History* (Cambridge: At the University Press, 1927), p. 11. I have paraphrased the remark.

[13]Dr. Henry Jackson, quoted by Herbert Paul in Acton, *Letters to Mary Gladstone*, p. lxv.

[14]Acton, "Inaugural Lecture," p. 25.

[15]Ibid., p. 5.

[16]Ibid., pp. 3-6, *passim*.

[17]Ibid., p. 27.

[18]Ibid., p. 28.

[19]Dr. Henry Jackson, quoted by Herbert Paul in Acton, *Letters to Mary Gladstone*, p. lxiii.

[20]Mrs. Mary (Gladstone) Drew, *Acton, Gladstone and Others*, p. 11.

[21]Acton, "Inaugural Lecture," p. 28.

[22]Fisher, "Acton's Lectures," p. 225.

[23]Trevelyan, *Present Position of History*, p. 12.

[24]Bell, "Acton Gets His Chair," p. 137.

[25]*Saturday Review*, 22 June 1895, p. 822. The whole paragraph reads as follows:

> Lord Acton's idea of a lecture on modern history appears to be that it should be sufficiently difficult to supply mental gymnastics to the most nimble mind; but we fear that the most persistent mental gymnast will often be unrewarded by reaching the meaning which this inarticulate teacher has cunningly concealed. Whatever his reputation for erudition, it is certain that Lord Acton has never learned to write English; and surely one of the indispensable qualifications for the Chair of Modern History at Cambridge is that the occupant should be intelligible. That the well digested knowledge and unfailing lucidity of Seeley, or even the brilliant historic imagination and splendid prose of his predecessor Kingsley, should be succeeded by these pretensions and confused fancies! . . . The Batavian splutterings of Lord Acton's awkward pen are not to be endured, and unless in his succeeding lectures the new Professor can find some means to give lucid expression to his reputed learning and thus justify his appointment, we sincerely hope he will resign his post, which, were we to judge merely from his inaugural lecture, he would seem in no way qualified to fill.

[26]*Spectator*, 15 June 1895, p. 807.

[27]J. L. Hammond, "Lord Acton," *Independent Review*, May 1904, pp. 652-53.

[28]Henry C. Lea, "Ethical Values in History," *Minor Historical Writing*, ed. A. C. Howland (Philadelphia: University of Pennsylvania Press, 1942), p. 60.

[29]Quoted in Herbert Butterfield, *Lord Acton*, Pamphlets of the English Historical Association, no. G9, p. 22.

[30]Lord Acton, *Lectures on Modern History*, ed. John N. Figgis and Reginald V. Laurence, p. xii.

[31]John Pollock, "Lord Acton at Cambridge," *Independent Review*, II (1904): 364.

[32]Ibid., p. 374.

[33]Thomas Thornely, *Cambridge Memories*, pp. 117-18.

[34]Acton, *Letters to Mary Gladstone*, p. lxii.

[35]Ibid., p. lxiv.

[36]Trevelyan, *Present Position of History*, p. 11.

[37]Acton, *Lectures on Modern History*, p. xvi.

[38]Drew, *Acton, Gladstone and Others*, p. 20.

[39]Acton, *Letters to Mary Gladstone*, p. lxvi.

[40]Gooch, *Under Six Reigns*, p. 47.

[41]Acton, *Lectures on Modern History*, pp. 315-18.

[42]Add. MSS. 5699. (See n.14 to chap. 1.)

[43]George E. Fasnacht, *Acton's Political Philosophy*, p. 141.

[44]G. N. Clark, "Origin of the *Cambridge Modern History*," *Cambridge Historical Journal*, VIII (1945): 63.

[45]Arnold J. Toynbee, *A Study of History* (London: Oxford University Press, 1934), vol. 1, *Introduction*, p. 46.

[46]Frederick W. Maitland, quoted in Blennerhassett, "The Late Lord Acton," p. 533.

9. Last Days:
Lord Acton in Retrospect

Whether or not the monumental *Cambridge Modern History* weighed him down physically as well as mentally, Acton did suffer a paralytic stroke in April 1901. His friend and fellow historian Frederick W. Maitland wrote to a mutual friend and contributor to the *History* at Oxford that "the Regius of Physic gave me on Friday a better account than I dreaded of the Regius of History. It is paralysis: one arm and one leg useless but mind unaffected ... [but] ... of course the Universal History cannot be talked of at present."[1]

Knowing that his work was almost certainly at end even if he should live a few years longer, Acton at the age of sixty-seven retired to his beloved country home at Tegernsee in Bavaria. There on 19 June 1902 he died and was buried by the side of the daughter who had preceded him and whose last days he had comforted with the words, "Be glad my child, you will soon be with Jesus Christ."[2]

His religion had always been the most important thing in the world to Acton. "The first of human concerns is religion," he had declared in his inaugural lecture, "and it

is the salient feature of the modern centuries. . . .³ The action of Christ who is risen on mankind whom he redeemed
fails not, but increases. . . . History is the true demonstration of religion."⁴

Acton had once written to his friend of forty years'
standing, Mr. Gladstone, that "all I write and all I think,
and all I hope, is based on the Divinity of Our Lord—the
one central hope of our poor wayward race."⁵

His friends were especially unhappy, therefore, to
watch his distress during these last years brought about by
the continuing struggle with the hierarchy of his church.
Although, as he often remarked, communion with Rome
was dearer to him than life itself, he could not help op-
posing arbitrary authority and concentration of power
wherever he found it. This brought him into constant conflict, first with Cardinal Wiseman, and then in later years
with Cardinal Manning, who wrote of Acton that he was
"learned in literature, of a German industry, cold, self-
confident, supercilious toward opponents, a disciple of
Döllinger and predisposed against me."⁶ Manning also
blamed Acton for turning Gladstone against him. His essays defending the ultramontane position were, Manning
believed, the basis of Acton's enmity, and he agreed with
Pius IX that Acton was not a Catholic at heart.

With the deaths of Pius IX and Cardinal Manning and
the installation of their successors, Leo XIII in the Vatican
and Herbert Cardinal Vaughan at Westminster, it
appeared that a new reign of conciliation was at hand. The
liberals within the Church were to be at least tolerated if
not encouraged. The new attitude was made clear to Acton
when Cardinal Vaughan congratulated him upon his Cambridge chair and added, perhaps pointedly, that the
Catholic Primate of England had complete confidence in
Acton's loyalty to the Church of Rome.

The English hierarchy, after all, had every reason to be
friendly toward Acton. In the first place, his piety and
deep sense of religion were acknowledged by all, even

those who maintained he was secretly a schismatic. Furthermore, Acton was one of the few Catholics to sit in either of the Houses of Parliament; he was the only Catholic on intimate terms with the cabinet; he was the only Catholic holding a chair at Oxford or Cambridge; and he was one of the leading scholars of Europe—Catholic, Protestant, Jew, or atheist. And, when all was said and done, he was the nephew of one cardinal and the great-grandnephew of another.*

When the foundation stone of Westminster Cathedral was laid, Vaughan invited Acton as one of his guests of honor. Still, relations between Acton and the church establishment could never be very close. Acton insisted on granting the popes every honor due them, but he reserved the right to criticize them when he believed they were guilty of corruption or abuse of power. As Miss Himmelfarb has noted,

> Acton had good reason for saying there was nothing heretical in this attitude. Catholic theologians of whose orthodoxy there is no suspicion have applied to the Pope the teaching of Aquinas on kingship, arguing that it is legitimate to disobey a Pope who orders the commission of a sin or passes a decree subversive of the Church. Generally, to be sure, they hasten to add that this eventuality has never come to pass and that no Pope has ever forfeited his right to obedience. But the implication remains: if the authority of a Pope must be justified by some more ultimate principle, it can be controverted by that principle.[7]

For Acton, of course, this principle was conscience. Even though he believed that his own salvation was dependent upon the Roman sacraments, he urged that Döllinger's

---

*Acton's uncle was Charles Edward, Cardinal Acton; see Chapter One. The uncle of Acton's grandfather was Karl Theodor von Dalberg, cardinal-prince-archbishop-elector of Mainz, arch-chancellor of the Holy Roman Empire, etc., etc.

wish to have the last rites from an Old Catholic instead of a Roman Catholic priest be respected. In Acton's eyes, if Döllinger went against the promptings of his own conscience, he would imperil, not save, his soul. This view, now generally accepted by Roman Catholic theologians, was at the time anathema to the ultramontanes, who never ceased to look for an opportunity to trap Acton into schism.

Despite the announced liberalism of the new pope, Acton remained wary. While he applauded the opening of the Vatican archives to Protestant scholars, he disagreed vehemently with the papal decree that added Hugo's *Les Misérables* to the Index. Although an era of good feeling kept relations between Acton and the hierarchy from reaching the breaking point during his tenure at Cambridge, the ultramontanes went over to the attack after Acton's death.

In fairness to the ultramontanes, it should be said that from their point of view they were merely responding to an attempt on the part of Abbot Francis Gasquet to rewrite history. Gasquet, a prominent English historian and future cardinal, was a good friend of Acton and had collaborated with him on the *Cambridge History*; in 1906 he published a selection of the Acton-Simpson correspondence.* From motives of friendship and regard for the Church, Gasquet carefully edited these letters (which dealt mostly with the controversial *Rambler* and *Home and Foreign Review* period) and omitted all but the mildest criticisms of the hierarchy. The overall effect was to portray Acton as a man who had been misunderstood to be a rebel but who was in fact a loyal and unquestioning son of the Church.

---

*The complete text of these letters is now being edited by Josef Altholz, Fr. Damian McElrath, and John C. Holland. The first and second volumes of *The Correspondence of Lord Acton and Richard Simpson* have been published; the third volume is still being prepared. See the entry in the Bibliography of Lord Acton's Works under "Books of Collected Essays and Correspondence" (section I) at the back of this book.

The Catholic journal *The Tablet* was happy to use Gasquet's selection as an excuse to celebrate Acton's orthodoxy. "All Catholics now alive," it declared, "have the benefit of Lord Acton's having lived and learned before them. He goes to the general credit of Catholicism; he is a great asset."[8]

A reply to this friendly article was not long in coming. A Jesuit priest, Father Herbert Thurston, wrote a blistering essay for *Catholic World*, entitled "The Late Lord Acton."[9] One priest, at least, was not disposed to forget Acton's many attacks on the church establishment and his close brushes with what Father Thurston considered heresy. Acton's letters to Mary Gladstone, published in 1904 with Acton's prior consent, added fuel, so to speak, to the ultramontane *auto de fé*. On the subject of Jesuits, for instance, Acton had calmly written to Mary Gladstone, in 1882, that "It is this combination of an eager sense of duty, zeal for sacrifice, and love of virtue, with the deadly taint of a conscience perverted by authority, that makes them so odious to touch and so curious to study."[10] If we assume that Father Thurston read this passage (among others), his irritation at Lord Acton becomes understandable.

Acton's son, the second Baron Acton, felt obliged to write a letter to the *Times*. Obviously motivated by filial loyalty, the second Baron noted that the *Letters to Mary Gladstone* had been published without the final approval of the Acton family. He carefully omitted the fact, however, that Lord Acton himself had approved the posthumous publication some years before his death. Acton obviously wished the world to know his opinions on certain matters, but he did not want to have his peace and quiet disturbed while he was still of the world. The son added that "In the last years of his life, when he was stricken by illness, and during what was almost our last conversation, he solemnly adjured me not to rash-judge others as he had done but to take care to make allowance for human weakness. And I was present at his farewell meeting with Cardinal New-man, the most moving scene I have ever witnessed."[11]

There is little doubt that Acton was always ambiguous on the subject of judgment as he was on many other subjects; he often urged a stern, unbending morality, but almost as often he advocated sympathy, tolerance, and respect for differing views. There is also little doubt that Acton was always a devout and loyal Catholic, no matter how much he might disagree with the ideas and actions of many of the leaders of the institution. The editor of the *Letters to Mary Gladstone* implied that Acton did not accept the infallibility dogma.

> Whether Lord Acton ought to have left the Church of Rome when Döllinger was excommunicated, or when the Vatican decrees were pronounced, is a question it would not become a Protestant to ask, much less to answer. He did not shrink from the risk of speaking out, and it was not his fault that he escaped. . . . The truths which all Christians hold in common, and the moral principles to which Sophocles ascribes an un-known antiquity, guided him in history as in life. His emphatic statement that he had never felt any doubt about any Roman doctrine was made some years before 1870, and the secession of the Old Catholics.[12]

Acton's editor is almost certainly recalling here the statement by Mountstuart Grant Duff in his autobiography, *Out of the Past*, that Acton had told him before 1870 that he had never questioned any Catholic dogma. The editor did not know, however, that Acton said much the same thing to another friend at Cambridge—forty years later and long after the infallibility decree had been adopted.[13] This is a subject on which certainty is impossible, but the weight of the evidence seems clearly to indicate that Acton did accept the doctrine of papal infallibility when speaking *ex cathedra* on faith and morals. There had always been a tradition in the Church of extensive consultation with theologians, bishops, abbots, and lay scholars before any major papal pronouncement was made. In view of Acton's great emphasis on the idea of development, it seems likely he was convinced that in time what appeared to be a new doctrine in 1870 would turn out to be no more than what the Church had always taught and believed.

Shortly after Acton's death, his friend F. W. Maitland wrote to R. L. Poole urging him to write a memoir, noting that Poole's disinterest in Catholic theology was an asset, since "Anyone, *if such there be* [emphasis supplied], who really knows the inside of the infallibility episode would be likely to make a deal too much of it."[14]

Despite the renewed controversy over Acton's orthodoxy, those who knew him were proud to tell of his personal qualities as well as paying tribute to his scholarship. A week earlier Maitland had written that "I shall never forget the talks I had with Acton. He seemed to know all the letters that ever were written, especially the most private. In a short time he did an enormous deal to improve the position of history here and I think the loss irreparable."[15] One of his editors, Herbert Paul, spoke of "the profundity of his knowledge, the generosity of his temper, and the humility of his soul."[16]

Of course, Acton has had his critics as well. Dr. Herman Finer of the University of Chicago has summed up what some scholars, at least, have regarded as the faults or shortcomings of Acton's career and character. "He was in his public aspect incomplete in every way," Dr. Finer notes.

> He was a member of the House of Commons and never spoke. He was a member of the House of Lords and hardly spoke. He opposed the Papacy, but was not, like his mentor, Döllinger, cut off. He encouraged Gladstone's liberal policy but stopped short. He coached Gladstone on the road to his polemic with the Vatican and then admonished him. He came to detest

the Holy See and in an historic view, Catholicism, but did not leave the Church. He ascribed to systems of ideas an all dominating force but for Catholicism and Ultramontanism repudiated their full logical consequences. He demonstrated that Protestantism could be as persecuting as Catholicism, yet managed to find an excuse for the latter. Having claimed that life was for the discovery of truth and being editor of a journal, he abandoned the journal rather than fight the Catholic Church on the high ground of truth. . . . His friends paid him the tribute of admiration, reverence; they expressed delight in his erudition, his wit and zesty wisdom; but one notes a curious absence of *affection* in their correspondence. . . . [There was nothing to kindle his passion.] He lacked the lash of everyday discipline. He was never compelled to make up his mind. . . . He lacked selectiveness, he had no reason for either beginning or ending a work; no spur pricked him to vow a hierarchy of decisions.[17]

On the other hand, his most recent biographer, Miss Gertrude Himmelfarb, maintains that

it is idle to bemoan the fact that Acton was not a Voltaire, a Gibbon, or a Turgot. He had hoped to be much more than any of them, to inaugurate a new era in history, where the techniques of a Ranke would be wedded to the vision of an Augustine, an Augustine with a new eschatology in which the plan of divine salvation would be identical with the history of human freedom. It was no spirit of the times that defeated Acton. It was his own restless, dissatisfied, ambitious mind, content with no small part of the whole, and for which no whole was quite good enough. To deplore the fact that he was not an eighteenth-century historian was to make of him not a tragic figure but a pathetic one.[18]

Dr. G. P. Gooch, the most distinguished of Acton's younger colleagues at Trinity College, has well defined his place in history:

Ordered liberty, he taught, was the highest prize of mankind, and the only method of winning it and keeping it was to cut up power into little bits. . . . No man, no class, no party, no country, no church, not even his own, was wise enough or unselfish enough to be entrusted with unlimited authority. . . .[19]

It was Acton's lifelong opposition to totalitarianism in every form which accounts for the spectacular revival of interest in the man and his writings in the middle decades of the twentieth century. Fifty years after his death the lonely scholar has come into his own. "He is of this age more than of his," declares Gertrude Himmelfarb. . . . "He is indeed one of our great contemporaries." It is above all as an apostle of liberty that his name and influence survive. . . .[20]

He ranks with Locke and Jefferson, Humboldt, Mill and Croce among the oracles of the Liberal faith.[21]

The very ambivalence for which Acton has been sometimes criticized is perhaps the most important reason why he repays careful study. Like his great teacher Burke, he knew that the mysteries at the root of the civil social order are infinitely complex and that there are no simple answers to the problems that have troubled men for centuries. Such great ideals and forces as democracy and nationalism, he knew, must be tempered by prudence and by the demand of a higher law. Though liberty itself must be the highest *political* end, it could not be the final end for humanity. While he was not afraid to admit that liberalism and democracy were not perfect and in practice often had grave faults, he still clung to the belief that no better system was likely to be invented. As Dr. Gooch has put it, "If he returned to the world of today and was told, as we have been assured from the Fascist and Marxist camps . . . that classical liberalism is dead, he would surely rejoin: So much the worse for the twentieth century."[22]

The remaining years of the twentieth century will be more bearable if more people put into practice some of the truths Acton tried to teach: that there is more to humankind than material nature; that every person is important; that every person's conscience must be respected; that the state was made for people, not people for the state; that the test of a free society is the treatment of its minorities; that duties are as important as rights and that liberty is necessary so that people may fulfill their duties; that ordered liberty is the most delicate fruit of a high civilization; that all persons need an area they can call their own so they can make the fullest use of their talents; and that since all power tends to corrupt, the best way to prevent its misuse is to "cut it up into little bits."

Notes

[1]Maitland to R. L. Poole, 6 May 1901. See A. Lane Poole, "The Maitland-Poole Correspondence," *Cambridge Historical Journal*, X, no. 3 (1952): 332. With the publication of part of the Maitland-Poole correspondence, it has recently come to light that Arthur Balfour, prime minister at the time of Acton's death, offered the Regius Professorship first to F. W. Maitland who apparently declined for a still unknown reason. Acton's successor was to be J. B. Bury, author of *The Idea of Progress* and *The History of Freedom of Thought.*

[2]Lord Acton, *Letters of Lord Acton to Mary . . . Gladstone*, ed. Herbert Paul, p. lxxv.

[3]Lord Acton, "Inaugural Lecture on the Study of History," in *Lectures on Modern History*, ed. John N. Figgis and Reginald V. Laurence, p. 8.

[4]Ibid., p. 12.

[5]Mrs. Mary (Gladstone) Drew, *Acton, Gladstone and Others*, p. 5.

[6]E. S. Purcell, *The Life of Cardinal Manning*, pp. 490-91.

[7]Gertrude Himmelfarb, *Lord Acton: A Study in Conscience and Politics*, p. 232.

[8]*Tablet* (London), CVII (22 September 1906).

[9]Herbert Thurston, "The Late Lord Acton," *Catholic World*, LXXXIV (1906): 357-72.

[10]Acton, *Letters to Mary Gladstone*, p. 114.

[11]Richard M. D. Acton, Letter to the Editor, *Times* (London), 28 October 1906.

[12]Herbert Paul, in Acton, *Letters to Mary Gladstone*, p. lxviii.

[13]Oscar Browning, *Memories of Sixty Years*, p. 16.

[14]Maitland to Poole, 27 June 1902, in Poole, "Maitland-Poole Correspondence," p. 337.

[15]Ibid., 22 June 1902.

[16]Acton, *Letters to Mary Gladstone*, p. 91.

[17]Herman Finer, "Acton as Historian and Political Scientist," *Journal of Politics*, X (1948): 607-608.

[18]Himmelfarb, *Lord Acton*, p. 228.

[19]G. P. Gooch, *Historical Surveys and Portraits* (New York: Barnes & Noble, 1966), p. 156.

[20]G. P. Gooch, *Under Six Reigns*, p. 46.

[21]Gooch, *Historical Surveys*, p. 156.

[22]G. P. Gooch, "Lord Acton: Apostle of Liberty," *Foreign Affairs*, July 1947, p. 630.

Selected Bibliography of Books and Articles about Lord Acton and His Thought

Acton, Richard Maximilian Dalberg, 2d Baron. Letter to the Editor. *Nation and Athenaeum* XXXII (1922): 194.

—— Letter to the editor. *The Times* (London), 28 October 1906.

Altholz, Josef L. "The Conscience of Lord Acton." *Smith History Lecture Monographs.* Houston, Texas: University of St. Thomas, 1970.

—— *The Liberal Catholic Movement in England: The Rambler and Its Contributors, 1848-1864.* London: Burns & Oates, 1962.

Auchumuty, James J. "Acton as a Member of the House of Commons." *The Bulletin of the Faculty of Arts.* Vol. 5. Alexandria: Farouk I University, 1950.

—— "Acton's Election as an Irish Member of Parliament." *English Historical Review* LXI (1946): 394-405.

—— "Acton: The Youthful Parliamentarian." *Historical Studies of Australia and New Zealand* IX, no. 34 (May 1960): 131-39.

Ausubel, H. "Cult of Acton." *Saturday Review.* 14 March 1953, pp. 22-23.

Banaschevski, Peter. *Macaulay und Acton.* Munich: Werk-Verlag E. Banaschewski, 1960.

Beloff, Max. "A Challenge to Historians." *Listener* (London) IX (1949): 816-18.

Blakiston, Noel, ed. *The Roman Question* (Extracts from the dispatches of Odo Russell from Rome 1858-1870). London: Chapman & Hall, 1962.

Blennerhassett, Charlotte. "Acton." *Biographisches Jahrbuch und deutscher Nekrolog* VII (1902): 16-22.

—— "The Late Lord Acton." *Edinburgh Review* CXCVII (1903): 501-34.

—— "Lord Acton." *Deutsche Rundschau* CXXII (1905): 64-92.

Blennerhassett, W. L. "Acton: 1834-1902." *Dublin Review* CXCIV (1934): 169-88.

Bottino, Edward. "The Rambler Controversy: The Positions of Simpson, Newman, and Acton, 1856-62." Unpublished Ph.D. thesis, St. John's University, N.Y., 1970.

Brinton, Crane. *English Political Thought in the Nineteenth Century*. London: E. Benn, 1933.

—— "Lord Acton's Philosophy of History." *Harvard Theological Review* XII (1919): 84-112.

Browning, Oscar. *Memories of Later Years*. London: D. Appleton & Co., 1923.

—— *Memories of Sixty Years*. London: John Lane, The Bodley Head, 1910.

—— "Personal Recollections of Sir John Seeley and Lord Acton." *Albany Review* II (1908): 548-56.

Bryce, James. "The Letters of Lord Acton." *North American Review* CLXXVIII (1904): 698-710.

—— "Lord Acton." *Proceedings of the British Academy* I (1903-4): 277-82.

—— *Studies in Contemporary Biography*. London: Macmillan & Co., 1903.

Bury, J. B. *History of the Papacy in the Nineteenth Century*. London: Macmillan & Co., 1930.

Butler, Abbot Edward Cuthbert. *Vatican Council*. 2 vols. London: Longmans, Green & Co., 1962.

Butterfield, Herbert. "Acton: His Training, Methods and Intellectual System." In *Studies in Diplomatic History and Historiography in Honour of G. P. Gooch, C.H.*, edited by A. O. Sarkissian, pp. 169-98. London: Longmans, Green & Co., 1961.

—— "Journal of Lord Acton: Rome 1857." *Cambridge Historical Journal* VIII (1946): 186-204.

—— *Lord Acton*. Pamphlets of the English Historical Association, no. G9. London: G. Philip, 1948.

—— "Lord Acton's Correspondence with Döllinger." *Historical Journal*, vol. 9, no. 1 (1966): 140-44.

—— Review of David Mathew's *Acton: The Formative Years.* *English Historical Review* LXI (1946): 414.

—— *Whig Interpretation of History.* London: G. Bell & Sons, 1931.

Cambridge Modern History: An Account of Its Origin, Authorship and Production. Cambridge: At the University Press, 1907.

Clark, Eugene. "Catholic Liberalism and Ultramontanism, Freedom and Duty: A Study of the Quarrels Over the Control of Catholic Affairs in England, 1858-66." Unpublished Ph.D. thesis, University of Notre Dame, 1965.

Clark, G. N. "Origin of the Cambridge Modern History." *Cambridge Historical Journal* VIII (1945): 57-64.

Conzemius, Victor. "Acton, Döllinger und Ketteler. Zum Verständnis des Ketteler Bildes in den Quirinusbriefen und zur Kritik an Vigeners Darstellung Kettelers auf dem Vaticanum 1." *Archiv für mittelrheinische Kirchengeschichte* XIV (1962): 194-258.

—— "Lord Acton and the First Vatican Council." *Journal of Ecclesiastical History* (U.K.) Vol. 20, no. 2 (1969): 267-94.

Coulton, G. G. "Mistaken Ascription to Acton?" *English Historical Review* XLVI (1931): 460.

—— *Papal Infallibility.* London: The Morehouse Publishing Co., 1932.

Cowling, Maurice. "Mr. Woodruff's Acton." *Cambridge Journal* VI (1952): 181-90.

Creighton, Louise. *Life and Letters of Mandell Creighton.* 2 vols. London: Longmans, Green & Co., 1904

Dean, S. F. "Lord Acton and Edmund Burke." *Journal of the History of Ideas,* April 1972, pp. 325-35.

Döllinger, Johann Ignaz von. *Briefwechsel mit Lord Acton 1850-1869,* and *Briefwechsel mit Lord Acton 1869-1870.* 2 vols. Edited by Victor Conzemius. Munich: Beck, 1963, 1965.

—— *Declarations and Letters on the Vatican Decrees.* Edited by F. H. Reusch. Edinburgh, 1891.

—— "Döllinger and the Temporal Power of the Popes." *Dublin Review* L (1861): 195-234.

—— "Döllinger on the Temporal Power." *Edinburgh Review* CXVI (1862): 261-93.

Downing, Francis. "The Mind of Lord Acton." Unpublished Ph.D. thesis, Fordham University, 1940.

Drew, Mrs. Mary (Gladstone). *Acton, Gladstone, and Others.* London: Nisbet & Co., 1924.

—— *Her Diaries and Letters.* Edited by Lucy Masterman. London: Methuen & Co., 1930.

────── "Lord Acton's Legacy to Liberals." *Optimist* III (1908): 34-39.

────── *Some Hawarden Letters, 1878-1913.* London: Nisbet & Co., 1917.

Drozdowski, Eugene, and Parker, Harold. "A Prophet for This Generation?" *South Atlantic Quarterly,* Vol. 52 (October 1953): 521-27.

Engel-Janosi, Frederic. "The Correspondence Between Lord Acton and Bishop Creighton." *Cambridge Historical Journal* VI (1940): 307-21.

────── "Reflections of Lord Acton on Historical Principles." *Catholic Historical Review* (Lancaster) XXVII (1941): 166-85.

────── "Some Notes on Lord Acton Suggested by a Recent Book." *Ibid.* XXIX (1943): 357-61.

Fasnacht, George E., ed. "Acton's Notes for a Romanes Lecture." *Contemporary Review* CLXXXII (December 1952): 348-53.

────── *Acton's Political Philosophy.* London: Hollis & Carter, 1952.

────── "Lord Acton on Freedom and Conscience." *Hibbert Journal,* Vol. 48 (April 1950): 278-81.

────── "Lord Acton on Socialism." *Contemporary Review* Vol. 176 (July 1949): 25-29.

Figgis, J. N. "Acton." *Dictionary of National Biography,* I, 2 and supplement, pp. 8-12. London: Smith, Elder & Co.

────── *Churches in the Modern State.* London: Longmans, Green & Co., 1914.

Finer, Herman. "Acton as Historian and Political Scientist." *Journal of Politics* X (1948): 603-35.

Fish, A. "Acton, Creighton and Lea: A Study in History and Ethics." *Pacific Historical Review* XVI (1947): 59-69.

Fisher, H. A. L. *James Bryce.* 2 vols. London, 1927.

────── "Lord Acton's Lectures." *Independent Review* XI (1906): 224-28.

────── *Studies in History and Politics.* Oxford: The Clarendon Press, 1920.

Fitzgerald, Percy H. *Fifty Years of Catholic Life and Progress.* 2 vols. London, 1901.

Fitzmaurice, Edmond. *Life of Granville George Leveson-Gower, 2nd Earl Granville.* 2 vols. London: Longmans, Green & Co., 1905.

Freeman, D. S. *Robert E. Lee.* Vol. IV, pp. 515-17. New York: C. Scribner's Sons, 1935.

Friedrich, Johann. *Geschichte des vatikanischen Konzils.* 3 vols. Bonn, 1877.

——*Ignaz von Döllinger*. 3 vols. Munich: Beck, 1901.

——"Römische Briefe über das Konzil." *Revue internationale de théologie* XI (1903): 621-28.

Gillow, Joseph, ed. *Bibliographical Dictionary of the English Catholics*. 5 vols. London: Burns & Oates, 1885-95.

Gladstone, William Ewart. *Correspondence on Church and Religion of W. E. Gladstone*. Edited by D. C. Lathbury. 2 vols. London: J. Murray, 1952.

——*The Political Correspondence of Mr. Gladstone and Lord Granville, 1868-1876*. Edited by Agatha Ramm. 2 vols. London: Office of the Royal Historical Society, 1952.

——"Robert Elsmere: The Battle of Belief." *Nineteenth Century* XXIII (1888): 766-88.

Gladstone, William Ewart, and Schaff, Philip. *The Vatican Decrees in Their Bearing on Civil Allegiance: A Political Expostulation*. London: J. Murray, 1874.

Gooch, G. P. *History and Historians in the Nineteenth Century*. London: Longmans, Green & Co., 1913.

——"Lord Acton: Apostle of Liberty." *Foreign Affairs*, July 1947, pp. 629-42.

——*Under Six Reigns*. London: Longmans, Green & Co., 1958.

——"Victorian Memories VII: Lord Acton." *Contemporary Review* CLXXXIX (April 1956): 204-9.

Grant Duff, Mountstuart E. "Lord Acton's Letters." *Nineteenth Century and After* LV (1904): 765-75.

——*Out of the Past*. 2 vols. London: J. Murray, 1903.

Greville Memoirs. Edited by Lytton Strachey and Roger Fulford. 8 vols. London: Macmillan & Co., 1938

Hales, E. E. Y. *Pio Nono*. London: Eyre & Spottiswoode, 1954.

Hansard. *Parliamentary Debates* (3rd series). Vols. CLVIII-CLXVI (1860-62).

Hammond, J. L. *Gladstone and the Irish Nation*. London: Longmans, Green & Co., 1938.

Hammond, J. L. and Foote, M. R. D. *Gladstone and Liberalism*. New York: Macmillan Co., 1953.

Himmelfarb, Gertrude. "The American Revolution in the Political Theory of Lord Acton." *Journal of Modern History* XXI (1949): 293-312.

——*Lord Acton: A Study in Conscience and Politics*. Chicago, 1952.

——*Victorian Minds*. New York: Knopf, 1968.

Hill, R. "Lord Acton and the Catholic Reviews." *Blackfriars* XXXVI (1955): 469-82.

―――"Reconsideration: Lord Acton." *History Today* II (1952): 551-57.

Hohl, Clarence L., Jr. "Lord Acton's Visit to America, 1853." *Proceedings of the American Catholic Historical Society of Philadelphia,* 1960, Vol. 71 (314): 73-84.

―――"Lord Acton on Church and State." Unpublished Ph.D. thesis, St. Louis University, 1951.

Holland, James C. "The Education of Lord Acton." Unpublished Ph.D. thesis, The Catholic University of America, 1968. In preparation for publication.

"Janus" (pseudonym for Ignaz von Döllinger, Johannes Friedrich, and Johannes Huber). *The Pope and the Council.* London: Rivingtons, 1873.

Janossi, Engel de. "The Acton-Creighton Correspondence." *Cambridge Historical Journal* VI, no. 3.

Kenrick, Peter Richard. *An Inside View of the Vatican Council.* Edited by Leonard W. Bacon. New York: American Tract Society, 1872.

Kirk, John. *Biographies of English Catholics in the Eighteenth Century.* Edited by J. H. Pollen and E. Burton. London: Burns & Oates, 1909.

Kirk, Russell. "Lord Acton's Opinions." *Yale Review* vol. 42, no. 4 (June 1953): 660-64.

Kobell, Louise von. *Conversations of Dr. Döllinger.* London: R. Bentley & Son, 1892.

Kochan, Lionel. *Acton on History.* London: Andre Deutsch, 1954.

―――"Lord Acton Fifty Years After." *Contemporary Review* vol. 181 (14 June 1952): 353-56.

Lally, Frank Edward. *As Lord Acton Says.* Newport (Rhode Island): R. Ward, 1942.

Leslie, Shane. *Cardinal Manning: His Life and Labours.* New York: P. J. Kennedy, 1954.

―――*Henry Edward Manning.* London: Burns, Oates & Washborne, 1921.

Letters of the Empress Frederick. Edited by Fredrick Ponsonby. London: Macmillan & Co., 1908.

Longford, Elizabeth. *Victoria R.I.* London: Weidenfeld & Nicolson, 1964.

MacDougall, Hugh. O.M.I. *The Acton-Newman Relations: The Dilemma of Christian Liberalism.* New York: Fordham University Press, 1962.

McElrath, Damian O.F.M. "Richard Simpson and John Henry Newman: The *Rambler,* Laymen and Theology," *Catholic Historical Review* LII, no. 4 (January 1967): 509-33.

McElrath, Damian, O.F.M. (in collaboration with James Holland and Ward White and Sue Katzman). *Lord Acton: The Decisive Decade, 1864-74.* Louvain: Publications Universitaires de Louvain, 1970.

MacRae, D. G. "The Politics of Lord Acton." *Political Quarterly* Vol. 24 (July 1953): 285-92.

Magnus, Philip. *Gladstone, A Biography.* London: J. Murray, 1954.

Maine, Henry Sumner. *Popular Government.* London: J. Murray, 1918.

Maitland, Frederic William. *Collected Papers.* Edited by H. A. L. Fisher. 3 vols. Cambridge: At the University Press, 1911.

Manning, Henry Edward. *Caesarism and Ultramontanism.* London, 1874.

―――― *The Ecumenical Council and the Infallibility of the Roman Pontiff.* London: Longmans, Green & Co. 1869.

―――― *The True Story of the Vatican Council.* 2d edition. London: Burns & Oates, 1877.

―――― *The Vatican Council and Its Definitions.* London: Longmans, Green & Co., 1870.

Massey, H. J. "Lord Acton's Theory of Nationality." *Review of Politics* vol. 31 (October 1969): 495-508.

Mathew, David. *Acton: The Formative Years.* London: Eyre & Spottiswoode, 1946.

―――― *Catholicism in England, 1535-1935.* London: Longmans, Green & Co., 1936.

―――― *Lord Acton and His Times.* London: Eyre & Spottiswoode, 1968.

Mill, John Stuart. *Three Essays on Religion.* New York: H. Holt & Co., 1874.

―――― *Utilitarianism, Liberty, and Representative Government.* London: J. M. Dent & Sons, 1871.

Morgan, John H. *John Viscount Morley.* New York: Houghton Mifflin Co., 1924.

Morley, John. *Critical Miscellanies.* 4 vols. London: Macmillan & Co., 1904.

―――― *Life of William Ewart Gladstone.* 3 vols. London: Macmillan & Co., 1904.

―――― *Recollections.* 2 vols. London: Macmillan & Co., 1917.

Mass, C. B. *The Old Catholic Movement, Its Origins and History.* 2d ed. London, 1964.

Murray, Robert H. *Studies in the English Social and Political Thinkers of the Nineteenth Century.* 2 vols. Cambridge: W. Heffer & Sons, 1929.

Newman, John Henry. *Essay on the Development of Christian Doctrine.* Edited by Charles F. Harrold. New York: Longmans, Green & Co., 1949.

——— *A Letter Addressed to His Grace the Duke of Norfolk on Occasion of Mr. Gladstone's Recent Expostulation.* New York: Catholic Publication Society, 1875.

——— *Letters and Correspondence.* Edited by Anne Mozley. 2 vols. London: Longmans, Green & Co., 1891.

Nielsen, Frederick. *History of the Papacy in the Nineteenth Century.* 2 vols. London: J. Murray, 1906.

Noack, Ulrich. *Geschichtswissenschaft und Wahrheit.* Frankfort: M. G. Schulte-Bulmke, 1935.

——— *Katholizität und Geistesfreiheit.* Frankfort: M. G. Schulte-Bulmke, 1936

——— *Politik als Sicherung der Freiheit.* Frankfort: M. G. Schulte-Bulmke, 1947.

Norman, E. R. *Anti-Catholicism in Victorian England.* New York: Barnes & Noble, 1968.

Nurser, John. "The Idea of Conscience in the Work of Lord Acton." Unpublished Ph.D. thesis. Cambridge University, 1957.

Petander, K. *Lord Acton och hans kritik an Leopold von Ranke.* Stockholm: Kfis bokförlag i distribution, 1955.

Plummer, Alfred. "Recollections of Dr. Döllinger." *Expositor* (4th series) I (1890): 212-25, 270-84, 422-35.

Pollock, John. "Lord Acton at Cambridge." *Independent Review* II (1904): 360-78.

Poole, R. L. "John Emerich, Lord Acton." *English Historical Review* XVII (1902): 692-99.

Purcell, E. S. *Life of Cardinal Manning.* 2 vols. London: Macmillan & Co., 1896.

Quirinus (pseud.). *Letters from Rome on the Council.* London: Rivingtons, 1870.

Raico, Ralph, "The Place of Religion in the Liberal Thought of Constant, Tocqueville and Lord Acton." Unpublished Ph.D. thesis, University of Chicago, 1971.

Russell, George W. E. *Portraits of the Seventies.* London: T. F. Unwin, 1916.

Ryan, Guy A. "The Acton Circle, 1864-71: The *Chronicle* and the *North British Review.*" Unpublished Ph.D. thesis, University of Notre Dame, 1969.

Saturday Review (London). Vols. XII-XV (1861-63), LXXIX (1895).

Schuettinger, Robert L. "The Accommodation of Political and Religious Values in the Thought of Lord Acton." *Il Politico* (University of Pavia) XXXIII, no. 1 (1968): 201-9.

—— "The Education of Lord Acton." In *Toward Liberty: Essays in Honor of Ludwig von Mises.* Vol. II, pp. 334-46. Menlo Park, Calif.: Institute for Humane Studies, 1971.

Scottino, Joseph Peter. "An Examination of the Concept of Liberty in the Political Thought of Lord Acton." Unpublished Ph.D. thesis, Fordham University, 1961.

Shaw, W. A. *A Bibliography of the Historical Works of Dr. Creighton, late Bishop of London; Dr. Stubbs, Dr. S. R. Gardiner, and the late Lord Acton.* London: Offices of the Royal Historical Society, 1903.

Shorter, Clement. "Lord Acton's Hundred Best Books." *Pall Mall Magazine.* XXXVI (July 1905): 3-10.

Smith, R. A. L. "Books in General" (Essay-review of Acton's works). *The New Statesman and Nation,* 27 May 1944, pp. 355-56.

—— *Collected Papers.* London: Longmans, Green & Co., 1947.

Spectator LXXIV (1895).

Strachey, Lytton, *Eminent Victorians.* London: G. P. Putnam's Sons, 1929.

Stephen, M. D. "Liberalism, Church and State: Gladstone's Relations with Manning and Acton, 1832-70." *Journal of Religious History,* December 1961, pp. 217-32.

Sullivan, William K. *University Education in Ireland: A Letter to Sir John Dalberg Acton.* Dublin: W. B. Kelly, 1866.

Tedder, H. L. "Lord Acton as a Book Collector." *Proceedings of the British Academy* I (1903-4): 285-88.

Temperley, Harold. "Lord Acton on the Origins of the War of 1870, with Some Unpublished Letters from the British and Viennese Archives." *Cambridge Historical Journal* II (1926): 68-82.

Thornely, Thomas. *Cambridge Memories.* London: H. Hamilton, 1936.

Thurston, Herbert. "The Late Lord Acton." *Catholic World* LXXXIV (1906): 357-72.

The Times (London). Obituary of Lord Acton. 20 June 1902.

Tonsor, S. J. "Ignaz von Doellinger: Lord Acton's Mentor." *Anglican Theological Review,* Vol. 41, no. 3 (1959): 211-15.

—— "Lord Acton on Döllinger's Historical Theology." *Journal of the History of Ideas,* Vol. 20 (June 1959): 329-52.

Trevelyan, G. M. *An Autobiography and Other Essays*. London: Longmans, Green & Co., 1949.

——— *The Present Position of History*. Cambridge (U.K.): Longmans, Green & Co., 1927.

Ullathorne, William Bernard. *The Council and Papal Infallibility: A Letter Addressed to the Clergy and the Laity of the Diocese of Birmingham*. London, 1870.

——— *A Letter on the "Rambler" and the "Home and Foreign Review,"* London, 1862.

——— *Mr. Gladstone's Expostulation Unravelled*. New York: Catholic Publication Society, 1875.

——— *See above*, Butler, Abbot Edward Cuthbert. *Vatican Council*. (Based on Bishop Ullathorne's letters.)

Vallette, J. "Un Catholique Liberal Anglais," *Mercure France* vol. 316 (October 1952): 333-37.

Wallace, Lillian P. *The Papacy and European Diplomacy 1869-1878*. Chapel Hill (N.C.): University of North Carolina Press, 1948.

Ward, Wilfrid. *Life of John Henry Cardinal Newman*. 2 vols. London: Longmans, Green & Co., 1912.

——— *Life and Times of Cardinal Wiseman*. 2 vols. London: Longmans, Green & Co., 1897.

Watkins, A. and Butterfield, H. "Gasquet and the Acton-Simpson Correspondence." *Cambridge Historical Journal* X (1950): 82.

Watt, E. D. "Acton's Concept of Freedom." Unpublished Ph.D. thesis, Duke University, 1961.

——— "Freedom as an Incantation: The Example of Lord Acton." *Journal of Politics*, Vol. 25 (August 1963): 461-71.

Weaver, Richard M. "Liberalism with a Ballast." *Sewanee Review*, Vol. 63 (April 1954): 334-41.

Woodruff, Douglas. "A Reply" (to the article by Maurice Cowling, *see above*). *Cambridge Journal* VI (1953): 436-39.

Woodward, E. L. "The Place of Lord Acton in the Liberal Movement of the Nineteenth Century." *Politica* IV (September 1939): 248-65.

Bibliography
of the Works of Lord Acton

PREFATORY NOTE

There are three published bibliographies of the works of
Lord Acton. The first of these (upon which the succeeding
studies are largely based) is by William A. Shaw and was
published under the title: *A Bibliography of the Historical
Works of Dr. Creighton, Dr. Stubbs, Dr. S. R. Gardiner and
the Late Lord Acton* (London: Royal Historical Society,
1903. Reprint. New York: Burt Franklin, 1969).

The preface to this bibliography states that Dr. Shaw was
assisted in identifying Acton's works (which are rarely
signed by his name or even an initial) by the Second Baron
Acton; a colleague of Acton's at Cambridge, Mr. Reginald
V. Laurence; and Mr. T. F. Wetherell (Acton's coeditor at
the *Rambler* and *Home and Foreign Review* and editor of
the *Chronicle* and *North British Review*).

The second bibliography was compiled by F. E. Lally and
published in his study of Acton, *As Lord Acton Says* (Newport, Rhode Island: Remington Ward, 1942). Mr. Lally was
aided by new information published in *Lord Acton and His*

Circle (an incomplete version of the Acton-Simpson correspondence), edited by Abbot Gasquet (London, 1906), and also by information in *The History of Freedom and Other Essays*, edited by John N. Figgis and Reginald V. Laurence (London, 1907).

The third bibliography was compiled by Bert F. Hoselitz and published in *Essays on Freedom and Power*, edited by Gertrude Himmelfarb (Glencoe, Illinois: The Free Press, 1948).

The present bibliographical study is, of course, much indebted to the previous work of the above mentioned scholars. In addition, the recently published Acton-Simpson correspondence (edited by Josef L. Altholz and Damian McElrath) has made a major contribution to Acton scholarship. By going far beyond Abbot Gasquet's incomplete work, they have made it possible definitely to identify several other articles as being the work of Acton or being the work of others.

The essay-review entitled "Mr. Buckle's Thesis and Method," for instance, was only recently attributed to Acton in William H. McNeill's edition of Acton's historical writings, *Essays in the Liberal Interpretation of History* (Chicago, 1967). With the publication of Altholz and McElrath's work in 1971, however, there can no longer be any doubt that this essay was almost entirely the work of Richard Simpson.

In addition to establishing the authorship of several disputed or mistakenly attributed articles, I have taken the opportunity of correcting, in this new bibliography, a few minor typographical errors of spelling and dating in the previous bibliographies.

I also thought it would be useful to subdivide the large number of Acton's writings into some kind of subject classification. Because a good many (probably most) of Acton's writings were concerned with more than one field of history or philosophy, this has not been easy. To cite just one example, Acton's review of Edward Vaughan Kenealy's poetical work "A New Pantomime" (*Home and Foreign Review* II, no. 4 [April 1863]: 669-74) might have been listed under "Irish History and Culture" because the author is Irish or under "British History and Culture" because he published in Britain or under "German History and Culture" because the poem under discussion is about Goethe's *Faust*. I have listed it under "Ecclesiastical History" because Acton chose to treat the poem as a theological statement and discussed its implications in relation to the Catholic Church. I have placed articles, in general, under the widest or broadest classification wherever possible. Thus, I have listed works about Bavaria or Austria under the heading "German History and Culture."

It will be apparent from a glance at this bibliography that Acton did in fact write a great deal even though he published little under his own name and authored no books in his lifetime. The subject classification will also reveal the range of Acton's interests. About a fifth of his work was directly concerned with Church or generally religious matters. Approximately a tenth of his articles and reviews were concerned with German history, and slightly smaller percentages were concerned with French and British history respectively. He also was substantially interested in Italian and American history. On the other hand, he had very little interest in philosophy (except philosophy of history), economics, or ancient history. He was, of course, primarily a historian of modern Western Europe.

I should stress that the subclassifications are not meant to be hard-and-fast because many of Acton's articles dealt with several of my listed categories at the same time. I hope, however, that this admittedly rough classification will give some idea of where Acton's interests and special abilities lay. It may also be of some help to scholars concerned with Acton's work in a particular area, such as modern French history.

The reader will also note that almost all of Acton's major articles have now been published in book form, in some cases in several different anthologies. The abbreviations used for these anthologies in citing republications are as follows: *Essays in the Liberal Interpretation of History* (LIH), *Essays on Church and State* (C&S), *Essays on Freedom and Power* (F&P), *Historical Essays and Studies* (HES), *The History of Freedom and Other Essays* (HOF).

UNPUBLISHED WORKS OF ACTON (MANUSCRIPTS)

Abingdon. Woodruff Manuscripts.
Birmingham. Oratory Archives. (Especially for the Acton-Newman Correspondence.)
Cambridge. University Library. Additional Manuscripts (Lord Acton).
Downside. Abbey Archives. Lord Acton Papers.
London. British Museum. Additional Manuscripts (Lord Acton and W. E. Gladstone).
Oxford. Pembroke College Archives. Lord Acton Papers.
Oxford. University Library. Viscount Bryce Papers.

BOOKS OF COLLECTED ESSAYS AND CORRESPONDENCE

Under the Authorship of Lord Acton and Edited by Others

Correspondence of Lord Acton and Richard Simpson. Edited by Josef L. Altholz and Damian McElrath. 2 vols. to date. Cambridge: At the University Press, 1971. Volume III is yet to be published.
Essays in the Liberal Interpretation of History. Edited by William H. McNeill. Chicago, 1967.

Essays on Church and State. Edited by Douglas Woodruff. London, 1952.

Essays on Freedom and Power. Edited by Gertrude Himmelfarb. Glencoe, Ill. 1948.

Historical Essays and Studies. Edited by John N. Figgis and Reginald V. Laurence. London, 1908.

The History of Freedom and Other Essays. Edited by John N. Figgis and Reginald V. Laurence. London, 1907.

Lectures on the French Revolution. Edited by John N. Figgis and Reginald V. Laurence. London, 1910.

Lectures on Modern History. Edited by John N. Figgis and Reginald V. Laurence. London, 1906. Republications: (1) *Renaissance to Revolution: The Rise of the Free State* (new title). Introduction by Hans Kohn. New York, 1961. (2) *Lectures on Modern History.* Introduction by Hugh Trevor-Roper. New York, 1961.

Letters of Lord Acton to Mary, Daughter of the Right Hon. W. E. Gladstone. Edited by Herbert Paul. London, 1904. Second revised edition. London, 1913.

Lord Acton and His Circle. Edited by Abbot Francis A. Gasquet. London, 1906.

Lord Acton on Papal Power. Edited by H. A. MacDougall. London, 1973.

Selections from the Correspondence of the First Lord Acton. Edited by John N. Figgis and Reginald V. Laurence. London, 1917.

Under the Authorship of Others but Including Works by Acton

Drew, Mary Gladstone. *Some Hawarden Letters, 1878-1913.* Edited by L. March-Phillipps and B. Christian. London, 1917. (Letters written to Mrs. Drew as edited by the above. Includes several letters from Acton, notably his list of one hundred best books.)

Döllinger, Johann Ignaz von. *Briefwechsel mit Lord Acton.* Edited by Victor Conzemius. Vol. I, 1850-1869; Vol. II, 1869-1870. Munich, 1963-65.

McElrath, Damian, in collaboration with Holland, James; White, Ward; and Katzman, Sue. *Lord Acton: The Decisive Decade, 1864-74, Essays and Documents.* Louvain, 1970. (Includes many letters and essays by Acton.)

ARTICLES, BOOK REVIEWS, AND ESSAYS BY LORD ACTON

Ancient History and Culture

Address delivered 26 February 1877. "The History of Freedom in Antiquity." (Bridgnorth, 1877.) Reprinted in F&P, pp. 30-57; HOF, pp. 1-29; LIH, pp. 243-70.

Article in the *Chronicle:*
"Ozanam on the Fifth Century." (1 February 1868): 106-8.

Book Reviews in the *Home and Foreign Review:*
C. Merivale. *History of the Romans under the Empire.* Vol. II, no. 4 (April 1863): 589-93.

F. D. Gerlach. *Vorgeschichte, &c., des Römischen Statts.* Vol. III, no. 6 (October 1863): 679-81.

Adolph Stahr. *Tiberius.* Vol. IV, no. 7 (January 1864): 276-81.

W. Forsyth. *Life of M. T. Cicero.* Vol. IV, no. 8 (April 1864): 705.

—— in the *Chronicle:*
C. Martha. *Les Moralistes sous l'Empire Roman.* Vol. I (30 March 1867): 43.

F. de Saulcy. *Les derniers jours de Jérusalem.* Vol. I (6 April 1867): 43.

"Professor Hergenröther's *Life of Photius.*" Vol. I (27 July 1867): 419-21.

—— in the *North British Review:*
C. Martha. *Le poème de Lucrèce; morale, religion, science.* Vol. LI, no. 101 (October 1869): 215-16.

Pamphlet: *Human Sacrifice.* London: printed privately by Robson, Levey, and Franklyn (probably 1863).

Belgian History and Culture

Book Review in the *Home and Foreign Review:*
J. J. Thonissen. *Vie du Comte Félix de Mérode.* Vol. II, no. 3 (January 1863): 268-70.

—— in the *North British Review:*
L. Hymans. *Histoire de la Belgique, 1814-30.* Vol. LI, no. 102 (January 1870): 570-71.

British History and Culture

Article in the *Home and Foreign Review*:
    "Secret History of Charles II." Vol. I, no. 1 (July 1862): 146-74. Reprinted in LIH, pp. 95-130; HES, pp. 85-122.

—— in the *Chronicle*:
    "Ranke" (on Ranke's *Englische Geschichte*). Vol. I (20 July 1867): 393-95.
    "The Early Years of H.R.H. The Prince Consort." Vol. I (10 August 1867): 470-71.
    "Mr. Goldwin Smith on the Political History of England." Vol. I (31 August 1867): 543-44. Reprinted in C&S, pp. 406-10.
    "The Queen's Journal." Vol. II (18 January 1868): 65-66.

—— in the *Quarterly Review*:
    "Letters and Papers, Foreign and Domestic, of the Reign of Henry VIII." Vol. CXLIII, no. 285 (January 1877): 1-51. Reprinted as "Wolsey and the Divorce of Henry VIII" in HES, pp. 1-64.

—— in the *Nineteenth Century*:
    "J. W. Cross's *Life of George Eliot*." Vol. XVII, no. 97 (March 1885): 464-85. Reprinted as "George Eliot's Life" in HES, pp. 273-304.

Book Reviews in the *Rambler, New Series*:
    Thomas Macknight. *History of the Life and Times of Edmund Burke*. Vol. IX, part 53 (April 1858): 268-73.

—— in the *Rambler, New Series* (i.e., Third Series):
    E. Arnold. *The Marquis of Dalhousie's Administration of British India*. Vol. VI, part 19 (May 1862): 534-36.

—— in the *Home and Foreign Review*:
    J. Spedding. *Letters and Life of Francis Bacon*. Vol. I, no. 1 (July 1862): 241-42.
    M. Napier. *Memorials of Graham of Claverhouse, Viscount Dundee*. Vol. II, no. 3 (January 1863): 236-37.
    T. Arnold. *A Manual of English Literature*. Ibid., pp. 250-54.
    C. Knight. *The Popular History of England*. Ibid., pp. 254-57.
    F. Arnold. *The Public Life of Lord Macaulay*. Ibid. pp. 257-60.
    T. Macknight. *Life of Henry St. John, Viscount Bolingbroke*. Vol. II, no. 4 (April 1863): 634-37.

S. R. Gardiner. *History of England, 1603-16.* Vol III, no. 5 (July 1863): 269-70.

W. Massey. *History of England during the Reign of George III. Ibid.,*pp. 312-14.

J. G. Phillimore. *History of England during the Reign of George III.* Vol. III, no. 6 (October 1863): 713-15. Reprinted in C&S, pp. 403-6.

T. E. May. *Constitutional History of England. Ibid.* pp. 715-18. Reprinted in C&S, pp. 397-400.

J. E. Doyle. *A Chronicle of England, B.C. 55–A.D. 1485.* Vol. IV, no. 7 (January 1864): 289-90.

L. von Ranke. *Englische Geschichte, Vol. IV.* Vol. IV, no. 8 (April 1864): 715-16.

—— in the *Chronicle:*

J. B. Mullinger. *Cambridge Characteristics in the 17th Century.* Vol. I (14 September 1867): 596-97.

A. Bisset. *History of the Commonwealth of England.* Vol. II (8 February 1868): 139-40.

—— in the *North British Review:*

W. Lee. *Life and Newly Discovered Writings of Daniel De Foe.* Vol. LI, no. 101 (October 1869): 249-51.

C. D. Yonge. *Life and Administration of the 6th Earl of Liverpool. Ibid.,* pp. 264-65.

M. Büdinger. *Wellington. Ibid.,* pp. 265-66.

Lord Stanhope. *Reign of Queen Anne.* Vol. LII, no. 104 (July 1870): 553-56.

Earl of Malmesbury. *Letters of the First Earl of Malmesbury.* Vol. LIII, no. 105 (October 1870): 273-75.

Sir. H. L. Bulwer. *Life of Henry John Temple, Viscount Palmerston.* Vol. LIII, no. 106 (January 1871): 586-89.

—— in the *Nineteenth Century:*

T. W. Reid. *Life, letters, and friendships of R. Monckton Milnes, 1st Lord Houghton.* Vol. XXVIII (December 1890): 993-1000. Reprinted in HES, pp. 414-25.

—— in the *English Historical Review:*

J. F. Bright. *History of England, 1837-80.* Vol. III (1888): 798-809. Reprinted in HES, pp. 472-90.

Edited by Lord Acton. *Letters of James II, to the Abbot of La Trappe.* (Introduction by Acton.) Miscellanies of the Philobiblion Society. Vol. XIV (London, 1872-76).

Correspondence:
> Letter on "Our Public Schools and Universities before the Reformation," in *the Rambler, New Series* (i.e., Third Series), VI, part 16 (November 1861): 119-24.
>
> On "Harpsfield's *Narrative of the Divorce*," in the *Academy, New Series*, IX, no. 216 (24 June 1876): 609-10.
>
> "Briefe Lord Acton's über George Eliot." Contributed by Rudolf Imelmann. Published in *Probleme der englischen Sprache und Kultur*, edited by Wolfgang Keller, pp. 195-207. Heidelberg, 1925. Letters were written between 19 October 1885 and 11 March 1886.

Ecclesiastical History

Address delivered 28 May 1877. "The History of Freedom in Christianity." (Bridgnorth, 1877.) Reprinted in HOF, pp. 30-60; F&P, pp. 58-87; LIH, 271-99.

Articles in the *Rambler, New Series:**
> "The Count de Montalembert." Vol. X, part 60 (December 1858): 421-28.
>
> "Political Thoughts on the Church." Vol. XI, part 61 (January 1859): 30-49. Reprinted in HOF, pp. 188-211.

---

*Miss Himmelfarb, in her biography of Acton, makes one addition to the bibliography of Acton's works compiled by Hoselitz in her previous anthology, *Essays on Freedom and Power*. On page 244 of *Lord Acton* she states that "only one addition need be made to that bibliography. The first item listed under 'The following articles appeared in the *Rambler, New Series*' should be:

' "Bossuet," X, part 54 (June 1858).' "

Neither Shaw nor Lally cited this essay on the French theologian Jacques Bénigne Bossuet as being the work of Acton. However, Josef Altholz in his *The Liberal Catholic Movement in England* (London, 1962) asserts that Acton was in trouble with the Church for identifying St. Augustine with Jansenism in an essay on Bossuet (p. 77). Douglas Woodruff, in his Acton anthology, *Essays on Church and State* (London, 1952), republishes the essay as Acton's without comment on pages 230-45.

According to the latest and most complete work of scholarship on the *Rambler* period, however, the author was most likely J. M. Capes, a convert who was editor of the *Rambler* from 1848 to 1858. According to Altholz and McElrath (*Acton-Simpson Correspondence*, Vol. I, p. 74), "There is better evidence, however, that the author was J. M. Capes. He is listed as the author in Simpson's notebook, the best source for attributions in the early *Rambler*."

"The Catholic Press." Vol. XI, part 62 (February 1859): 73-90. Reprinted in C&S, pp. 260-78.

—— in the *Rambler, New Series* (i.e., Third Series):
"Historical Annotations to the Foregoing Article." ("The Abbé de Lamennais," by the Baron d'Eskstein.) Vol. I, part 1 (May 1859): 70-77.
"The Roman Question." Vol. II, part 5 (January 1860): 136-54.
"The Political System of the Popes." Vol. II, part 5 (January 1860): 154-65; Vol. III, part 7 (May 1860): 27-38; Vol. IV, part 11 (January 1861): 183-93. Reprinted in C&S, pp. 123-58.
"The States of the Church." Vol. II, part 6 (March 1860): 291-323. Reprinted in C&S, pp. 86-122.
"Hefele's Life of Ximenes." Vol. III, part 8 (July 1860): 159-70. Reprinted in C&S, pp. 381-94.
"Döllinger's History of Christianity." Vol. IV, part 11 (January 1861): 145-75. Reprinted in C&S, pp. 374-81.
"The Catholic Academy." Vol. V, part 15 (September 1861): 291-302. Reprinted in C&S, 279-90.
"Döllinger on the Temporal Power." Vol. VI, part 16 (November 1861): 1-62. Reprinted in HOF, pp. 301-74.
"The Protestant Theory of Persecution." Vol. VI, part 18 (March 1862): 318-51. Reprinted in HOF, pp. 150-87; F&P, pp. 88-127.

—— in the *Home and Foreign Review:**
"Cardinal Wiseman and the *Home and Foreign Review*." Vol. I, no. 2 (October 1862): 501-20. Reprinted in HOF, pp. 436-60.
"Ultramontanism." Vol. III, no. 5 (July 1863): 162-206. Reprinted in C&S, pp. 37-85; LIH, pp. 165-214.
"Mediaeval Fables of the Popes." Vol. III, no. 6 (October 1863): 610-37. Reprinted in C&S, pp. 200-229.
"The Munich Congress." Vol. IV, no. 7 (January 1864): 209-44. Reprinted in C&S, pp. 159-99.

*Shaw lists "The Waldensian Forgeries," in the *Home and Foreign Review*, Vol. II, no. 4 (April 1863): 504-30, as being the work of Acton. Both Lally and Hoselitz cite the article but explain that it was actually the work of Döllinger with Acton probably acting as translator and editor. In a letter to Simpson on 20 January 1863 Acton refers to a prospective article on the Waldensian Forgeries written by Döllinger. (*Lord Acton and His Circle*, p. 298).

"Conflicts with Rome." Vol. IV, no. 8 (April 1864): 667-96. Reprinted in F&P, pp. 269-98; HOF, pp. 461-91.

—— in the *Chronicle:*
"Material Resources of the Papacy." Vol. I (30 March 1867): 7-8.
"Fra Paolo Sarpi." *Ibid.*, pp. 14-17. Reprinted in C&S, pp. 251-59.
"The Case of Monte Cassino." Vol. I (6 April 1867): 33.
"Döllinger on Universities." Vol. I (13 April 1867): 57-59.
"The Secret Bull." Vol. I (4 May 1867): 124-25.
"The Next General Council." Vol. I (13 July 1867): 368-70.
"Essays in Academical Literature." ("Essays in Religion and Literature," edited by Archbishop Manning.) Vol. I (5 October 1867): 664-67.
"The Acta Sanctorum." Vol. I (2 November 1867): 756-58.

—— in the *North British Review:*
"The Pope and the Council." Vol. LI, no. 101 (October 1869): 127-35.
"The Vatican Council." Vol. LIII, no. 105 (October 1870): 183-229. Reprinted in F&P, pp. 299-356; HOF, pp. 492-550.
"The Borgias and Their Latest Historian." Vol. LIII, no. 106 (January 1871): 351-67. Reprinted in HES, pp. 65-84.

Book Reviews in the *Rambler, New Series:*
R. P. Félix. *Le progrès par le Christianisme: Conférences de Notre Dame de Paris.* Vol. X, part 55 (July 1858): 70-72.
A. Theiner. *Documents inédits relatifs aux affaires réligieuses de France.* Vol. X, part 58 (October 1858): 265-67.

—— in the *Rambler, New Series* (i.e., Third Series):
P. Charles of St. Aloysius. *Statistisches Jahrbuch der Kirche.* Vol. III, part 8 (July 1860): 262-64.

—— in the *Home and Foreign Review:*
Le Père J. M. Prat. *Histoire du père Ribadeneyra.* Vol. I, no. 1 (July 1862): 242-43.
H. Formby. *Pictorial Bible and Church History Stories.* Vol. II, no. 3 (January 1863): 215-19.
B. Niehues. *Geschichte des Verhältnisses zwischen Kaiserthum und Papstthum im Mittelalter. Ibid.*, pp. 220-21.
E. H. J. Reusens. *Anecdota Adriani Sexti. Ibid.*, pp. 230-31.
Hugo Laemmer. *Monumenta vaticana historiam*

ecclesiasticam saeculi XVI illustrantia. Ibid., pp. 231-33.
L. Schauer and Alp Chuquet, *La correspondance inédite de L. C. Saint Martin et Kirchberger baron de Liebistorf, 1792-97. Ibid.*, pp. 240-42.

Zeitgenossen ... von A. von Reumont. *Ibid.*, pp. 270-72.

J. A. Gerth von Wijk. *Specimen historico-theologicum exhibens historiam ecclesiae ultrajectinae Romano-Catholicae male Jansenisticae dictae. Ibid.*, pp. 277-78.

Die kirchliche Frage und ihre protestantische Lösung ... mit Beziehung auf die Schriften J. J. I. von Döllinger's und Bischof von Ketteler's. *Ibid.*, pp. 281-83.

F. J. Buss. *Oesterreichs Umbau im Verhältniss des Reichs zur Kirche. Ibid.*, pp. 283-84.

J. C. Morison. *The Life and Times of St. Bernard, Abbot of Clairvaux. Vol. II*, no. 4 (April 1863): 608-12.

P. Villari. *History of Girolamo Savonarola. Ibid.*, pp. 616-17.

J. J. I. von Döllinger. *Beiträge sur politischen, kirchlichen und Cultur-Geschichte der sechs letzten Jahrhunderte. Ibid.*, pp. 625-29.

Edward Vaughan Kenealy. *A New Pantomime. Ibid.*, pp. 669-74.

M. C. Debombourg. *Atlas chronologique des Etats de l'Eglise. Vol. III*, no. 5 (July 1863): 279.

G. F. Maclear. *A History of Christian Missions during the Middle Ages. Ibid.*, pp. 279-82.

M. l'Abbé Alliez. *Histoire du Monastère de Lérins. Ibid.*, pp. 282-83.

A. de Brimont. *Un Pape au Moyen Age. Ibid.*, pp. 284-85.

L'Abbé Magnan. *Histoire d'Urbain V. Ibid.*, pp. 285-86.

L'Abbé J. B. Christophe. *Histoire de la Papauté pendant le XVme Siècle. Ibid.*, pp. 287-89.

E. H. J. Reussens. *Syntagma Doctrinae Theologicae. Ibid.*, p. 290.

E. Stähelin. *Johannes Calvin: Leben und ausgewählte Schriften. Ibid.*, pp. 290-91.

Jakob Maehly. *Sebastian Castellio. Ibid.*, pp. 291-92.

F. Brandes. *John Knox. Ibid.*, p. 292.

R. R. Madden. *Galileo and the Inquisition. Ibid.*, p. 295.

M. Roux. *Mémoires de l'Abbé Le Gendre. Ibid.*, pp. 303-5.

W. Herbst. *Matthias Claudius der Wandsbecker Bote. Ibid.*, p. 309.

J. Carnaudet. *Acta Sanctorum. Vol. III*, no. 6 (October 1863): 682-85.

M. Joël. *Verhältniss Albert des Grossen zu Moses Maimonides. Ibid.*, pp. 689-90.

W. A. Hollenberg. *Studien su Bonaventura. Ibid.*, p. 690.

Mgf. Jager. *Histoire de l'Eglise Catholique en France. Ibid.*, pp. 693-94.

J. Friedrich. *Johann Wessel. Ibid.*, pp. 696-97.

C. Nitsch. *Die evangelische Bewegung in Italien. Ibid.*, pp. 724-26.

J. F. Maguire. *Father Matthew—A Biography.* Vol. IV, no. 7 (January 1864): 305-8.

H. E. Manning. *Sermons on Ecclesiastical Subjects. Ibid.*, pp. 310-12.

Sylvester Malone. *A Church History of Ireland.* Vol. IV, no. 8 (April 1864): 708-15.

Baum, Cunitz, et al. *Corpus Reformatorum.* Vol. XXIX. *Ibid.*, p. 715.

F. Laurent. *Etudes sur l'histoire de l'Humanité. Ibid.*, p. 715.

———— in the *Chronicle:*

L. Chodzko. *Le Métropolitain K. G. C. Cieciszowski et son temps.* Vol. I (30 March 1867): 19.

K. Werner. *Geschichte der katholischen Theologie in Deutschland.* Vol. I (11 May 1867): 164-65.

E. E. Marcy. *Christianity and Its Conflicts, Ancient and Modern.* Vol. I (3 August 1867): 450.

B. Hübler. *Die Constanzer Reformation und die Concordate von 1418.* Vol. I (24 August 1867): 523.

Notizie intorno alla vita ed alle opere di Monsignor Celestino Cavedoni. Vol. I (12 October 1867): 692.

Th. von Karajan. *Abraham à Sancta Clara.* Vol. I (14 December 1867): 906.

C. von Schätzler. *Neue Aufersuchungen über das Dogma von der Gnade und das Wesen des christlichen Glaubens.* Vol. II (18 January 1868): 68-69.

———— in the *North British Review:*

Arabella G. Campbell. *The Life of Fra Paolo Sarpi.* Vol. LI, no. 101 (October 1869): 238-39.

F. Williams. *Memoirs and correspondence of Bishop Atterbury. Ibid.*, pp. 247-49.

Augustus Theiner. *Histoire des deux Concordats. Ibid.*, pp. 262-63.

J. Crétineau-Joly. *Bonaparte, le concordat de 1801, &c.*
    Ibid., pp. 263-64.
P. Le Page Renouf. *The Case of the Pope Honorius.* Vol. LI,
    no. 102 (January 1870): 525-26.
Trois documents de l'église du 15me siècle. Ibid., p. 544.
F. Sclopis. *Le Cardinal Jean Morone. Ibid.*, pp. 546-47.
P. A. Carayon. *Le Père Ricci, Général des Jésuites. Ibid.*,
    pp. 558-62.
J. Waddington. *Congregational History.* Vol. LII, no. 103
    (April 1870): 245.
G. Baguenault de Purchèse. *Jean de Morvillier évêque
    d'Orléans.* Vol. LII, no. 104 (July 1870): 537-40.
*The pontifical decrees against the motion of the earth.
    Ibid.*, pp. 546-47.
J. Stroughton. *Ecclesiastical History of England. Ibid.*,
    pp. 550-51.
Documents Magistri Johannis Hus vitam illustrania. Vol.
    LIII, no. 105 (October 1870): 243.
E. de Rozière. *Liber diurnus, ou recueil des formules
    usitées par la Chancellerie Pontificale du Ve au XIme
    siècle. Ibid.*, pp. 252-53.
H. H. Milman. *Savonarola, Erasmus, &c.* Vol. LIII, no. 106
    (January 1871): 603-4.

——— in the *Academy:*
Mandell Creighton. *History of the Papacy during the
    Period of the Reformation. Vols. I and II (1378-1464).*
    Vol. XXII (1882): 407-9.

——— in the *English Historical Review:*
Creighton's *History of the Papacy, Vols. III and IV.* Vol. II
    (1887): 571-81. Reprinted in HES, pp. 426-41.
H. C. Lea. *A History of the Inquisition of the Middle Ages.*
    Vol. III (1888): 773-88. Reprinted in HOF, pp. 551-74.

Correspondence:*
Letter on "The Danger of Physical Science" (signed N. N.),
    in the *Rambler, New Series* (i.e., Third Series), VI, part
    19 (May 1862): 526-34.

———

*Previous Acton bibliographies have attributed the Quirinus Letters to
Acton. Bert F. Hoselitz records the following citation:
    Römische Briefe vom Concil, by Quirinus, four parts (Munich,
1870). P. 710. English translation, *Letters from Rome on the Council*,

Sendschreiben an einen deutschen Bischof des vaticanischen Concils, p. 19. Nördlingen, September 1870.

Letters to the *Times* on the Vatican Decrees. *Times*, 9 November 1874; 24 November 1874; 30 November 1874; and 12 December 1874. Reprinted in *Selections from the Correspondence of the First Lord Acton*, edited by J. N. Figgis and R. V. Laurence, pp. 119-44. London, 1917.

Extracts from letters to Mandell Creighton on Creighton's *History of the Papacy*. Reprinted in HES, pp. 503-7.

Speech:
"The Roman Government Question." Sir John Acton's speech in the House of Commons as reported by Hansard, *Parliamentary Debates*, Vol. CLVIII (Third Series), cols. 679-81 (23 Victoria) 1860.

---

three series (London, 1870). P. 856. These Letters appeared originally in the *Augsburger Allgemeine Zeitung* during December 1869 and the first part of 1870.

F. E. Lally adds the warning, "In reality, Lord Acton only collaborated in these Letters." W. A. Shaw, however, adds no such qualification.

They were actually written by Döllinger, based on letters sent to him from several friends at the Council. Acton was certainly one of these reporters, as was Dr. J. Friedrich (theologian to Cardinal Hohenlohe and later Döllinger's biographer). Other reporters may have been Bishop Dupanloup and Graf Louis Arco-Valley. David Mathew sees evidence of Acton's style in some of the letters, but concludes that although Acton supplied some information he cannot be called the author of these letters. (*Lord Acton and His Times*, pp. 184-85).

In a recently published letter, Acton explicitly denied authorship. He wrote to Thomas Wetherell, one of his journalistic colleagues, from Tegernsee on 25 July 1870 that, "If Renouf, or anybody, reviews Quirinus, he ought to know that I am not Quirinus, as Blenner [Hassett] seems to have reported. I inspired much of what he wrote, and much was prepared from my notes. But there is much in the letters over which I had no influence, and do not at all approve of; and not one of the letters ever passed through my hands before going to Augsburg; so that I had no real control, and have no general responsibility. If you read them you would often be able to tell the difference." (Woodruff MSS., published in McElrath, *Lord Acton: The Decisive Decade*, p. 95)

The *Chronicle*, under the head of "Current Events," published a number of journalistic reports on the political situation of the Papal States in Italy by Acton from 1867 to 1868.

Current Events: The Temporal Power, 1867-68.

1867: 30 March, p. 2, from "Decentralisation checked" to
p. 3, "called on to support."

6 April, p. 27, from "The Roman papers of the 23rd of
March" to p. 28, "not easily overcome."

11 May, p. 148, Rome and Italy.

18 May, p. 171, Rome and Italy.

15 June, pp. 266-67, Italy and Rome.

29 June, pp. 314-15, Rome.

6 July, pp. 339-40, Rome.

13 July, p. 362, Rome.

20 July, pp. 386-87, Italy.

3 August, p. 435, The Revolution in Rome.

28 September, pp. 625-26, Rome and Italy.

5 October, p. 650, Rome and Italy.

12 October, p. 673, Rome.

19 October, pp. 697-98, Rome.

26 October, p. 721, The Roman Question.

2 November, pp. 745-46, The Roman Question.

9 November, pp. 769-70. Italy and France.

16 November, pp. 793-94, Italy and Rome.

23 November, p. 819, Italy and Rome.

30 November, pp. 841-42, Rome.

7 December, pp. 865-66, The Roman Question and the
Conference.

14 December, p. 889, The Roman Question.

21 December, p. 914, The Roman Question.

29 December, p. 937, The Roman Question.

1868: 4 January, p. 2, Italy.

11 January, p. 25, Italy.

18 January, p. 50, Italy.

25 January, p. 73, The Italian Budget.

8 February, p. 122, Letter of General della Marmora.

Economics

Book Reviews in the *Home and Foreign Review:*

W. Roscher. *Die deutsche Nationalökonomie.* Vol. II, no. 3
(January 1863): 233-35.

G. de Molinari. *Cours d'économie politique.* Vol. IV, no. 7
(January 1864): 313-15.

———— in the *Chronicle:*

J. G. Courcelle-Seneuil. *Traité théorique et pratique
d'économie politique.* Vol. I (1 June 1867): 235.

—— in the *North British Review:*
Jules de Vroil. *Etude sur Cliquot-Blervache, économiste du 18me siècle.* Vol. LII, no. 103 (April 1870): 262-63.
L. de Lavergne. *Les économistes français du 18me siècle.* Vol. LII, no. 104 (July 1870): 556-58.

French History and Culture
Article in the *Chronicle:*
"The Massacre of St. Bartholomew." Vol. I (15 February 1868): 158-60.

—— in the *North British Review:*
"The Massacre of St. Bartholomew." Vol. LI, no. 101 (October 1869): 30-70. Reprinted in HOF, pp. 101-49.

Book Reviews in the *Rambler, New Series:*
M. Villemain. *La Tribune Moderne.* Vol. X, part 56 (August 1858): 140-42.

—— in the *Rambler, New Series* (i.e., Third Series):*
Schmidt-Weissenfels. *Geschichte der französischen Revolutions-Literatur.* Vol. II, part 4 (November 1859): 104-7.

—— in the *Home and Foreign Review:*
H. d'Arbois de Jubainville. *Histoire des ducs de Champagne.* Vol. I, no. 2 (October 1862): 538-40.
V. Fournel. *La Littérature indépendante. Ibid.,* pp. 542-43.
M. Mortimer-Ternaux. *Histoire de la Terreur. Ibid.,* pp. 547-48.
Mémoires sur Carnot, par son fils. Ibid., pp. 548-50.
Mémoires de M. Dupin. Ibid., pp. 550-51.
Recueil de documents sur l'histoire de Lorraine. Vol. II, no. 3 (January 1863): 237-38.
L. Dussieux and E. Soulié. *Mémoires du Duc de Luynes, 1735-58. Ibid.,* pp. 238-39.
A. Thiers. *Histoire de Consulat et de l'Empire, Ibid.,* pp. 244-48.

---

*Shaw, Lally, and Hoselitz all erroneously attribute the review of F. Guizot, *The Christian Church and Society in 1861*, Vol. VI, part 17 (January 1862): 265-68, to Acton. Simpson wrote to Acton on 10 December 1861: "By all means let [Henry Nutcombe] Oxenham [a convert who studied under Döllinger] do the short notices of Guizot." (*Acton-Simpson Correspondence*, Vol. II, p. 223.)

Mémoires de Canler, ancien chef du service de la Sûreté.
Ibid., pp. 276-77.

Honoré Bonhomme. *Madame de Maintenon et sa famille.*
Vol. II, no. 4 (April 1863): 631-32.

Edmund et Jules de Goncourt. *La femme au dix-huitième*
sieclè. Ibid., pp. 632-34.

M. Guizot. *Histoire parlementaire de France. Ibid.*, pp. 650-
51.

E. Augier. *Le fils de Giboyer. Ibid.*, pp. 666-69.

M. A. Huguenin. *Histoire de royaume Mérovingien.*
Vol. III, no. 5 (July 1863): 283-84.

M. C. Hippeau. *Mémoires inédits du Comte Leveneur de*
Tillières. Ibid., pp. 297-98.

A. Coquerel fils. *Voltaire, lettres inédites sur la tolérance.*
Ibid., pp. 305-6.

C. Desmaze. *Le Châtelet de Paris. Ibid.*, p. 306.

Dom Devienne. *Histoire de la ville de Bordeaux. Ibid.*,
p. 307.

Silvestre de Sacy. *Dacier: tableau historique de l'Erudition*
française depuis 1789. Ibid., pp. 309-10.

F. Colincamp and M. Naudet. *J. F. Boissonade, critique*
littéraire sous le premier Empire. Ibid., pp. 310-11.

Alexandre Sorel. *Le Couvent des Carmes et le Séminaire*
de Saint-Sulpice pendant la Terreur. Ibid., pp. 311-12.

A. Nettement. *Histoire de la Restauration. Ibid.*, pp. 316-18.

C. A. Sainte-Beuve. *Nouveaux Lundis. Ibid.*, pp. 318-19.

V. Fournel. *Les contemporains de Molière.* Vol. III, no. 6
(October 1863): 697-98.

Ch. Marty-Laveaux. *Oeuvres de P. Corneille. Ibid.*, pp. 698-
99.

F. Lachat. *Oeuvres complètes de Bossuet. Ibid.*, pp. 699-701.

M. le Cte. de Seilhac. *L'Abbé Dubois. Ibid.*, pp. 701-2.

H. Nadault de Buffon. *Buffon; sa Famille, &c. Ibid.*, pp. 704-
11.

Léon Verdier. *Histoire politique et littéraire de la*
Restauration. Vol. IV, no. 8 (April 1864): 722-23.

M. Guizot. *Mémoires pour servir à l'histoire de mon temps.*
Ibid., pp. 723-24.

Ed. Laboulaye. *Le parti libéral, son programme, et son*
avenir. Ibid., 724-25.

—— in the *Chronicle:*

A. Nettement. *Histoire de la Restauration.* Vol. I (30 March
1867): 19.

P. Clément. *Jacques Coeur et Charles VII*. Vol. I (13 April 1867): 65.

M. le Marquis de Sainte-Aulaire. *Correspondance complète de Madame du Deffand*. Vol. I (20 April 1867): 90.

Mémoires du Comte Beugnot, ancien ministre (1783-1815). *Ibid.*, pp. 90-91.

A. Desplanque. *Projet d'assassinat de Philippe le Bon par les Anglais*. Vol. I (27 April 1867): 115.

P. Clément. *Lettres, instructions et mémoires de Colbert*. *Ibid.*, pp. 115-16.

C. A. Sainte-Beuve. *Nouveaux Lundis*. Vol. I (4 May 1867): 140-41.

J. Crétineau-Joly. *Histoire des trois derniers Princes de la Maison de Conde*. Vol. I (11 May 1867): 165-66.

Le Comte de Christen. *Journal de ma Captivité*. Vol. I (18 May 1867): 189.

J. Vapereau. *L'annee littéraire et dramatique*. Vol. I (1 June 1867): 234.

M. W. Freer. *The Regency of Anne of Austria, Mother of Louis XIV*. Vol. I (8 June 1867): 259.

E. Hatin. *Bibliographie historique et critique de la presse périodique*. Vol. I (29 June 1867): 332.

C. Kingsley. *Three lectures on the Ancien Régime*. Vol. I (13 July 1867): 379-80. Reprinted in C&S, pp. 411-13.

M. Guizot. *Mémoires pour servir à l'histoire de mon temps*. *Ibid.*, p. 380.

M. Saint-Marc Girardin. *La Fontaine et les Fabulistes*. *Ibid.*, p. 380.

Guide de Paris, par les principaux Ecrivains et Artistes de la France. Vol. I (20 July 1867): 405.

A. de Pontmartin. *Nouveaux Samedis*. Vol. I (27 July 1867): 426.

M. Lenient. *La Satire en France au XVIme Siècle*. Vol. I (10 August 1867): 475.

A. Moreau de Jonnès. *Etat économique et social de la France depuis Henri IV*. Vol. I (24 August 1867): 523-24.

T. Juste. *Le Comte le Hon*. Vol. I (7 September 1867): 572-73.

M. Nourrisson. *La politique de Bossuet*. Vol. I (14 September 1867): 596.

L. Ratisbonne. *Alfred de Vigny: Journal d'un poète*. *Ibid.*, p. 597.

W. Wattenbach. *Algier*. Vol. I (12 October 1867): 692-93.

W. L. Holland. *Briefe der Herzogin Elisabeth Charlotte von Orléans, 1676-1706*, Vol. I (19 October 1867): 716-17.

L. Passy. *Histoire Administrative, 1789-1815.* Vol. I
(9 November 1867): 788.

M. Guizot. *M. de Barante.* Vol. I (16 November 1867): 810-
11.

S. Smiles. *The Huguenots.* Vol. I (28 December 1867): 953-
54.

Le Marquis de Noailles. *Henri de Valois et la Pologne en
1572.* Vol. II (25 January 1868): 90.

Major B. B. Malleson. *History of the French in India, 1674-
1761.* Vol. II (15 February 1868): 163-64.

—— in the *North British Review:*

Alphonse Jobez. *La France sous Louis XV.* Vol. LI, no. 101
(October 1869): 252-53.

Le Comte de la Boutetière. *Le Chevalier de Sapinaud et les
chefs Vendéens. Ibid.,* pp. 256-57.

C. de Cherrier. *Histoire de Charles VIII, roi de France.* Vol.
LI, no. 102 (January 1870): 541-44.

The Baron Carl de Ketschendorf. *Archives Judicaires . . .
des grands procès politiques en France, 1792-1840. Ibid.,*
pp. 565-66.

R. Lavollée. *Portalis, sa vie et ses oeuvres. Ibid.,* pp. 566-67.

C. Asselineau. *Charles Baudelaire, sa vie et son oeuvre.
Ibid.,* p. 578.

A. Cucheval-Clarigny. *Histoire de la Constitution de 1852.
Ibid.,* pp. 582-83.

C. A. Sainte-Beuve. *Nouveaux Lundis. Ibid.,* pp. 594-95.

T. Feuillet de Conches. *Louis XVI, Marie-Antoinette et
Madame Elisabeth.* Vol. LII, no. 103 (April 1870): 259-62.

Le Baron de la Morinerie. *Souvenirs d'émigration de
Madame la Marquise de Lâge de Volude.* Vol. LII, no. 104
(July 1870): 558-60.

Oeuvres de Charles Dunoyer. Ibid., pp. 569-70.

Karl Eugen von Ujfalvy. *Alfred de Musset. Ibid.,* pp. 573-74.

M. Mortimer-Ternaux. *Histoire de la Terreur.* Vol. LIII, no.
105 (October 1870): 259-61.

C. A. Dauban. *Paris en 1794 et en 1795. Ibid.,* pp. 261-63.

M. Büdinger. *Lafayette. Ibid.,* pp. 271-72.

La Strage di San Bartolomeo. Vol. LIII, no. 106 (January
1871): 561-62.

*Lettres du Marquis A. de Custine à Varnhagen d'Ense.
Ibid.,* pp. 591-92.

———— in the *Nineteenth Century:*
  Talleyrand's Memoirs. Vol. XXIX (April 1891): 670-84.
  Reprinted in HES, pp. 393-413.
  Souvenirs d'Alexis de Tocqueville. Vol. XXXIII (May
  1893): 883-86. Reprinted in C&S, pp. 419-20.

———— in the *English Historical Review:*
  J. R. Seeley. *A Short History of Napoleon the First.* (and)
  John C. Ropes. *The First Napoleon.* Vol. II (1887): 593-603.
  Reprinted in HES, pp. 442-58.
  Emmanuel de Broglie. *Mabillon et la Société de l'Abbaye
  de Saint-German-des-Prés à la fin du XVIIme siècle.* Vol.
  III (1888): 585-92. Reprinted in HES, pp. 459-71.
  H. M. Stephans. *A History of the French Revolution.* Vol.
  VII (1892): 381-84. Reprinted in HES, pp. 491-95.

German History and Culture

Article in the *Rambler, New Series* (i.e., Third Series):
  "Notes on the Present State of Austria." Vol. IV, part 2
  (January 1861): 193-205. Reprinted in C&S, pp. 339-52.

———— in the *Home and Foreign Review:*
  "Confessions of Frederick the Great." Vol. II, no. 3
  (January 1863): 152-71. Reprinted in C&S, pp. 353-73.

———— in the *Chronicle:*
  "Maurice of Saxony." Vol. I (19 October 1867): 710-11.

———— in the *English Historical Review:*
  "Wilhelm von Giesebrecht." Vol. V, no. 18 (April 1890):
  306-10. Reprinted in HES, pp. 496-502.

Book Reviews in the *Rambler, New Series:*
  Thomas Carlyle. *History of Frederick II of Prussia, called
  Frederick the Great.* Vol. X, part 60 (December 1858):
  429.

———— in the *Rambler, New Series* (i.e., Third Series):
  "The Tyrolese Patriots of 1809 by the Author of Du
  Guesclin." Vol. IV, part 10 (November 1860): 126-28.

———— in the *Home and Foreign Review:*
  A. F. DeCareil. *Oeuvres de Leibniz.* Vo. I, no. 2 (October
  1862): 543-45.
  F. Hülskamp and H. Rump. *Literarischer Handweiser für
  das katholische Deutschland. Ibid.,* pp. 561-62.

H. Holland. *Geschichte der altdeutschen Dichtkunst in Bayern.* Vol. II, no. 3 (January 1863): 221-23.

Jos. Beck. *Freiherr I. Heinrich von Wessenberg. Ibid.,* pp. 248-50.

T. L. Kington. *History of Frederick II.* Vol. II, no. 4 (April 1863): 613-14.

F. von Hurter. *Wallenstein's vier letzte Lebensjahre. Ibid.,* pp. 629-31.

L. Hausser. *Deutsche Geschichte, Vols. II and III. Ibid.,* pp. 642-45.

H. Brockhaus (Ersch und Grüber). *Allgemeine Encyclopädie.* Vol. III, no. 5 (July 1863): 269-70.

J. Janssen. *Frankfurt's Reichscorrespondenz, 1376-1439. Ibid.,* pp. 289-90.

M. Kayserling. *Moses Mendelssohn. Ibid.,* pp. 307-9.

Alfred Ritter von Arneth. *Maria Theresia's erste Regierungsjahre.* Vol. III, no. 6 (October 1863): 702-3.

C. H. Gildemeister. *Johann Georg Hamann's des 'Magus in Norden' Autorschaft. Ibid.,* pp. 703-4.

A. Springer. *Geschichte Oesterreichs seit 1809. Ibid.,* pp. 711-13.

O. Klopp. *Kleindeutsche Geschichtsbaumeister. Ibid.,* p. 713.

H. Richelot. *Goethe, ses mémoires, &c.* Vol. IV, no. 8 (April 1864): 720-21.

——in the *Chronicle:*

S. Sugenheim. *Geschichte des deutschen Volkes.* Vol. I (13 April 1867): 64-65.

M. Deutinger. *Der gegenwärtige Zustand der deutschen Philosophie. Ibid.,* p. 67.

Dr. von H——st. *Das Attentat vom 4 April, 1866.* Vol. I (15 June 1867): 284.

Lizzie S. Eden. *A Lady's Glimpse of the late War in Bohemia.* Vol. I (22 June 1867): 307.

H. Mendelssohn-Bartholdy. *Friedrich von Gentz.* Vol. I (20 July 1867): 403

W. L. Gage. *Life of Professor Carl Ritter. Ibid.,* pp. 403-4.

J. G. Droysen. *Geschichte der preussischen Politik—Friedrich I, König von Preussen.* Vol. I (7 September 1867): 572.

O. Klopp. *Die preussische Politik des Fridericianismus nach Friedrich II.* Vol. I (5 October 1867): 692. Reprinted in C&S, pp. 413-14.

M. Ritter. *Geschichte der deutschen Union . . . 1598-1612.* Vol. I (19 October 1867): 716.

M. Wohl. *Mahnruf zur Bewahrung Suddeutschlands.* Ibid., p. 717.

E. H. Meyer. *J. M. Lappenberg.* Vol. I (26 October 1867): 740.

T. Toeche. *Kaiser Heinrich VI.* Vol. I (2 November 1867): 764-65.

Maistre de Roger de la Lande. *Histoire de la Prusse, 1815-67.* Vol. II (4 January 1868): 18.

Officieller Ausstellungs-Bericht des Oesterreicheschen Central-Comités. Ibid., p. 20.

T. Bernhardt. *Preussens moderne Entwickelung.* Vol. II (11 January 1868): 41-42.

W. H. Riel. *Neues Novellenbuch.* Vol. II (18 January 1868): 68.

————in the *North British Review:*

L. von Ranke. *Zur deutschen Geschichte vom Religionsfrieden bis zum dreissigjährigen Krieg.* Vol. LI, no. 101 (October 1869): 239-40.

E. Reimann. *Geschichte des Bayrischen Erbfolgekrieges.* Ibid., pp. 253-55.

A. von Arneth. *Joseph II, und Katarina von Russland.* Ibid., p. 255.

E. von Cosel. *Geschichte des preussischen Staats und Volkes.* Ibid., pp. 255-56.

G. von S. N. *Geschichte Oesterreichs.* Ibid., pp. 269-70.

H. Ewald. *Die zwei Wege in Deutschland.* Ibid., p. 275.

L. von Ranke. *Geschichte Wallensteins.* Vol. LI, no. 102 (January 1870): 551-53.

B. Erdmannsdörfer. *Graf Georg Friedrich von Waldeck.* Ibid., pp. 553-54.

J. G. Droysen. *Friedrich Wilhelm I., König von Preussen.* Ibid., pp. 556-58. Reprinted in C&S, pp. 395-97.

G. H. Klippel. *Das Leben des Generals von Scharnborst.* Ibid., pp. 568-69.

Briefe von Alexander von Humboldt an Bunsen. Ibid., pp. 577-78.

L. von Ranke. *Briefwechsel Friedrich des Grossen mit dem Prinzen Wilhelm IV von Oranien.* Vol. LII, no. 103 (April 1870): 258-59.

F. von Ompteda. *Politischer Nachlass des Ludwig von Ompteda, 1804-13.* Ibid., pp. 263-65.

G. H. Pertz. *Das Leben des Feldmarschalls Grafen Neithardt von Gneisenau. Ibid.*, pp. 265-67.

E. Kelchner and K. Mendelssohn-Bartholdy. *Briefe des K. F. Friedrich von Nagler. Ibid.*, pp. 271-72.

G. Freitag. *Karl Mathy: Geschichte seines Lebens. Ibid.*, pp. 277-78.

K. Goedeke. *Emanual Geibel. Ibid.*, pp. 279-80.

W. Wattenbach. *Peter Luder.* Vol. LII, no. 104 (July 1870): 536-37.

Anton Springer. *Friedrich Christoph Dahlmann, Ibid.*, pp. 568-69.

Der Staatsstreich vom 2. December 1851. Vol. LIII, no. 105 (October 1870): 282-84.

O. Stobbe. *Hermann Conring.* Vol. LIII, no. 106 (January 1871): 564-65.

A. von Arneth. *Maria Theresia. Ibid.*, pp. 575-79.

H. Baumgarter. *Wie wir wieder ein Volk geworden sind. Ibid.*, pp. 597-98.

Edited by Lord Acton. *Les matinés royales, ou l'art de régner, opuscule inédit de Frédéric II, dit le Grand, Roi de Prusse.* (London and Edinburgh, 1863).

History (General)
Book Review in the *Rambler, New Series* (i.e., Third Series):
J. B. Robertson. *Lectures on Ancient and Modern History.* Vol. II, part 6 (March 1860): 396-98.

—— in the *Home and Foreign Review:*
Dr. Hoefer. *Nouvelle Biographie Générale,* Vol. XL. *Ibid.*, pp. 274-76.

Modern Greek History and Culture
Book Review in the *Rambler, New Series* (i.e., Third Series):
G. Finlay. *History of the Greek Revolution.* Vol. VI, part 18 (March 1862): 404-8.

—— in the *Home and Foreign Review:*
H. W. J. Thiersch. *Griechenlands Schicksale.* Vol. II, no. 4 (April 1863): 652-55.

Irish History and Culture
Articles in the *Rambler, New Series* (i.e., Third Series):
"Irish Education." Vol. III, part 9 (September 1860): 418-19.
"Mr. Goldwin Smith's Irish History." Vol. VI, part 17 (January 1862): 190-220. Reprinted in HOF, 232-69.

Italian History and Culture

Articles in the *Rambler, New Series* (i.e., Third Series):

"Cavour." Vol. V, part 14 (July 1861): 141-65. Reprinted in HES, pp. 174-203.

——— in the *Chronicle:*

"The Ministerial Changes in Italy." Vol. I (20 April 1867): 81-83.

"Secret History of the Italian Crisis." Vol. I (27 April 1867): 102-3.

"Reminiscences of Massimo d'Azeglio." Vol. I (11 May 1867): 158-59.

"The Situation at Florence." Vol. I (27 July 1867): 415-16.

Book Reviews in the *Home and Foreign Review:*

E. Benoist. *Guichardin.* Vol. III, no. 5 (July 1863): 292-93.

A. Reumont d'Aquisgrana. *Bibliografia dei lavori pubblicati in Germania sulla Storia d'Italia. Ibid.,* pp. 293-95.

Bonamy Price. *Venetia and the Quadrilateral. Ibid.,* pp. 321-22.

——— in the *Chronicle:*

Instruzione del Duca di Savoia Carlo Emmanuele I. al Marchese Fr. Villa inviato alla Maestà del Re d'Inghilterra. Vol. I (30 March 1867): 18-19.

A. Cappelli. *Lettere di Ludovico Ariosto.* Vol. I (6 April 1867): 43-44.

H. Taine. *Philosophie de l'art en Italie. Ibid.,* p. 44

E. Ricotti. *Storia della Monarchia Piemontese.* Vol. I (13 April 1867): 66.

Oeuvres complètes de P. Rossi. Ibid., pp. 66-67.

Pietro de Donato Giannini. *Della vita e delle opere di Massimo d'Azeglio. Ibid.,* p. 67.

Casare Cantù. *Storia della Letterature Italiana.* Vol. I. (20 April 1867): 89-90.

C. Milanesi. *Il sacco di Roma del 1527.* Vol. I (4 May 1867): 138-39.

M. Amari. *La Guerra del Vespro Siciliano.* Vol. I (11 May 1867): 165.

A. von Reumont. *Geschichte der Stadt Rom.* Vol. I (18 May 1867): 187-88.

P. Emiliani-Giudici. *Storia dei Comuni Italiani. Ibid.,* p. 188.

A. Coppi. *Annali d'Italia dal 1750.* Vol. I (8 June 1867): 259-60.

P. Clément. *L'Italie en 1671.* Vol. I (27 July 1867): 426.

―――in the *North British Review:*
   Carl Peter. *Geschichte Roms.* Vol. LI, no. 101 (October 1869): 217-18.
   M. Gachard. *La Bibliothèque des Princes Corsini à Rome.* Vol. LI, no. 102 (January 1870): 544-45.
   G. Carcano. *Lettere di Massimo d'Azeglio.* Vol. LIII, no. 105 (October 1870): 284-86.

Latin American History and Culture
Article in the *Bridgnorth Journal.* "The Rise and Fall of the Mexican Empire." (14 March 1868.) Reprinted in LIH, pp. 214-42; HES, pp. 143-72.

Book Reviews in the *Home and Foreign Review:*
   A. M. du Gratry. *La République de Paraguay.* Vol. III, no. 5 (July 1863): 319-20.
   Charles Calvo. *Recueil complet de Traités de tous les états de l'Amérique Latine. Ibid.,* pp. 320-21.
   F. Wolf. *Histoire de la littérature Brésilienne. Ibid.,* pp. 722-24.

―――in the *North British Review:*
   Paul Gaffarel. *Etude sur les rapports de l'Amerique et de l'ancien continent avant Christophe Colomb.* Vol. LI, no. 101 (October 1869): 232-33.

Medieval History and Culture
Articles in the *Chronicle:*
   "M. Littré on the Middle Ages." Vol. I (3 August 1867): 443-44.
   "Nicholas of Cusa." Vol. I (7 September 1867): 565-67. Reprinted in C&S, pp. 246-50.

Book Review in the *Rambler, New Series* (i.e., Third Series):
   J. F. A. Peyré. *Histoire de la Première Croisade.* Vol. V, part 15 (September 1861): 403-6.

―――in the *Home and Foreign Review:*
   A. Potthast. *Bibliotheca Historica Medii Aevi.* Vol. III, no. 6 (October 1863): 681-82.
   F. Gregorovius. *Geschichte der Stadt Rom im Mittelalter. Ibid.,* pp. 694-95.

Modern European History and Culture

Articles in the *Rambler, New Series* (i.e., Third Series):*
> "National Defense." Vol. III, part 9 (September 1860): 289-300.
> "Note on Events in Italy, Mexico, and Prussia." (In the Foreign Events section.) Vol. VI, part 19 (May 1862): 526-34.

———in the *Home and Foreign Review:*
> "Nationality." Vol. I, no. 1 (July 1862): 1-25. Reprinted in F&P, pp. 166-95; LIH, pp. 131-59; HOF, pp. 270-300.

———in the *Chronicle:*
> "Mr. Bergenroth's Introduction." (To Vol. II of the *Calendar of State Papers, Spanish*.) Vol. I. (14 September 1867): 587-89.
> "Mr. Grant Duff's *Glance Over Europe*." Vol. II (11 January 1868): 31-32.

———in the *Quarterly Review:*
> "Sir Erskine May's *Democracy in Europe*." Vol. CXLV, no. 289 (January 1878): 112-42. Reprinted in F&P, pp. 128-65; HOF, pp. 61-100.

Other Articles:
> "The Causes of the Franco-German War." A paper read before the Trinity Historical Society at Cambridge, the "Eranus" society at Cambridge, and the S. Catharine's College Historical Society at Cambridge in 1899. Reprinted as "The Causes of the Franco-Prussian War" in HES, pp. 204-25.
> Introduction to *Annals of Politics and Culture*, by G. P. Gooch (Cambridge, 1901.

Book Reviews in the *Home and Foreign Review:*
> F. Beckman. *Zur Geschichte des Kopernikanischen Systems*. Vol. I, no. 1 (July 1862): 240-41.

---

*Shaw and Lally do not mention the article "Note on Events in Italy, Mexico, and Prussia" at all and Hoselitz is apparently the victim of a typographical error for he substitutes "Russia" for "Prussia." Besides the *Rambler* itself, we have Acton's letter to Simpson (18 April 1862) in which he refers to his "25 pages of foreign events ... on Italy, Mexico and Prussia." (*Acton-Simpson Correspondence*, Vol. II, p. 277.)

Alex. Teulet. *Relations politiques de la France et de l'Espagne avec l'Ecosse au XVIme siècle. Ibid.*, p. 241.

Le Baron Kervyn de Lettenhove. *Commentaires de Charles Quint.* Vol. I, no. 2 (October 1862): 540-42.

G. A. Bergenroth. *Calendar of State Papers, Spanish.* Vol. II, no. 3 (January 1863): 227-30.

A. Gindely. *Meine Forschungen in fremden und einheimischen Archiven. Ibid.*, pp. 235-36.

C. von Martens. *Vor fünfzig Jahren. Tagebuch meines Feldzugs in Russland, 1812. Ibid.*, pp. 242-43.

M. Bogdanowitsch. *Geschichte des Feldzugs im Jahre 1812. Ibid.*, pp. 243-44.

W. N. Sainsbury. *Calendar of Colonial State Papers, 1513-16.* Vol. II, no. 4 (April 1863): 617-19.

Armand Baschet. *La diplomatie Vénitienne. Les princes de l'Europe au XVIme siècle. Ibid.*, pp. 622-23.

N. W. Senior. *Biographical Sketches. Ibid.*, pp. 645-47.

B. Carneri. *Demokratie, Nationalität und Napoleonismus. Ibid.*, pp. 655-56.

Maximilian Ritter von Thielen. *Erinnerungen aus dem Kriegerleben &c.* Vol. III, no. 5 (July 1863): 314-15.

S. Sugenheim. *Geschichte der Aufhebung der Leibeigenschaft in Europa.* Vol. III, no. 6 (October 1863): 691-92.

E. Scherer. *Etudes critiques sur la littérature contemporaine. Ibid.*, pp. 718-20.

W. Raymond. *Corneille, Shakespeare et Goethe.* Vol. IV, no. 8 (April 1864): 721.

Kleine historische Schriften von H. von Sybel. Ibid., p. 722.

———in the *Chronicle:*

Ch. A. Dauban. *Precis d'histoire contemporaine.* Vol. I (6 April 1867): 44.

G. Campori. *Lettere artistiche inedite.* Vol. I (4 May 1867): 138.

A. Bardonnet. *Procès-verbal de délivrance à Jean Chandos, Commissaire du Roi d'Angleterre, des places françaises abandonnées par le traité de Bretigny.* Vol. I (8 June 1867): 258-59.

G. Rosa. *Storia generale delle Storie.* Vol. I (22 June 1867): 306.

O. Hamst. *A Martyr to Bibliography.* Vol. I (27 July 1867): 426.

E. Quinet. *Histoire de la Campagne de 1815.* Vol. I
(3 August 1867): 451.

A. Geffroy. *Gustave III et la cour de France.* Vol. I
(10 August 1867): 475-76.

J. R. Browne. *The Land of Thor.* Vol. I (26 October 1867):
740-41.

T. Martin. *Memoir of W. E. Aytoun.* Vol. I (16 November
1867): 811.

Sir H. L. Bulwer. *Historical Characters.* Vol. I (30 November 1867): 860.

Emma Sophia, Countess Brownlow. *Slight Reminiscences
of a Septuagenarian.* Vol. I (7 December 1867): 883.

———in the *North British Review:*

Paul Friedmann. *Les dépêches de Giovanni Michiel,
1554-7.* Vol. LI, no. 101 (October 1869): 233-35.

F. P. Perrens. *Les Mariages Espagnols, 1602-15. Ibid.,*
pp. 237-38.

S. R. Gardiner. *Prince Charles and the Spanish Marriage.
Ibid.,* pp. 240-46.

Dispacci di Giovanni Michiel. Vol. LI, no. 102 (January
1870): 545-46.

S. R. Gardiner. *Narrative of the Spanish Marriage Treaty.
Ibid.,* pp. 549-50.

J. J. Honegger. *Grundesteine einer allgemeinen
Kulturgeschichte der neuesten Zeit. Ibid.,* p. 575.

W. H. Riehl. *Wanderbuch. Ibid.,* p. 589.

H. von Sybel. *Historische Zeitschrift.* Vo. LII, no. 104 (July
1870): 560-62.

K. von Klinkowstrom. *Aus der alten Registratur der
Staatskanzlei. Ibid.,* pp. 565-66.

T. Juste. *Le soulèvement de la Hollande en 1813. Ibid.,*
p. 567.

A. L. W. *Der Feldzug am Mittelrhein, 1794.* Vol. LIII, no. 105
(October 1870): 263-65.

General C. Mercer. *Journal of the Waterloo Campaign.
Ibid.,* pp. 272-73.

J. Stevenson. *Calendar of State Papers, Foreign, Elizabeth.*
Vol. LIII, no. 106 (January 1871): 561.

Dr. Philippson. *Heinrich IV und Philipp III. Ibid.,* p. 564.

G. Fischbach. *Die Belagerung von Strassburg. Ibid.,*
pp. 595-97.

J. Schmidt. *Bilder aus dem geistigen Leben unserer Zeit.
Ibid.,* pp. 605-6.

Lecture. "The War of 1870." (London, 1871). Reprinted in HES, pp. 226-72.

North American History and Culture

Articles in the *Rambler, New Series* (i.e., Third Series):

"Political Causes of the American Revolution." Vol. V, part 8 (May 1861): 17-61. Reprinted in C&S, pp. 291-338; F&P, pp. 196-250; LIH, 41-94.

"Foreign Affairs: Notes on Italy and America." Vol. VI (January 1862): 277-92.*

——in the *Bridgnorth Journal:*

"The Civil War in America, Its Place in History." (20 January 1866). Reprinted in HES, pp. 123-42.

Book Reviews in the *Home and Foreign Review:*

E. M. Hudson. *The Second War of Independence in America.* Vol. II, no. 4 (April 1863): 656-59.

Thirteen Months in the Rebel Army: By an impressed New Yorker. Vol. III, no. 5 (July 1863): 325-26.

Two Months in the Confederate States: By an English Merchant. Ibid., pp. 326-27.

C. J. Reithmüller. *Alexander Hamilton and His Contemporaries.* Vol. IV, no. 8 (April 1864): 718-19.

Max von Eelking. *Die deutschen Hülfstruppen im Nordamerikanischen Befreiungskriege. Ibid.*, pp. 719-20.

G. Ticknor. *Life of W. H. Prescott. Ibid.*, pp. 725-26.

——in the *Chronicle:*

G. Sander. *Geschichte des vierjährigen Bürgerkrieges in den Vereinigten Staaten von Amerika.* Vol. I (30 March 1867): 19.

Lucia Norman. *A Youth's History of California.* Vol. I (9 November 1867): 787-88.

H. Ruttimann. *Das nordamerikanische Bundesstaatsrecht.* Vol. I (21 December 1867): 929.

——in the *North British Review:*

Horace Greeley. *Recollections of a Busy Life.* Vol. LI, no. 101 (October 1869): 268-69.

---

*Not cited in Shaw, Lally, or Hoselitz, but referred to in a letter from Simpson to Acton (10 December 1861). (*Acton-Simpson Correspondence,* p. 224.)

R. G. Gillett. *Democracy in the United States. Ibid.*, pp. 273-74.

H. Blankenburg. *Die innern Kämpfe der nordamerikanischen Union. Ibid.*, p. 274.

G. T. Curtis. *Life of Daniel Webster, Vol. I.* Vol. LII, no. 103 (April 1870): 268-71.

G. T. Curtis. *Life of Daniel Webster, Vol. II.* Vol. LII, no. 104 (July 1870): 571-73.*

M. Bernard. *A Historical Account of the Neutrality of Great Britain During the American Civil War. Ibid.*, pp. 578-79.

———in the *English Historical Review*:
J. Bryce. *The American Commonwealth.* Vol. IV (1889): 388-96. Reprinted in HOF, pp. 575-87.

Correspondence: Letter of Sir John Acton to General Robert E. Lee (Bologna, 4 November 1866). Reprinted in D. S. Freeman, *Robert E. Lee.* (New York and London, 1935) Vol. IV, pp. 515-17.

Diaries: "Lord Acton's American Diaries," in the *Fortnightly Review, New Series.* Vol. CX, no. 659 (November 1921): 727-42; Vol. CX, no. 660 (December 1921): 917-34; Vol. CXI, no. 661 (January 1922): 63-83.

Philosophy
Book Reviews in the *Home and Foreign Review*:
M. Matter. *Saint Martin, le philosophe inconnu.* Vol. I, no. 2 (October 1862): 538-40.
M. Matter. *Swedenborg.* Vol. IV, no. 8 (April 1864): 717.
Pensées et fragments divers de Charles Neuhaus. Ibid., pp. 733-34.

———in the *Chronicle*:
E. Geruzez. *Mélanges et Pensées.* Vol. I (6 April 1867): 44.
J. E. Erdmann. *Grundriss der Geschichte der Philosophie.* (4 May 1867): 140.
A. Schwegler. *Handbook of the History of Philosophy.* Vol. I (30 November 1867): 858-59.

*Hoselitz erroneously cites pages 573-74.

———in the *North British Review:*
   E. Pffleiderer. *Gottfried Wilhelm Leibniz.* Vol. LII, no. 103
       (April 1870): 255-58. Reprinted in C&S, pp. 415-18.
   A. Desjardins. *Les moralistes français du seizième siècle.*
       Vol. LII, no. 104 (July 1870): 540-41.
   A. Pichler. *Die Theologie des Leibniz. Ibid.,* pp. 551-52.

Philosophy of History
Article in the *Rambler, New Series:**
   "Mr. Buckle's Philosophy of History." Vol. X, part 56
       (August 1858): 88-104. Reprinted in HES, pp. 324-43; in
       LIH, pp. 22-40.

———in the *English Historical Review:*
   "German Schools of History." Vol. I, no. 1 (June 1886): 7-42.
       Reprinted in HES, pp. 344-92.
   "Döllinger's Historical Work." Vol. V, no. 20 (October
       1890): 700-744. Reprinted in HOF, pp. 375-435.

Book Review in the *English Historical Review:*
   R. Flint. *Historical Philosophy in France and French*

---

*Bert Hoselitz includes the following citation:
   "Mr. Buckle's Thesis and Method," Vol. X, part 55 (July 1858),
   pp. 27-42. Acton's co-editor, Richard Simpson, probably wrote the
   major part of this article. Republished in HES, pp. 305-23.
Both Shaw and Lally do not cite this article as part of Acton's work at all.
However, Figgis and Laurence included the article in their collection,
Historical Essays and Studies, and William H. McNeill has included it in
his recent anthology, *Essays in the Liberal Interpretation of History,*
without any mention of the controversy over the authorship.
   It is clear that Richard Simpson was the author of this article; Acton and
Simpson usually discussed each other's articles in advance and so most of
their work at this time included ideas suggested by the other. In that
sense, Acton may be said to have contributed a few paragraphs to this essay.
   On 31 May 1858, Simpson wrote to Acton outlining the contents for the
next issue of the *Rambler,* the July issue. He refers to "3 RS—with your
[Acton's] introduction & end as aforesaid—on Buckle." He goes on to say
". . . could you not write a long introduction about Buckle, containing your
ideas of what the philosophy of history should be; then you could make
the transition to my contribution, which shows what Buckle's idea of it is;
& end with promising an article to show what his erudition amounts to."
(This future article was Acton's essay entitled "Mr. Buckle's Philosophy
of History" which appeared in the August 1858 *Rambler.*) The Simpson
letter is published in *The Correspondence of Lord Acton and Richard
Simpson,* Vol. I, p. 28.

Belgium and Switzerland. Vol. X (1895): 108-13. Reprinted in HOF, pp. 588-96.

Correspondence:

Letters to the Syndicate of the Cambridge University Press on the plan of its proposed Universal History. Published as a pamphlet, *The Cambridge Modern History, etc.,* (Cambridge, 1907). These letters were written in the late 1890s.

Printed circular to the contributors "From the Editor of the Cambridge Modern History," dated Cambridge, 12 March 1898. Published in *Lectures on Modern History* (London, 1907), pp. 315-18. Reprinted in LIH, pp. 396-99.

Polish History

Book review in the *Chronicle.* A. Mickiewicz. *Histoire populaire de la Pologne.* Vol. I (1 June 1867): 233.

Political Philosophy*

Book Reviews in the *Home and Foreign Review:*

E. A. Freeman. *History of Federal Government.* Vol. II, no. 4 (April 1863): 587-89. Reprinted in C&S, pp. 400-403.

Sir G. C. Lewis. *A Dialogue on the best Form of Government. Ibid.,* pp. 651-52.

_____ in the *North British Review:*

C. Frantz. *Die Naturlehre des Staats.* Vol. LIII, no. 105 (October 1870): 295-96.

*Both the Shaw and Lally bibliographies attribute to Acton an essay on John Stuart Mill's *On Liberty.* Lally gives the following citation:

In the *Rambler* (New Series) "Mill on Liberty". Vol. ii, pp. 62-75, 376-385, Nov. 1859 and March 1860.

In fact, as Hoselitz points out, this essay was written by Thomas Arnold, Jr. (son of the Headmaster of Rugby and the brother of Matthew Arnold), who taught English literature at the Catholic University of Dublin and later at University College, Dublin. Shaw and Lally were doubtless confused because the article was signed with an *A.* Herbert Paul makes the same mistake in his introduction to *Letters of Lord Acton to Mary Gladstone.*

Acton refers to the forthcoming article on Mill by Arnold in letters to Simpson on 23 and 28 August 1859 and on 30 September 1859. ("I have asked Arnold for Mill's Liberty ... ," *Acton-Simpson Correspondence,* Vol. I, p. 217).

Hoselitz erroneously cites letters written by Acton referring to the Arnold essay on 24, 28 and 30 August 1859. The actual dates are 23, 28 August (as Hoselitz correctly notes) and 30 September 1859.

_____in the Nineteenth Century:
L. A. Burd's Edition of Machiavelli's "Il Principe."
Vol. XXXI (April 1892): 696-700.

Introduction: Introduction to Il Principe by Niccolo Machiavelli,
edited by L. A. Burd (Oxford, 1891). Reprinted in HOF,
pp. 212-31. New edition: Oxford, 1968.

Portuguese History and Culture
Book Review in the Chronicle: M. Kayserling. Geschichte der
Juden in Portugal. Vol. I (10 August 1867): 475.

Russian History and Culture
Book Reviews in the Home and Foreign Review:
P. Gagarin. Oeuvres choisies de Pierre Tchadaïef. Vol. I,
no. 2 (October 1862): 551-52.
F. Bodenstedt. Russische Fragmente. Vol. II, no. 3 (January
1863): 284-86.
Count Macdonnel. Diary of an Austrian Secretary of Lega-
tion at the Court of Czar Peter the Great. Vol. III, no. 5
(July 1863): 300.

_____in the Chronicle:
Die vorgebliche Tochter der Kaiserin Elisabeth Petrowna.
Vol. I (2 November 1867): 765.

_____in the North British Review:
Aus den Memoiren eines Russischen Dekabristen. Vol. LI,
no. 102 (January 1870): 570-71.
C. Schirren. Livländische Antwort an Herrn Juri Samarin.
Ibid., pp. 584-85.
A. R. von Vivenot. Korsakoff. Vol. LII, no. 104 (July 1870):
562-64.
W. H. Dixon. Free Russia. Ibid., pp. 584-89.

Spanish History and Culture
Book Review in the Home and Foreign Review:
C. de Moüy. Don Carlos et Philippe II. Vol. II, no. 4 (April
1863): 623-25.

_____in the Chronicle:
G. de Leva. Storia documentata di Carlo V. Vol. I (13 April
1867): 65-66.
M. Gachard. Don Carlos et Philippe II. Vol. I (4 May 1867):
139-40.

J. G. Magnabal's translation of le Marquis de Pidal's *Philippe II, Antonio Perez, et le royaume d'Aragon*. Vol. I (20 July 1867): pp. 402-3.

E. Chasles. *Michel de Cervantes*. Vol. I (3 August 1867): 450-51.

——— in the *North British Review*:

W. Wattenbach. *Eine Ferienreise nach Spanien und Portugal*. Vol. LI, no. 101 (October 1869): 275-76.

Cinco Cartas de D. Diego Sarmiento de Acuna, primer Conde de Gondomar. Vol. LII, no. 103 (April 1870): 253-54.

Swedish History and Culture

Book Review in the *Home and Foreign Review*:

H. Woodhead. *Memoirs of Christina, Queen of Sweden*. Vol. III, no. 5 (July 1863): 300.

——— in the *North British Review*:

G. Droysen. *Gustaf Adolf*. Vol. LI, no. 102 (January 1870): 550-51.

Swiss History and Culture

Book Review in the *Home and Foreign Review*:

J. C. Kopp. *Geschichte der eidgenössischen Bünde*. Vol. II, no. 4 (April 1863): 615-16.

Travel

Book Review in the *Home and Foreign Review*:

J. W. Jones. *The Travels of Ludovico di Varthema*. Vol. IV, no. 8 (April 1864): 707-8.

——— in the *Chronicle*:

G. Pertot. *L'Ile de Crète, souvenirs de voyage*. Vol. I (6 April 1867): 44.

G. Peacock. *Handbook of Abyssinia*. Vol. I (9 November 1867): 788.

——— in the *North British Review*:

J. van Lennep. *Travels in Little-known Parts of Asia Minor*. Vol. LII, no. 104 (July 1870): 579-81.

Appendix
Lord Acton's Hundred Best Books

In their correspondence, Lord Acton and Mary Gladstone frequently discussed what should constitute "the hundred best books." Acton eventually sent her his own list, which, in 1883, she recorded in her diary. The list was first published in July 1905 in *Pall Mall Magazine* (Volume XXXVI, No. 147) with an introduction and critique by Clement Shorter. Here is the list as it appeared there.

1. Plato's Laws—Steinhart's Introduction.
2. Aristotle's Politics—Susemihl's Commentary.
3. Epictetus' Encheiridion—Commentary of Simplicius.
4. St. Augustine's Letters.
5. St. Vincent's Commonitorium.
6. Hugo of S. Victor—De Sacramentis.
7. S. Bonaventura—Breviloquium.
8. S. Thomas Aquinas—Summa contra Gentiles.
9. Dante—Divina Commedia.
10. Raymund of Sabunde—Theologia Naturalis.
11. Nicholas of Cusa—Concordantia Catholica.
12. La Bible de Reuss.
13. Pascal's Pensées—Havet's Edition.
14. Malebranche, De la Recherche de la Vérité.
15. Baarder—Spekulativ Dogmatik.
16. Molitor—Philosophie der Geschichte.
17. Astié—Esprit de Vinet.

18. Pünjer—Geschichte der Religions-philosophie.
19. Rothe—Theologische Ethik.
20. Martensen—Die Christliche Ethik.
21. Oettingen—Moralstatistik.
22. Hartmann—Phenomenologie des sittlichen Bewusstseyns.
23. Leibniz—Letters edited by Klopp.
24. Braniss—Geschichte der Philosophie.
25. Fisher—Franz Bacon.
26. Zeller—Neuere Deutsche Philosophie.
27. Bartholomess—Doctrines Religieuses de la Philosophie Moderne.
28. Guyon—Morale Anglaise.
29. Ritschl—Entstehung der Altkatholischen Kirche.
30. Loening—Geschichte des Kirchenrechts.
31. Baur—Vorlesungen über Dogmengeschichte.
32. Fénelon—Correspondence.
33. Newman's Theory of Development.
34. Mozley's University Sermons.
35. Schneckenburger—Vergleichende Darstellung.
36. Hundeshagen—Kirchenvorfassungsgeschichte.
37. Schweizer—Protestantische Centraldogmen.
38. Gass—Geschichte der Lutherischen Dogmatik.
39. Cart—Histoire du Mouvement Religieux dans le Canton de Vaud.
40. Blondel—De la Primenté.
41. Le Blanc de Beaulieu—Theses.
42. Thiersch—Vorlesungen über Katholizismus.
43. Möhler—Neue Untersuchungen.
44. Scherer—Mélanges de Critique Religieuse.
45. Hooker—Ecclesiastical Polity.
46. Weingarten—Revolutionskirchen Englands.
47. Kliefoth—Acht Bücher von der Kirche.
48. Laurent—Etudes de l'Histoire de l'Humanité.
49. Ferrari—Révolutions de l'Italie.
50. Lange—Geschichte des Materialismus.
51. Guicciardini—Ricordi Politici.
52. Duperron—Ambassades.
53. Richelieu—Testament Politique.
54. Harrington's Writings.
55. Mignet—Négotiations de la Succession d'Espagne.
56. Rousseau—Considérations sur la Pologne.
57. Foncin—Ministère de Turgot.
58. Burke's Correspondence.
59. Mémorial de Ste. Hélène.

60. Holtzendorf—Systematische Rechts-encyklopädie.
61. Thering—Geist des Römischen Rechts.
62. Geib—Strafrecht.
63. Maine—Ancient Law.
64. Gierke—Genossenschaftsrecht.
65. Stahl—Philosophie des Rechts.
66. Gentz—Briefwechsel mit Adam Müller.
67. Vollgraff—Polignosie.
68. Frantz—Kritik aller Parteien.
69. De Maistre—Considérations sur la France.
70. Donoso Cortes—Ecrits Politiques.
71. Périn—De la Richesse dans les Sociétés Chrétiennes.
72. Le Play—La Reforme Sociale.
73. Riehl—Die Bürgerliche Sociale.
74. Sismondi—Etudes sur les Constitutions des Peuples Libres.
75. Rossi—Cours du Droit Constitutionnel.
76. Barante—Vie de Roger Collard.
77. Duvergier de Hauranne—Histoire du Gouvernement Parlementaire.
78. Madison—Debates of the Congress of Confederation.
79. Hamilton—The Federalist.
80. Calhoun—Essay on Government.
81. Dumont—Sophismes Anarchiques.
82. Quinet—La Révolution Française.
83. Stein—Sozialismus in Frankreich.
84. Lasselle—System der Erworbenen Rechte.
85. Thomissen—Le Socialisme depuis l'Antiquité.
86. Considérant—Destinée Sociale.
87. Rosher—Nationalökonomik.
[88.]*
89. Mill—System of Logic.
90. Coleridge—Aids to Reflection.
91. Radowitz Fragmente.
92. Gioberti—Pensieri.
93. Humboldt—Kosmos.
94. De Candolle—Histoire des Sciences et des Savants.
95. Darwin—Origin of Species.
96. Littré—Fragments de Philosophie.
97. Cournot—Enchaînements des Idées fondamentales.
98. Monatsschrift des wissenschaftlichen Vereins.

*Number 88 is missing from the *Pall Mall* list, which also lists no number
99 or number 100.

Index